经济合作与发展组织（OECD）

Arrangement on
Officially Supported Export Credits
2015 Revision

# 官方支持
# 出口信贷的安排
# 2015 修订版

中国出口信用保险公司　译

中国金融出版社

责任编辑：肖　炜
责任校对：刘　明
责任印制：丁淮宾

**图书在版编目（CIP）数据**

官方支持出口信贷的安排（Guanfang Zhichi Chukou Xindai de Anpai）/经济合作与发展组织编；中国出口信用保险公司译．—2015修订版．—北京：中国金融出版社，2015.6

ISBN 978-7-5049-7891-2

Ⅰ．①官…　Ⅱ．①经…②中…　Ⅲ．①出口信贷—国际信贷—经济协定　Ⅳ．①F831.6

中国版本图书馆CIP数据核字（2015）第054954号

出版发行　中国金融出版社
社址　北京市丰台区益泽路2号
市场开发部　(010)63266347，63805472，63439533（传真）
网上书店　http://www.chinafph.com
　　　　　(010)63286832，63365686（传真）
读者服务部　(010)66070833，62568380
邮编　100071
经销　新华书店
印刷　保利达印务有限公司
尺寸　140毫米×210毫米
印张　14.375
字数　306千
版次　2015年6月第1版
印次　2015年6月第1次印刷
定价　38.00元
ISBN 978-7-5049-7891-2/F.7451

经济合作与发展组织（OECD）翻译和再版授权编号：
P－2015－018－T

原版以英语和法语出版，其中英语版名称为：
Arrangement on Officially Supported Export Credits
法语版名称为：
Arrangement sur les Crédits à l'Exportation Bénéficiant d'un Soutien Public



中文版翻译质量和与原文的一致性仅由译者负责。如出现原文与译文不一致的情况，则以原文内容为准。译者名单（按姓氏拼音排序）：丛从、韩羽时、姜超、康和意、刘晓慧、王鲁广、谢茜、杨世新、恽之瑜、张法、张友迅。

# 序　言

自20世纪60年代起，世界主要发达国家均通过参加经济合作与发展组织（OECD）来协调各自的出口信贷和出口信用保险政策，并于1978年制定出台了第一版《官方支持出口信贷的安排》，即通常所说的“君子协定”，以保障成员国之间对外经济贸易、特别是资本性货物贸易的有序发展，避免可能出现的恶性竞争。由于OECD国家的对外贸易和投资总额在国际贸易中占有很大份额，“君子协定”自推出后便在国际出口信贷业内产生了广泛影响，成为了许多发展中国家后续建立出口信用机构并制定相关政策的重要参考依据。

近十年来，全球经贸环境发生了深刻变化，特别是2008年的金融危机对世界各国的经济贸易造成了严重冲击。后危机时代，大部分发达经济体仍受困于诸多危机遗留问题并陷入高赤字困境，而发展中国家经济复苏情况相对良好、贸易回升速度相对较快、国际经贸地位亦得到明显提升；同时，绿色能源、低碳化成为全球产业发展的新趋势。为应对这场危机的后续影响，包括OECD成员国在内的多国出口信用机构均采取了更加灵活多样的支持政策和措施，以帮助本国出口企业摆脱困境、助力本国经济的复苏和发展。因此，为与时俱进地反映出口信贷和出口信用保险领域出现的新情况、新变化，应对并协调所产生的新问题，OECD每年根据最新形势发展并结合业务实践对“君子协定”文本进行不同程度地修改和调整，以求继续促进各国对出口信贷和出口信用保险的规范、有序使用，维护官方支持下的公平竞争。

中国出口信用保险公司（以下简称中国信保）是由中国政府

出资设立的政策性保险机构，在成立以来的十余年间对中国外经贸事业的支持作用日益凸显。尤其是在2008年国际金融危机发生后，中国信保在业务经营遵守本国法律、法规，符合国际惯例的前提下，勇于担当、积极作为，进一步提升服务水平，有效支持了中国对外经贸的稳定增长，自身业务亦实现了快速发展。2009—2014年，中国信保累计支持中国企业开展对外贸易、对外工程承包和对外投资1.6万亿美元，帮助出口企业获得银行融资1.9万亿元人民币，为全国数万家出口企业、数百个中长期项目提供了出口信用保险支持和服务。据伯尔尼协会（Berne Union）统计，自2010年起中国信保的承保总规模（含中长期出口信用保险、海外投资保险和短期出口信用保险）已连续多年位列全球官方ECA前列，国际影响力日渐提升。

“他山之石，可以攻玉”。除认真履行国家使命、积极发挥政策性作用外，中国信保亦一直注重汲取国际信用保险业界的有益经验，促进自身业务发展。为此，我们在2006年翻译并出版了《官方支持出口信贷的安排（2005修订版）》。随着近年来国内外环境及自身业务的最新发展变化，我们更加深刻地认识到，及时了解和掌握最新国际出口信贷和出口信用保险政策及其规则变化的重要性。我们只有不断地学习和借鉴才能进一步开阔视野、拓展思路，并实现更快的成长与进步。为此，中国信保再次组织力量对OECD“君子协定”最新版本（2015年1月修订版）进行了翻译。

2015年修订版共包括四章和十四个附件。与2005年修订版相比，体系更加完善，内容更加丰富，特别体现在附件部分。一是增加了“铁路出口信贷的行业谅解”、“对于涉及第0类国家交易的市场基准”、“买方风险分类的定性描述”三个附件；二是对民用航空器、可再生能源、气候变化减缓和水资源项目等行业的谅解内容进行了大幅充实。

再度翻译出版“君子协定”表明中国信保不仅一如既往地坚持博采众长，而且愿意与国内同行分享成果，以促进共同发展。希望这是一本对出口信贷和出口信用保险的理论与实务工作者有价值、有帮助、有裨益的参考书，同时也有助于为我们做好中国的出口信用保险事业奠定更加坚实的基础！

中国出口信用保险公司

二〇一五年六月

# 目　录


第一章　一般规定 …………………………………………… 1
第二章　出口信贷的融资条款 ………………………………… 7
第三章　关于约束性援助的规定 …………………………… 27
第四章　程序 ……………………………………………… 39
附件 1　船舶出口信贷的行业谅解 ……………………… 55
附件 2　核电站出口信贷的行业谅解 …………………… 63
附件 3　民用航空器出口信贷的行业谅解 ……………… 71
附件 4　可再生能源、气候变化减缓和水资源项目出口信贷的行业谅解 ……………………………………… 129
附件 5　铁路出口信贷的行业谅解 ……………………… 147
附件 6　适用于项目融资交易的条款 …………………… 153
附件 7　通知中应提供的信息 …………………………… 159
附件 8　最低保费费率的计算 …………………………… 173
附件 9　对于涉及第 0 类国家交易的市场基准 ………… 181
附件 10　关于适用第三国还款担保以及多边或区域性机构分类的标准和条件 …………………………………… 185
附件 11　买方风险分类的定性描述 ……………………… 191
附件 12　关于适用国别风险降低技术和买方信用增进的标准和条件 …………………………………………… 201
附件 13　开发性特点清单 ………………………………… 209
附件 14　定义表 …………………………………………… 213
ARRANGEMENT ON OFFICIALLY SUPPORTED EXPORT CREDITS—2015 REVISION ………………………… 219

# 第一章

# 一 般 规 定

## 1. 目的

(a)《官方支持的出口信贷安排》(以下简称《安排》) 的主要目的是为官方支持出口信贷的规范使用提供一个基本框架。

(b)《安排》旨在培育在官方支持(如第5条(a)款所定义)下的公平竞争环境,以鼓励出口商开展竞争的基础是所出口货物和服务的质量和价格,而不是所获得的最优惠的官方支持融资条件。

## 2. 地位

《安排》在经济合作与发展组织(以下简称经合组织)框架下形成并发展,1978年生效且永不失效。《安排》只是各加入国之间的"君子协定",尽管得到经合组织秘书处(以下简称秘书处)的行政支持,但并非经合组织的法令①。

## 3. 加入国

目前,《安排》的加入国有:澳大利亚、加拿大、欧盟、日本、韩国、新西兰、挪威、瑞士和美国。其他经合组织成员国和非成员国可经现有加入国的邀请加入。

## 4. 非加入国可获得的信息

(a) 加入国应以通知的方式,与非加入国分享第5条(a)款所指的有关官方支持的信息。

(b) 任一加入国应在互惠的基础上,与答复其他加入国的询问一样,答复与其在官方支持的融资条件上有竞争关系的非加入国的询问。

---

① 经合组织公约第5条规定了相关定义。

## 5. 适用范围

《安排》适用于由政府或代表政府为货物和/或服务出口（包括融资租赁）提供的、还款期在2年或2年以上的所有官方支持。

（a）官方支持可采取以下不同方式：

（1）出口信用担保或保险（纯保险）。

（2）官方融资支持：

——直接信贷/融资和再融资，或

——利率支持。

（3）上述形式的任意组合。

（b）《安排》适用于约束性援助；第四章规定的程序同样适用于与贸易有关的非约束性援助。

（c）《安排》不适用于军用设备和农产品的出口贸易。

（d）若有明确证据显示，合同买方所在国并非货物的最终进口国，买方的目的主要是为获取更优惠的还款条件，则不得提供官方支持。

## 6. 行业谅解

（a）以下《行业谅解》是《安排》的组成部分：

——船舶（附件1）

——核电站（附件2）

——民用航空器（附件3）

——可再生能源、气候变化减缓和水资源项目（附件4）

——铁路（附件5）

（b）对于《行业谅解》所包含的货物和/或服务出口，《行业谅解》的加入国可根据《行业谅解》的规定提供官方支持。若《行业谅解》未作相应规定的，《行业谅解》的加入国则适用《安排》的规定。

## 7. 项目融资

（a）对于满足附件6附录1所列标准的货物和/或服务出口，加入国可适用附件6规定的条款。

（b）上述（a）款适用于《核电站出口信贷的行业谅解》《可再生能源、气候变化减缓和水资源项目出口信贷的行业谅解》《铁路出口信贷的行业谅解》中规定的货物和服务出口。

（c）上述（a）款不适用于《民用航空器出口信贷的行业谅解》和《船舶出口信贷的行业谅解》中规定的货物和服务出口。

## 8. 退出

加入国可通过书面的即时通讯方式，如经合组织在线信息系统（OLIS），通知秘书处而退出《安排》。退出将在秘书处收到通知的180个公历日后生效。

## 9. 监督

秘书处负责监督《安排》的执行情况。

# 第二章

# 出口信贷的融资条款

出口信贷的融资条款包括本章列出的所有规定，并应贯通理解各条款。

《安排》对可获官方支持的条款作出了限制。加入国认识到，在实践中对特定贸易或行业适用的融资条款比《安排》中的规定更为严格。加入国应继续尊重这些融资条款的惯例，特别是还款期不得超过货物使用寿命的原则。

## 10. 预付款、官方支持的最大限度和当地费用

（a）加入国应要求接受官方支持的货物和服务的买方在附件14规定的信用起始日当天或之前，支付不低于出口合同金额15%的预付款。在计算预付款时，若交易中包含未接受官方支持的第三国货物和服务时，出口合同金额可按比例降低。保费允许进行100%的融资/保险。保费可计入也可不计入出口合同金额。在信用起始日之后支付的质保金在本文中不被视为预付款。

（b）对此类预付款提供的官方支持仅可采用出运前风险保险或担保的形式。

（c）除（b）款和（d）款规定外，加入国提供的官方支持不得超过出口合同金额的85%，包括来自第三国的货物和服务，但不包括当地费用。

（d）加入国可对当地费用提供官方支持，条件是：

（1）对当地费用提供的官方支持不得超过出口合同金额的30%。

（2）对当地费用的官方支持条件不得比其他相关出口获得的官方支持条件更优惠/更宽松。

（3）若对当地费用的官方支持超过出口合同金额的15%，则

应按照第48条的要求进行先期通知，详细说明接受官方支持的当地费用的情况。

## 11. 最长还款期的国别分类

（a）第Ⅰ类国家是高收入[①]的经合组织国家。其他所有国家都属于第Ⅱ类国家。

（b）进行国别分类时，应采用下列操作标准和程序：

（1）《安排》的国别分类根据世界银行为借款国进行国别分类而测算的人均国民收入来确定。

（2）在世界银行未获得足够的信息以公布一国人均国民收入的情况下，世界银行应估算该国的人均国民收入是高于还是低于当前的门槛标准。除非加入国另有决定，否则将根据估算结果进行分类。

（3）在按照第11条（a）款对一国进行重新分类的情况下，该国最新分类情况应在秘书处将世界银行相关数据和结论通报给所有加入国两周后生效。

（4）当世界银行修改有关数据时，该修改应被视为与《安排》无关。尽管如此，加入国可通过达成共同谅解的方式调整一国的国别分类。加入国如在秘书处首次发布数据的同一公历年内发现相关数据错误或遗漏，加入国可积极考虑调整一国的国别分类。

（c）仅当世界银行对一国的国别分类连续两年保持不变的情况下，方可调整该国最长还款期的国别分类。

---

① 依据世界银行每年按照人均国民收入的划分来判定。

## 12. 最长还款期

在不影响第 13 条效力的前提下，最长还款期根据按照第 11 条标准来确定的进口国国别分类情况而变化。

（a）对于第Ⅰ类国家，最长还款期为 5 年；在遵循第 48 条规定的先期通知程序后，最长还款期可为 8.5 年。

（b）对于第Ⅱ类国家，最长还款期为 10 年。

（c）对于涉及一个以上进口国的合同，加入国应按照第 58 条至第 63 条的有关程序寻求建立一个共同谅解，并就适当的还款期达成一致意见。

## 13. 非核电站的还款期

（a）对于非核电站，最长还款期为 12 年。若某加入国欲支持比第 12 条规定更长的还款期，则该加入国应按照第 48 条的程序给予先期通知。

（b）非核电站是指不用核能作燃料的成套电站或其组成部分；其包括建设和调试此类非核能电站所直接需要的所有配件、设备、原料和服务（包括人员培训），但不包括通常由买方负责的事项，尤其是涉及土地开发、道路、乡村建设、输电线、调试厂和供水系统等不在核电站界限范围内的有关费用，以及买方所在国因官方审批程序（如工地许可、建设许可和燃料装卸许可）所产生的费用，除非：

（1）若调试厂的买方即为电站的买方，新建调试厂的最长还款期应与非核电站的最长还款期（12 年）相同；以及

（2）电压在 100 千伏以上的变电站、变压器和传输线的最长

还款期应与非核电站相同。

## 14. 本金的偿还和利息的支付

（a）出口信贷的本金应等额分期偿还。

（b）应至少每6个月偿还一次本金并支付一次利息。第一次本金偿还和利息支付应不迟于信用起始日之后的6个月。

（c）在为租赁交易提供出口信贷支持的情况下，可采取本金和利息等额共还的方式，而无须按照上述（a）款的规定等额分期偿还本金。

（d）在特殊且有正当理由的情况下，可不按上述（a）款至（c）款规定提供出口信贷。如债务人的资金状况与还款表规定的每半年等额还款计划在时间上不一致，则可适用于其他还款条件，但应满足以下标准：

（1）6个月内单笔或多笔本金偿还数额不得超过信贷本金总额的25%。

（2）应至少每12个月偿还一次本金。第一次偿还时间不得迟于信用起始日之后的12个月；在信用起始日之后的12个月内，本金偿还数额不低于信贷本金总额的2%。

（3）应至少每12个月支付一次利息。第一次支付时间不得迟于信用起始日之后的6个月。

（4）还款期的加权平均期限最长不得超过：

——对于主权买方（或有主权还款担保）的交易，第I类国家是4.5年，第II类国家是5.25年。

——对于非主权买方（或没有主权还款担保）的交易，第I

类国家是 5 年，第 II 类国家是 6 年。

——尽管有上述两点的具体规定，但按照第 13 条，对于非核电站项目的支持是 6.25 年。

（5）加入国应按照第 48 条给予先期通知，对不按照（a）款至（c）款规定提供信贷支持的原因作出解释。

（e）信用起始日之后的到期利息不得资本化。

## 15. 利率、保费费率和其他费用

（a）利息不包括：

（1）为卖方信贷或其他融资信贷提供保险或担保而收取的保费或其他费用；

（2）整个还款期内应支付的除银行年费或半年年费之外的，与出口信贷相关的银行费用或佣金；以及

（3）进口国征收的预提税。

（b）如果采取直接信贷/融资或再融资方式提供官方支持，保费既可计入利息票面价值中，也可作为一项单独收费；但应向加入国分别列明两部分费用情况。

## 16. 出口信贷的有效期

除第 21 条规定的商业参考利率（CIRRs）有效期之外，单笔出口信贷或信贷额度融资条件的有效期，在作出最终承诺前不能超过 6 个月。

## 17. 避免或最小化损失的措施

如果是在合同生效后（当出口信贷协议和附属文件皆已生效）

采取的措施，且其意图仅在于避免或最小化可能导致拒付或索赔的事件所造成的损失时，《安排》并不禁止出口信贷机构或融资机构接受比《安排》规定更宽松的融资条款。

## 18. 匹配

考虑到加入国的国际义务及其与《安排》目的的一致性，加入国可按照第 45 条规定所述的程序，对加入国或非加入国提供的融资条款进行匹配。根据本条款提供的融资条款将被视为符合第一章、第二章，以及附件 1、2、3、4、5、6（若适用）的规定。

## 19. 官方融资支持下的最低固定利率

(a) 对固定利率贷款提供官方融资支持的加入国应采用相关的商业参考利率（CIRRs）作为最低利率。商业参考利率是根据下列原则确定的利率：

(1) 商业参考利率应代表相关货币国内市场上的最终商业贷款利率；

(2) 商业参考利率应接近对国内一流借款人适用的利率；

(3) 商业参考利率应以固定利率融资的筹资成本为基础；

(4) 商业参考利率不得扭曲国内竞争条件；以及

(5) 商业参考利率应接近国外一流借款人可获得的利率。

(b) 官方融资支持条款不得部分或全部抵消或补偿投保人按照第 23 条交纳的防范不还款风险且合适的信用风险保费。

## 20. 商业参考利率的确定

(a) 每个希望确立商业参考利率的加入国应首先在以下两种

基准利率体系中为其本国货币选择其一：

（1）对于还款期不超过5年（含5年）的信贷，适用3年政府债券收益率；对于还款期在5年以上、不超过8.5年（含8.5年）的信贷，适用5年政府债券收益率；而对于还款期超过8.5年的信贷，适用7年政府债券收益率。或

（2）对于各种信贷，都适用5年政府债券收益率。

对基准利率体系作例外安排须经加入国同意。

（b）除非加入国另有约定，商业参考利率应在各加入国基准利率上加100个基点的固定利差来确定。

（c）其他加入国如决定以某种特定货币提供融资，则应使用该种货币的商业参考利率。

（d）加入国在提前6个月给予通知并与其他加入国协商后，可以变动基准利率体系。

（e）加入国或非加入国可要求为非加入国货币建立商业参考利率。在与有权益的非加入国磋商后，代表该非加入国的加入国或秘书处可按照第58条至第63条规定的共同谅解程序，提出使用该货币构建商业参考利率的建议。

## 21. 商业参考利率的有效期

适用于单笔交易的利率有效期不得超过120天。若官方融资支持的条款在合同签署日之前确定，则应在有关商业参考利率的基础上再加上20个基点。

## 22. 商业参考利率的适用

（a）在为浮动利率贷款提供官方融资支持的情况下，银行和

其他融资机构不得提供商业参考利率（初始合同签订时）和贷款期间短期市场利率中的较低者。

（b）在自愿、提前全部或部分偿还贷款的情况下，借款人应向提供官方融资支持的政府机构赔偿因提前还款而产生的所有费用和损失，包括政府机构替换因提前还款而受影响的固定利率现金流所产生的成本。

## 23. 信用风险的保费

除收取利息外，加入国还应收取承保出口信贷中不付款风险的保费。加入国收取的保费费率应根据风险情况厘定，并足以覆盖长期运营成本和损失。

## 24. 信用风险的最低保费费率

加入国收取的保费应不低于所适用信用风险的最低保费费率（MPR）。

（a）可适用的最低保费费率根据以下几个因素确定：

——可适用的国别风险分类；

——风险期间（即风险期或 HOR）；

——已确定的债务人的买方风险分类；

——官方出口信用保险产品的政治和商业风险承保比例及产品特质；

——任何已应用的国别风险降低技术；及

——任何已应用的买方风险信用增进的方法。

（b）最低保费费率以信贷本金金额的百分比表示，保费在第一次信贷提款日全额支付。附件 8 对计算最低保费费率的数学公式进行了解释。

（c）对于涉及债务人属于第 0 类国家、高收入经合组织国家和高收入欧元区国家①的交易，不设定最低保费费率。加入国对在这些国家的交易收取的保费费率应按照个案予以确定。为确保对这些国家债务人所进行交易而收取的保费费率不削弱私营市场定价，加入国应遵循以下程序：

——考虑到市场信息的可获得性和基础交易的特点，加入国在确定保费费率时，应按照附件 9 提出的一个或几个市场基准点，选择最适合特定交易的市场基准点。

——尽管上述条款有具体规定，若由于流动性或其他原因而使相关的市场信息受限，或交易的规模较小（信用价值低于 1000 万特别提款权），加入国收取的保费费率不应低于第 1 类国别风险分类中相应买方风险分类的最低保费费率。

——暂时性地②，若任何交易的债务人/担保人是第 0 类国家、高收入经合组织国家或高收入欧元区国家，且信用价值超过 1000 万特别提款权，加入国应按照第 48 条给予先期通知。

（d）对第 7 类“最高风险”国家适用的保费费率原则上应高于对该类国家确定的最低保费费率；具体费率由提供官方支持的

① 每年审查一国地位时需考虑：（1）是否是高收入国家（依据世界银行每年按照人均国民收入对国别分类的评审）；（2）在经合组织中的成员资格；（3）是否属于欧元区国家。在一国的收入分类（高收入或其他）连续 2 年保持不变后，其被列入或移除第 25 条（c）款中的高收入经合组织国家或高收入欧元区国家名单的行为才能生效。若因一国变更在 OECD 的成员资格或加入欧元区，导致其“高收入经合组织国家”或“高收入欧元区”的称号变更或移除，则在国家地位年度审议时立即生效。

② 第 24 条（c）款第 3 点规定的先期通知要求将于 2015 年 6 月 30 日终止。

加入国确定。

(e) 在计算一笔交易的最低保费费率时，可适用的国别风险分类应为债务人所在国的分类，可适用的买方风险分类应为债务人①的分类，除非：

——可对被担保债务金额有担保能力的第三方，将在整个信贷期间对全部还款义务提供不可撤销、无条件的、见索即付、有法律效力和执行力的担保。如果是第三方担保，加入国可选择适用担保人所在国家的国别风险分类，以及担保人的买方风险分类②；或

——第28条规定的多边或区域性机构作为交易的借款人或担保人，则可适用的国别风险分类和买方风险分类是所涉多边或区域性机构的风险分类。

(f) 附件10规定了根据第24条（e）款第1点和第2点所述情形，第三方担保应用的有关标准和条件。

(g) 计算最低保费费率时使用的风险期惯例是1/2提款期加上整个还款期，并假定一个常规的出口信贷还款模式，即以每半年一次的等额分期还款方式偿还本金加上自信用起始日后6个月起计的利息。对于非标准性的出口信贷还款模式，使用如下公式计算相应的还款期（每半年一次的等额分期还款方式）：相应还款期 =（加权平均还款期 - 0.25）/0.5。

(h) 若按照第三方担保人所在国而非债务人所在国确定适用

---

① 第24条（c）款规定了对于高收入经合组织国家或高收入欧元区国家作为第三方担保人的交易所收取的保费费率。

② 在涉及第三方作为担保人的交易中，适用的国家风险分类和买方风险分类必须与同一实体相关，抑或担保人或债务人中的任何一方。

的最低保费费率时，加入国则应按照第 47 条予以先期通知。若按照多边或区域性机构作为担保人确定适用的最低保费费率，加入国则应按照第 48 条予以先期通知。

## 25. 国别风险分类

除了高收入经合组织国家和高收入欧元区国家，其他国家应根据是否偿还其外债的可能性（亦即国家信用风险）来进行分类。

（a）国家信用风险包括以下五类：

——由债务人/担保人政府或还款生效必经的第三国机构颁布的延期付款命令；

——在通知国境外发生的政治事件和/或经济困境，或在通知国境外采取的立法/行政措施；这些事件或措施禁止或延迟有关信贷项下资金的汇兑；

——债务人/担保人所在国采取法律措施，宣布使用当地货币作为对债务的合法清偿，而不管因汇率波动出现当地货币兑换成信贷货币时的还款额不足以清偿资金汇兑时的债务额的情况；

——外国政府为禁止偿还贷款所采取的其他任何措施或决定；及

——在通知国境外发生的不可抗力，如战争（包括内战）、征用、革命、暴乱、内乱、飓风、洪水、地震、火山爆发、海啸及核事故。

（b）各国被划分为 8 种国别风险分类（第 0 ~ 7 类）。仅对 1 ~ 7 类国家确立最低保费费率，而第 0 类国家没有最低保费费率标准，因为这类国家的国别风险可被视为忽略不计。在涉及第 0 类国家的交易中，信用风险主要来自于债务人/担保人。

（c）各国按照国别风险分类方法进行分类①，这种方法包括：

——国别风险评估模型（以下简称模型）是基于三组风险指标，对每个国家的国家信用风险作出的定量分析。三组指标包括：国家的还款经验、财政状况和经济状况。模型的使用方法由对三组风险指标的评估，以及对风险指标组的综合分析和灵活加权等不同步骤组成。

——对模型评估结果的定性分析结果应在逐个国家的基础上，结合考虑本模型未全部或部分考虑的政治风险和/或其他风险因素。若适当，可对定量模型评估进行调整，以反映对国家信用风险的最终评估。

（d）应对国别风险分类进行持续监督，并至少每年审议一次，对国别风险分类方法进行的调整应立即通知秘书处。当一国被重新划分为更高或更低的国别风险分类时，加入国应在通告秘书处该重新分类后的5个工作日内，比照或高于与新国别风险分类相关的最低保费费率来确定费率。

（e）国别风险分类应由秘书处予以公开发布。

## 26. 主权风险评估

（a）所有按照第25条（d）款的国别风险分类方法进行分类的国家，都应进行主权风险评估，以在特殊情况下识别/确认这些主权：

——不是该国风险最低的债务人；及

① 为了管理方便，一些可被划入8种国别风险分类之一的国家如果通常不接受官方出口信贷支持，则它们有可能未被分类。对于这样的未分类国家，加入国可按照自己认为合适的标准对其国别风险进行分类。

——信用风险明显高于国别风险。

（b）符合上述（a）款列出标准的主权情况，应按照加入国开发并同意的主权风险评估方法予以确认。

（c）应对符合上述（a）款列出标准的主权名单进行持续监督，且至少每年审议一次；按照主权风险评估方法进行的调整应立即通知秘书处。

（d）按照上述（b）款列出的主权情况名单应由秘书处予以公开。

## 27. 买方风险分类

在国别风险分类中第 1 类至第 7 类国家的债务人，或酌情而定的担保人，应被归类到与债务人/担保人所在国家有关的买方风险分类中的一种①。附件 8 规定了应对债务人和担保人进行分类的买方风险分类矩阵。附件 11 则列出了买方风险分类的定性描述。

（a）买方风险分类应根据在加入国对债务人/担保人确定的优先无担保信用评级上确定。

（b）尽管有上述（a）款的规定，但在应用买方信用增进方法后，按照附件 6 列明的条款和条件支持的交易以及信用价值不超过 500 万特别提款权的交易则应根据交易情况进行分类；在针对这些交易时，不论分类如何，即使是买方信用增进后，在费率上也不能给予任何折扣。

（c）主权债务人和担保人被划入买方风险分类中 SOV/CC0 类别。

---

① 买方风险分类的规则应被理解为制订可适用的最优分类，亦即一个主权买方可能被划分到非最优的买方风险分类中。

(d) 在特殊情况下，非主权债务人/担保人可被划入买方风险分类中“优于主权”(SOV +) 类别①，如果：

——认可的信用评级机构 (CRA)② 对债务人/担保人使用的外币评级优于该机构对它们各自的主权评级；或

——债务人/担保人所在国的主权风险被认为明显高于其国别风险。

(e) 按照第 48 条规定，加入国对于下列交易应给予先期通知：

——向非主权债务人/担保人收取的费率低于买方风险分类中 CC1 (即为 CC0 或 SOV +) 类别中确定的相应费率；

——非主权债务人/担保人的信用价值高于 500 万特别提款权，且加入国对于该非主权债务人/担保人买方风险的评估优于认可的信用评级机构的评级③。

(f) 在对特定交易开展竞争的情况下，若参与竞争的加入国对债务人/担保人的买方风险分类不一致，则加入国之间应寻求就该买方风险的分类达成共识。若不能达成共识，则不禁止那些将债务人/担保人买方风险归类较高的加入国使用较低的买方风险分类。

---

① 按照“优于主权”(SOV +) 的买方风险分类确定的最低保费费率比按照“等同主权”(CC0) 的买方风险分类确定的最低保费费率要低 10%。

② 秘书处应对这类认可的信用评级机构进行编纂并保留名录。

③ 若不止一家认可的信用评级机构对非主权借款人进行评级，则只需在买方信用风险评级优于评级机构的最优信用评级的情况下予以通知。

## 28. 多边和区域性机构的分类

多边和区域性机构的分类应归入国别风险分类中 0 ~7 类①中的某一类，并适时审议。上述分类应由秘书处予以公开。

## 29. 官方出口信贷产品的承保比例和特质

按照附件 8 的规定，根据加入国提供的出口信贷产品的不同特质和承保比例，适用的最低保费费率有所区分。这种差别是从出口商的角度出发的（即为了中和因向出口商/金融机构提供不同质量的产品所引起的竞争影响）。

（a）出口信贷产品的特质是指该产品的功能是保险、担保或直接信贷/融资；若其为保险产品，是否覆盖赔偿等待期（即从债务人的还款到期日至保险人有责任向出口商/金融机构偿付之日的时间区间）的利息，而不收取附加费。

（b）加入国提供的所有现行出口信贷产品应被划入以下三类中的一类：

——次标准产品，即不覆盖赔偿等待期利息的保险，和覆盖赔偿等待期利息但另适当收取保费附加费的保险；

——标准产品，即覆盖赔偿等待期利息而无须另收保费附加费的保险和直接信贷/融资；及

——超标准产品，即担保。

## 30. 国别风险降低技术

（a）加入国可采用以下国别风险降低技术，具体方法已在附

① 考虑到买方风险的存在，各类多边和区域性机构应被划入买方风险分类中 SOV/CC0 类别。

件 7 中列出：

——离岸未来现金流结构与离岸监管账户结合使用；

——当地货币融资。

（b）按照第 47 条，若加入国采用了反映其运用国别风险降低技术的最低保费费率，则应予以先期通知。

## 31. 买方信用增进方法

（a）加入国可应用下列买方信用增进（BRCE）方法；在这些方法使用下信用增进因子（CEF）可大于 0：

——合同收益或应收账款的转让；

——资产抵押担保；

——固定资产担保；

——监管账户。

（b）附件 12 中规定了买方信用增进方法的定义和最大信用增进因子的价值。

（c）买方信用增进方法可单独使用或与下列限制结合使用：

——通过买方信用增进方法获得的信用增进因子最大不超过 0.35；

——资产抵押担保和固定资产担保不能在一笔交易中同时使用；

——在可应用的国别风险分类已通过离岸未来现金流结构与离岸监管账户结合使用而提高的情况下，不可再使用买方信用增进方法。

（d）在买方信用增进方法使信用增进因子大于 0 的情况下，若交易中非主权债务人/担保人的信用价值大于 500 万特别提款权，则加入国应按照第 48 条予以先期通知。

## 32. 对信用风险的最低保费费率有效期的审议

（a）为评估最低保费费率的适用性，并允许必要情况下将其调高或调低，应定期使用保费反馈工具（PFTs）对最低保费费率进行监督和调整。

（b）保费反馈工具（PFTs）应结合提供官方支持机构的实际经验以及信用风险定价的私营市场信息两方面因素，评估最低保费费率的适用性。

（c）对《安排》中涉及保费的所有规定的综合审议不得迟于 2015 年 12 月 31 日进行。

# 第三章

# 关于约束性援助的规定

## 33. 一般原则

（a）各加入国同意就出口信贷和约束性援助形成的补充政策。出口信贷政策应建立在公开竞争和自由发挥市场作用的基础上。约束性援助政策应为没有渠道或少有渠道获得市场融资的国家、经济部门或项目提供所需的外部资源。约束性援助政策应确保所提供资金价值的最大化、贸易扭曲的最小化，并使这些资源在促进发展方面产生实效。

（b）《安排》中关于约束性援助的规定不适用于多边或区域性机构的援助方案。

（c）本条中的原则并不预判发展援助委员会（DAC）对约束性或非约束性援助质量的评估。

（d）加入国可就任何形式援助的约束地位要求有关方面提供更多的信息。当无法确定某种融资操作是否符合附件 14 中所列关于约束性援助的定义范围时，援助提供国如主张某项援助按照附件 14 的定义实际上是“非约束性”的，则应提供证据来支持这一主张。

## 34. 约束性援助的形式

约束性援助可采取下述方式：

（a）官方开发性援助（ODA）贷款，其定义援引《DAC 关于相关融资、约束性与部分非约束性官方发展援助的指导原则（1987）》的相关规定；

（b）官方开发性援助（ODA）赠与，其定义援引《DAC 关于相关融资、约束性与部分非约束性官方发展援助的指导原则（1987）》的相关规定；及

（c）其他官方资金流（OOF），包括赠与和贷款，但不包括符合本《安排》要求的官方支持出口信贷；或

（d）任何其他相关援助（例如混合援助），该援助在法律上或事实上处于援助提供国的控制下，贷款方或借款方涉及上述两种或两种以上的援助方式，和/或涉及下述融资成分：

（1）以本《安排》适用的直接信贷/融资、再融资、利率支持、担保或保险等形式提供的官方支持出口信贷；

（2）以市场条件或类市场条件提供的其他资金，或来自买方的预付款。

## 35. 关联融资

（a）关联融资可采取多种形式，包括混合信贷、混合融资、联合融资、平行融资或单个一体化交易等。它们共同的主要特点是：

——优惠成分在法律或事实上与非优惠成分相联系；

——“一揽子”融资方案全部或其中一部分事实上是约束性援助；及

——优惠资金只有在相关的非优惠成分被受援国接受的前提下方可获得。

（b）“事实上”的关联或联系由以下因素决定：

——受援国和援助提供国之间存在非正式的谅解；

——援助提供国具有通过提供官方开发性援助来促进受援国接受“一揽子”融资方案的意向；

——“一揽子”融资方案与在援助提供国进行采购的有效挂钩；

——官方开发性援助的地位和每笔融资交易的招标或签约方式相挂钩；或

——任何其他被发展援助委员会或加入国认为在两种或两种以上的融资成分中存在事实上联系的做法。

（c）下列做法不应妨碍对“事实上”的关联或联系进行认定：

——通过对同一合同组成部分的分别通知来分割合同；

——对分阶段融资合同的分割；

——对同一合同中相互依存的几个部分不予通知；和/或

——由于“一揽子”融资方案的一部分不具有约束性而不予通知。

## 36. 接受约束性援助的国家资格

（a）根据世界银行的数据，人均国民总收入高于中低收入水平国家上限的国家，不应得到约束性援助。世界银行每年重新计算该划分标准①。只有一国在世界银行的评级连续两年不变后，该国才能被重新分类。

（b）进行国别分类时，应适用下列操作标准和程序：

---

① 为辨别某国是否具有约束性援助的资格，依据世界银行每年通过的人均国民收入临界值对国别分类进行年度审议。该临界值在经合组织网站上可以查到（http：//oecd. org/trade/exportcredits/classification. htm）。

(1)《安排》的分类根据世界银行为借款国进行国别分类而测算的人均国民收入来确定；该分类应由秘书处予以公布。

(2) 在世界银行未获得足够的信息以公布某国人均国民收入的情况下，应请世界银行估算该国的人均国民收入是高于还是低于当前的门槛标准。除非加入国另有决定，否则将根据估算结果对该国进行分类。

(3) 若一国获得约束性援助的资格按照（a）款发生变化，在秘书处将从上述世界银行数据得到的结论通报给所有加入国两周后，该重新分类方生效。在重新分类生效之前，不应对取得新资格的国家提供约束性援助融资；在生效日期之后，不应对新获升级的国家提供约束性援助融资，除非是包含在以前承诺过信贷额度内的单笔交易，在信贷额度到期前可继续提供（提供该援助融资的效期不应超过自新生效日起1年）。

(4) 当世界银行修改有关数据时，该修改应被视为与《安排》无关。尽管如此，一国分类的调整可通过共同谅解的方式并按照第58条至第63条规定的程序来实现；在秘书处首次发布数据的同一公历年内如发现相关数据有错误或遗漏，加入国可积极考虑调整该国的分类。

## 37. 接受约束性援助的项目资格

(a) 对于那些按照市场条件或《安排》中的条件进行融资，一般而言在商业上是可行的公共或私营项目，不应提供约束性援助。

(b) 有资格获得援助的主要评判标准是：

——该项目在财务上是否不可行，即该项目是否无法依据市场原则合理定价，以产生足够的现金流来弥补项目运行成本及服

务使用的资本，这是第一个标准；或

——基于与其他加入国的协商结果，是否能作出合理的结论，认为该项目不可能按市场条件或本《安排》中的条件进行融资，这是第二个标准。对于金额大于 5000 万特别提款权的受援项目，在考虑援助合理性时，应对根据市场条件或本《安排》中的条件融资的可获得性进行特别权衡。

（c）上述（b）款的主要评判标准旨在说明应该如何评估一个项目，以确定其是否应该通过援助来融资，或可按市场条件或《安排》中的条件进行出口信贷融资。通过第 51 条～第 53 条所述的协商程序，经过一段时间的经验累积，将针对这两类项目的划分标准为出口信贷机构和援助机构提供更为精确的事前指导。

## 38. 最低优惠水平

加入国提供的约束性援助的优惠水平不应低于 35%；当受益国为最不发达国家（LDC）时，优惠水平不应低于 50%，但下列情况除外，且这些情况同时免予适用第 49 条（a）款和第 50 条（a）款规定的通知程序：

（a）技术协助：约束性援助中的官方开发性援助成分只涉及技术合作，且该技术合作的金额小于交易总金额的 3%，或不足 100 万特别提款权（取二者较低者）；及

（b）小型项目：完全由开发性援助捐款资助的小于 100 万特别提款权的资本性项目。

## 39. 接受约束性援助国家或项目资格的例外情况

（a）第 36 条和第 37 条的规定不适用于优惠水平为 80% 或更高的约束性援助，除非该约束性援助构成第 35 条所述的“一揽子”相关融资方案的一部分。

（b）第 37 条的规定不适用于价值小于 200 万特别提款权的约束性援助，除非该约束性援助构成第 35 条所述的“一揽子”相关融资方案的一部分。

（c）对联合国确定的最不发达国家的约束性援助不受第 36 条和第 37 条的约束。

（d）在以下特定情况下，加入国应积极考虑加快约束性援助的程序：

——对于导致严重跨境污染的核事故或重大工业事故，受其影响的加入国希望提供约束性援助以消除或减缓此不利影响，或

——存在发生上述事故的显著风险，可能受到潜在影响的加入国希望提供约束性援助以阻止该风险发生。

（e）尽管有第 36 条和第 37 条的规定，加入国在例外情况下，可通过下述一种方式提供支持：

——附件 14 所定义、第 58 条至第 63 条所述的共同谅解程序；或

——按照第 51 条和第 52 条所述，援助理由得到加入国的实质支持；或

——按照第 53 条所述向经合组织秘书长的致函，加入国应视此为非通常情况和非常用方式。

## 40. 约束性援助优惠水平的计算

约束性援助优惠水平的计算与发展援助委员会计算赠与成分时所使用的方法相同，但不包括：

（a）计算某一给定币种贷款的优惠水平时所采用的贴现率，

即差别贴现率（DDR），应于每年 1 月 15 日按照以下计算方法调整：

——平均商业参考利率 + 溢价；

溢价（M）随还款期（R）变动如下：

| 还款期 | 溢价 |
| --- | --- |
| 少于 15 年 | 0.75 |
| 15（含）~20（不含）年 | 1.00 |
| 20（含）~30（不含）年 | 1.15 |
| 30 年（含）以上 | 1.25 |

——对于所有币种，平均商业参考利率的计算方法是：自前一年度 8 月 15 日至本年度 2 月 14 日的 6 个月期间内，每月有效商业参考利率的平均值。计算利率，包括溢价，应四舍五入为最近的 10 个基点。如果该货币的商业参考利率多于一个，则计算中应采用第 20 条（a）款中规定的还款期最长的商业参考利率。

（b）优惠水平计算的基准日为附件 14 中所规定的信用起始日。

（c）为计算“一揽子”相关融资方案的整体优惠水平，下列信贷、资金和支付的优惠水平应被视为零：

——符合本《安排》规定的出口信贷；

——以市场利率或接近市场利率提供的其他资金；

——其他优惠水平低于第 38 条所允许的最低优惠水平的官方资金，但排除匹配的情形；及

——来自买方的预付款。

在信用起始日当天或之前、未考虑预付款的支付款项应包括在优惠水平计算之内。

(d) 匹配中适用的贴现率：在对援助进行匹配时，完全匹配是指以一致的优惠水平进行匹配，该优惠水平以匹配时的有效贴现率重新计算。

(e) 只有当当地费用和第三国采购由援助提供国提供融资时，方可包括在优惠水平的计算当中。

(f) “一揽子”方案的总体优惠水平的计算方法：将方案中每一个组成部分的名义价值乘以各自部分的优惠水平，然后把乘积的结果相加，再把相加的结果除以各组成部分名义价值之和。

(g) 某个特定援助贷款的贴现率是指通知时的有效贴现率。然而在即时通知的情况下，该贴现率是指该援助贷款的条款确定时的贴现率。贷款期限内贴现率的变化并不改变其优惠水平。

(h) 如果合同签订前发生币种变化，则须对通知作出修正。用于计算优惠水平的贴现率为修正日当天可适用的贴现率。如果备选币种和所有计算优惠水平的必要信息都在原通知中得到说明，则上述修正不是必需的。

(i) 虽然上述 (g) 款有规定，但计算援助信贷额度下各笔交易优惠水平所使用的贴现率应为该信贷额度中原来通知的贴现率。

## 41. 约束性援助的有效期

(a) 加入国不应固定约束性援助的条款超过 2 年，无论援助是针对单笔交易融资、援助协定，还是援助信贷额度或类似的协议。在涉及援助协定、援助信贷额度或类似协议的情况下，有效期应始于该协定或协议的签署日，并按照第 50 条的规定予以通知；信贷额度期限的延长，应被视为一笔新交易，需要予以通知并说明其为延期，以及延期情况通知日所允许的条件。在涉及单笔交易的情况下，包括在援助协定、援助信贷额度或类似的协议中通知过的单笔交易，有效期在适用的情况下，应始于按第 49 条或第 50 条所做承诺的通知日。

（b）当一国首次丧失使用世界银行 17 年期贷款的资格时，现存和新的援助协定与信贷额度的有效期应被限制为 1 年，自按照第 36 条（b）款所述程序中确定的可能重新分类日起算。

（c）此类协定和信贷额度只有在满足下列符合《安排》中第 36 条和第 37 条规定的条件下，才能被延期：

——国别分类的重新调整；及

——《安排》中的规定变更。

在这些情况下，尽管按照第 40 条确定的贴现率有所变化，但现行的条款可以保持不变。

**42. 匹配**

考虑到加入国的国际义务及与《安排》目的的一致性，按照第 45 条所述的程序，加入国可对加入国或非加入国提供的融资条款进行匹配。

# 第四章

## 程　序

## 第一节 出口信贷和与贸易相关援助的共同程序

### 43. 通知

《安排》中相关程序规定的通知应按照且包括附件 7 中所含的信息，并应抄送给秘书处。

### 44. 官方支持的信息

（a）一旦加入国按照第 47 条至第 50 条所述程序承诺提供其已予以通知的官方援助，则应在相关报告表格上注明通知编号，以此方式通知其他所有加入国。

（b）按第 55 条至第 57 条规定进行信息交换的过程中，加入国应就其预期支持某特定交易的信贷条款通知其他加入国，并可要求其他加入国提供类似信息。

### 45. 匹配程序

（a）在加入国或非加入国按照第 18 条和第 42 条规定提出匹配融资条款之前，加入国应作出所有合理努力，包括适当使用第 57 条所述的当面磋商，来确认上述条款为官方支持的，并符合下列要求：

（1）加入国应按照已匹配条款要求的相同通知程序，就其意向支持的条款通知其他所有加入国。在对非加入国进行匹配时，实施匹配的加入国应遵循与已进行过匹配的加入国同样的通知程序。

（2）尽管有上述（1）款的规定，若适用的通知程序要求实施匹配的加入国在投标截止日后仍然保留其承诺，则实施匹配的加入国应就其匹配意向尽快予以通知。

（3）若发起匹配的加入国降低或收回其已通知的期限与条件的支持意向，则应立即就此通知其他所有加入国。

（b）若加入国想提供与按照第 47 条和第 48 条已通知过的条款完全一致的融资条款，应待通知时保证的等待期结束后方可实行。该加入国应就此意向尽快予以通知。

**46. 特别磋商**

（a）加入国如有合理的原因认为另一加入国（发起匹配的加入国）提供的融资条款比《安排》中规定的更优惠，则其应通知秘书处；秘书处应立即使各加入国知晓该信息。

（b）秘书处发布信息后的 2 个工作日内，发起匹配的加入国应澄清说明其提供的融资条款。

（c）发起匹配的加入国作出澄清说明后，任何加入国均可在 5 个工作日内要求秘书处组织特别磋商会议来讨论该问题。

（d）若加入国之间的特别磋商会议结果未决，则受益于官方支持的融资条款不应生效。

## 第二节　出口信贷的程序

**47. 先期通知并讨论**

（a）按照附件 7 要求，加入国在作出任何承诺前至少 10 个公历日通知其他所有加入国，如果：

——计算最低保费费率时，适用的国别风险分类及买方风险分类为债务人所在国之外的第三方担保人所在国别风险分类和买方分类（即依照第24条（e）款第1点所规定）；

——通过运用第30条所列出的国别风险降低技术，已调低适用的最低保费费率；

——打算按照附件4第10条（a）款第2点或（d）款提供支持；

——按照附件5第5条（a）款提供支持。

（b）如在此期间内其他任何加入国要求进行磋商，则发起的加入国应再等10个公历日。

（c）加入国在磋商后应就其最终决定通知其他所有加入国，以利于按照第69条所述进行的经验审议。加入国应按照上述（a）款保留已予通知的保费费率的经验记录。

## 48. 先期通知

（a）如加入国要采取下述行动，其应按照附件7要求，在作出任何承诺前至少10个公历日通知其他所有加入国：

（1）按照第10条（d）款第3点提供支持；

（2）对Ⅰ类国家中还款期超过5年的项目提供支持；

（3）按照第13条（a）款提供支持；

（4）按照第14条（d）款提供支持；

（5）当信贷额度高于1000万特别提款权①时，按照第24条

① 第24条（c）款第3点规定的先期通知要求将于2014年12月31日终止。

(c) 款提供支持；

(6) 按照第24条(e)款第2点使用的保费费率，即用于计算最低保费费率的可适用的国别风险分类和买方风险分类是根据多边或区域性机构作为债务人或担保人的分类确定的。

(7) 按照第27条(e)款使用的保费费率，即根据已选定的买方风险分类来计算交易的最低保费费率：

——非主权债务人/担保人评级低于CC1级(即CC0或SOV+级)；

——非主权债务人/担保人有高于500万特别提款权的授信额度且评级高于认可的信用评级机构的评级。

(8) 按照第31条(a)款使用的保费费率，即买方风险信用增进方法导致信用增进因子大于0。

(9) 按照附件2第8条(a)款提供支持。

(10) 按照附件4第10条(a)款第1点提供支持。

(11) 按照附件5第5条(b)款提供支持。

(b) 若发起加入国降低或收回其为此类交易提供支持的意向，其应立即通知其他所有加入国。

## 第三节　与贸易相关援助的程序

### 49. 先期通知

(a) 加入国若意向为下述项目提供官方援助，则应按照附件7予以先期通知：

——与贸易相关的非约束性援助，其价值等于或超过 200 万特别提款权，且优惠水平低于 80%；

——与贸易相关的非约束性援助，其价值不足 200 万特别提款权，其中赠与成分（由开发援助委员会定义）低于 50%；

——与贸易相关的约束性援助，其价值等于或超过 200 万特别提款权，且优惠水平低于 80%；

——与贸易相关的约束性援助，其价值不足 200 万特别提款权，且优惠水平低于 50%；第 38 条（a）款和（b）款所述情况除外。

——按照第 39 条（d）款提供的约束性援助。

（b）先期通知应在投标截止日或承诺日（择两者中较早的日期）前至少 30 个工作日作出。

（c）若发起加入国降低或收回其对已通知期限及条件的支持，其应立即通知其他所有加入国。

（d）本条之规定适用于如第 35 条所述的构成相关融资方案一部分的约束性援助。

**50. 即时通知**

（a）若加入国为约束性援助提供的官方支持的价值为以下情况，则其应按照附件 7 要求，在作出承诺的 2 个工作日内通知其他所有加入国：

——价值等于或超过 200 万特别提款权，且优惠水平等于或超过 80%；或

——价值低于 200 万特别提款权，且优惠水平等于或超过

50%；第38条（a）款和（b）款所述情况除外。

（b）当签订援助协定、信贷额度和类似协议时，加入国应即时通知其他所有加入国。

（c）若加入国打算匹配应即时通知的融资期限和条款，则不必予以先期通知。

## 第四节　约束性援助的磋商程序

### 51. 磋商目的

（a）寻求澄清约束性援助的贸易动机的加入国，可要求提供全面的《援助质量评估》（详见附件8）。

（b）此外，加入国可按照第52条规定要求与其他加入国进行磋商，包括第57条所述的旨在讨论以下事项的当面磋商：

——首先，提供的援助是否符合第36条和第37条的要求；以及

——如有必要，提供的援助在不符合第36条和第37条的要求时是否正当。

### 52. 磋商的范围及时间

（a）磋商过程中，加入国可要求包括下列内容在内的各种信息：

——对详尽的可行性研究/项目测评的评估；

——是否存在非优惠或援助性融资的竞争性报价；

——项目产生或节约外汇的预期；

——是否存在同世界银行等多边机构的合作；

——如存在国际竞争性招标（ICB），特别是援助提供国的卖方是否为报价最低的投标人；

——对环境的影响；

——任何私营部门的参与；以及

——对优惠或援助性信贷进行通知的时间（例如在投标截止日或承诺日前6个月）。

（b）在投标截止日或承诺日（择两者中较早的日期）前至少10个工作日，应完成磋商程序并由秘书处把第51条全部问题的磋商结果通知给其他所有加入国。若磋商各方存在分歧，秘书处应在5个工作日内邀请其他加入国发表意见。秘书处应把这些意见通报给进行通知的加入国；若各国对提供援助没有表示实质性支持，该加入国则应重新考虑是否给予援助。

## 53. 磋商结果

（a）如在无法得到其他加入国实质性支持的情况下，援助提供国仍打算实施某一项目，则应在不晚于磋商结束后的60个公历日内就其意向通知其他加入国，接受主席国的结论。援助提供国同时应致函经合组织秘书长，简要说明磋商的结果并解释促使援助该项目是与贸易无关的重大国家利益。加入国期望此种情况是个别和偶然的。

（b）援助提供国应立即就其向经合组织秘书长致函一事通知其他加入国，并将函件副本附在通知后。该通知发出10个工作日后，援助提供国和其他加入国才可作出约束性援助承诺。对在磋商过程中讨论的援助项目出现竞争性商业报价的情况，前述的10个工作日应延长至15天。

（c）秘书处应监督该过程及磋商结果。

## 第五节 出口信贷和与贸易相关援助的信息交换

### 54. 交换站

所有的沟通都应在各国指定的交换站通过及时通讯的方式（即在线信息系统）保密进行。

### 55. 询问的范围

（a）加入国可询问另一加入国对第三国的看法、第三国的某项制度或开展业务的某种特定方法。

（b）收到要求官方支持申请的加入国，可向另一加入国提出询问，并向其通报自己愿意提供的最优惠的信贷条件。

（c）若一项询问涉及多个加入国，则该询问中应包含一张所涉加入国的名录。

（d）所有询问的副本都应提交秘书处。

### 56. 答复的范围

（a）被询问的加入国应在7个公历日内答复询问并提供尽可能多的信息。答复内容应包括加入国可能采取措施决定的最佳指示。如有必要，随后应尽快提供全面答复。答复副本应提交给其他被询问国及秘书处。

（b）若对某项询问的答复出于任何原因变为无效，例如因为：

——提出、变更或撤销申请；或

——正在考虑其他条款。

答复应尽快作出，并将副本抄送询问函上列出的所有其他加入国及秘书处。

## 57. 当面磋商

(a) 加入国应在10个工作日内同意当面磋商的要求。

(b) 进行当面磋商的要求应通知加入国和非加入国。在10天限期结束后，应尽快安排磋商。

(c) 加入国的主席国应和秘书处协调必要的后续行动，例如达成共同谅解。秘书处应迅速通报磋商结果。

## 58. 共同谅解的程序和格式

(a) 达成共同谅解的提议只能向秘书处提出。提议应散发给所有加入国；当涉及约束性援助时，提议应同时由秘书处散发到所有开发性援助委员会的交换站。在线信息系统布告栏的共同谅解登记处不予披露提议发起人的身份。但应加入国或开发性援助委员会成员国要求，秘书处可进行口头披露，并对此类要求进行登记。

(b) 共同谅解的提议应标明日期并遵循下列格式：

——编号，后面注明“共同谅解”；

——进口国和买方的名称；

——尽量精确的项目名称或描述，以便清楚地识别该项目；

——发起国预期的条款；

——共同谅解提议正文；

——已知竞标者的国籍和名称；

——商业和财务竞标截止日和已知的标书号码；

——其他相关信息，包括提议共同谅解的原因，可供查阅的项目研究和/或特殊情况材料。

（c）按照第36条（b）款第4点提出的共同谅解提议应提交给秘书处并抄送给其他加入国。提议国应提供原因以全面解释某国的分类为何应与第36条（b）款所述的程序不同。

（d）秘书处应予以公布达成的共同谅解。

### 59. 共同谅解提议的答复

（a）答复应在20个公历日内作出，但鼓励加入国尽快答复。

（b）答复可以是要求提供其他信息、接受提议、拒绝提议、建议修改共同谅解或提出另一份共同谅解提议。

（c）若加入国因没有与出口商接触，或在项目援助的情况下没有和接受当局接触而因此不表示立场的，则视该国接受提议。

### 60. 对共同谅解的接受

（a）20个公历日结束后，秘书处应就共同谅解提议的状态通知所有加入国。若在不是所有加入国都接受提议，但又没有加入国反对的情况下，则该提议将再延长公示8个公历日。

（b）延长期结束后，未明确反对该提议的加入国视为接受该提议。然而，任一加入国，包括发起国，都可对一个或多个加入国明确接受的共同谅解提议提出有条件的接受。

(c) 如果加入国不接受共同谅解中的一项或多项内容，即暗示其接受共同谅解中其他所有内容。这种部分接受可能导致其他加入国改变对共同谅解提议的态度。所有加入国均可自由提供或匹配共同谅解没有规定的条款。

(d) 未获接受的共同谅解可按照第 58 条和第 59 条规定的程序进行重新讨论。在此情况下，加入国不受其原先决定的约束。

## 61. 对共同谅解的异议

若发起加入国，以及建议修改或提出替代提议的加入国无法在延长的 8 个公历日内达成一致，则这一期限可在双方均同意的情况下继续延长。秘书处应把该延期通知所有加入国。

## 62. 共同谅解的生效日

秘书处应通知所有加入国共同谅解将生效或已被否决。共同谅解将在此项通告作出后 3 个公历日后生效。秘书处将在在线信息系统上，对所有已达成或未决的共同谅解予以记录并不断更新。

## 63. 共同谅解的有效期

(a) 达成后的共同谅解从其生效日起持续两年有效，除非秘书处得到该谅解已无价值且所有加入国同意该观点的通知。若某加入国在原到期日前 14 个公历日内寻求延长共同谅解的有效期，则有效期应再延长两年。后续的再延期可按照同样的程序予以确定。按照第 36 条 (b) 款第 4 点达成的共同谅解在世界银行公布次年数据前一直有效。

(b) 秘书处应通过维护在线信息系统上的“有效共同谅解状态”清单，监督共同谅解的状态并据此通知有关加入国。相应地，除完成其他事项以外，秘书处应：

——添加加入国已达成的新的共同谅解；

——当某加入国要求延期时，更新到期日；

——删除到期的共同谅解；

——每季度公布下一季度将到期的共同谅解。

## 第六节　最低利率（CIRRS）通告的操作规定

### 64. 最低利率的通告

（a）按照第 20 条确定的各币种的商业参考利率应以及时通告的方式，每月至少报送给秘书处一次，并由秘书处通知所有加入国。

（b）此通知应在每月结束后的 5 天内送达秘书处。秘书处应立即通知各加入国适用的利率并公开相关信息。

### 65. 利率适用的生效日

商业参考利率的任何变化应在每月结束后的第 15 天生效。

### 66. 利率的即时修改

当市场情况的变化要求在某个月内就商业参考利率的修改进行通知时，修改后的利率应在秘书处收悉该修改通知后的 10 天内予以执行。

## 第七节 审议

### 67. 《安排》的定期审议

（a）加入国应定期审查《安排》的执行情况。在审议中，除审议其他事项之外，加入国应检查通知程序，差别贴现率制度的执行和运行，约束性援助的规则和程序，匹配的问题，先期承诺及更广泛参与《安排》的可能性等问题。

（b）审议应基于加入国的有关经验以及他们对改善《安排》运作及有效性的建议。加入国应考虑到《安排》的目标和当前的经济与货币形势。加入国为审议提供的信息和建议应在不晚于审议日期前45天送达秘书处。

### 68. 最低利率的审议

（a）加入国应定期审议确定商业参考利率的制度以确保公布的利率反映当前的市场情况，并达到构建这种利率制度的目标。审议也应包括适用相关利率时的溢价。

（b）当加入国认为一种或多种货币的商业参考利率不再反映当前的市场情况时，可向加入国的主席国提交申请，要求进行特别审议。

### 69. 最低保费费率和相关事项的审议

加入国应定期监督和审议保费规则和程序的所有方面，包括：

（a）针对国别风险分类以及主权风险评估方法，根据相关经验审议其有效性；

（b）最低保费费率的水平，该水平综合考虑机构在提供官方出口信贷的实际经验和关于信用风险定价的私营市场信息，并确保它们保持一套精确的信用风险度量方法；

（c）最低保费费率的差异，包括提供的出口信贷产品的承保比例和特质的差别；及

（d）与国别风险降低技术和买方信用增进方法有关的经验，以及对最低保费费率特定影响的有效性和适当性。

# 附件 1

# 船舶出口信贷的行业谅解

# 第一章　行业谅解的范围

## 1. 加入国

本行业谅解的加入国为：澳大利亚、欧盟、日本、韩国、新西兰和挪威。

## 2. 适用范围

本行业谅解作为《安排》的补充，为与下列出口合同相关的官方支持出口信贷列出了专门的指导原则：

（a）任何吨位达到或超过100总吨的新造海船。该船须用于运载货物或旅客，或具有某项特殊用途（例如，渔船、渔场用船、破冰船、挖泥船等，通过其动力和操控能力，这些船类可以持续显示其在公海上的适航性），且拖力达到或超过365千瓦；若船体外壳尚未完工，则必须可漂浮和移动。本行业谅解不适用于军用船只。浮动码头和可移动离岸器具不包括在本行业谅解内，但是当相关出口信贷出现问题时，本行业谅解的加入国（以下简称加入国）在仔细考虑过任何加入国的实质性请求后，可以决定是否包括此类项目。

（b）船只的任何改造。船只改造是指任何吨位超过1000总吨的海船，对其载货计划图、船体或动力系统进行显著的改造。

（c）（1）虽然气垫船类的船只不包括在本行业谅解中，但允许加入国以本行业谅解中同等的条件为气垫船类船只提供出口信贷。加入国必须承诺合理使用该条件，在本行业谅解条件下没有竞争的基础上，不对气垫类船只提供该条件。

（2）在本行业谅解中，“气垫船”的定义如下：吨位至少达到100吨的水陆两用交通工具，并完全由自身的喷气推动，且喷气在该工具外围环绕的可活动外沿内形成高气压，下方则是地面或水面。而且，该工具可以由螺旋桨或鼓风机等类似设备产生的管喷气流推进和控制。

（3）各加入国理解，与本行业谅解中相同的出口信贷条件仅可提供给，用于海上航线和非陆路航线，即不包括停靠基地位于距水域1公里以内陆地的气垫船类船只。

## 第二章　出口信贷和约束性援助的规定

### 3. 最长还款期

无论进口国的国别分类，最长还款期一律为交付后12年。

### 4. 现金支付

加入国应要求在交付时以现金方式支付20%的合同金额。

### 5. 本金的偿还及利息的支付

（a）出口信贷的本金应以等额分期的方式偿还，通常为每6个月偿还一次，最长为每12个月偿还一次。

（b）利息的支付不少于每6个月一次，且第一笔利息的支付应不晚于信用起始日之后的6个月。

（c）为租赁交易提供的出口信贷，等额偿还本金和利息总额的做法可替代（a）款中等额偿还本金的做法。

（d）信用起始日后到期的利息不应资本化。

（e）按照《安排》附件7的规定，若加入国打算按照与（b）

款规定不同的方式支付利息，需在作出任何承诺前至少10个公历日予以先期通知。

### 6. 最低保费

《安排》中关于最低保费基准的规定在本行业谅解的加入国进一步审议前不予适用。

### 7. 项目融资

《安排》中第7条和附件6中的规定在本行业谅解的加入国进一步审议前不予适用。

### 8. 援助

任何拟提供援助的加入国，除《安排》相关规定外，还应确认：在还款期内该船舶在公开注册下不投入运营，可确定该船舶的最终所有人居住在援助接受国且不是某外国利益方的非运营性附属机构，同时保证未获得其政府批准不会出售该船舶。

## 第三章 程序

### 9. 通知

为保持透明性，除应按照《安排》和国际复兴开发银行/伯尔尼协会/经合组织“债权人报告系统”的相关规定外，加入国每年还应在其系统中提供下列信息：官方支持以及本行业谅解实施方式的规定（包括正在执行的方案）。

### 10. 审议

（a）本行业谅解应每年审议一次，或依据任何加入国的要求在经合组织船舶建造工作组框架内进行审议，审议报告须提交给

《安排》加入国。

(b) 为保证《安排》与本行业谅解的连贯、一致，并考虑到船舶制造行业的特点，本行业谅解和《安排》的加入国将进行适当的磋商和协调。

(c)《安排》的加入国一旦决定修改《安排》，本行业谅解的加入国将审阅此项决定并考虑其与本行业谅解的相关性。未确定的上述考虑的《安排》修改将不适用于本行业谅解。本行业谅解的加入国在可以接受《安排》修改的情况下，应将此情况书面通知所有《安排》加入国。本行业谅解的加入国在无法接受《安排》修改中关于船舶建造内容的情况下，应将其反对意见通知给《安排》的加入国，并与之进行磋商以寻求对相关问题的解决方案。在双方无法达成一致的情况下，本行业谅解的加入国将决定《安排》修改中船舶建造的内容是否适用。

附录

## 对未来工作的承诺

除了《安排》的未来工作之外，本行业谅解的加入国同意：

(a) 列出一份被普遍认为在商业上不可行的船舶种类说明性清单，并考虑《安排》中所述的约束性援助的规定。

(b) 审议《安排》中关于最低保费基准的规定，以整合到本行业谅解中。

(c) 根据相关国际谈判的进度，讨论将最低利率，包括特殊商业参考利率和浮动利率的其他准则涵盖到本行业谅解中。

(d) 审议《安排》中与项目融资相关的规定对本行业谅解的适用性。

（e）讨论以下两点用于本行业谅解第 5 条关于本金偿还及利息支付有关规定的可能性：

——第一笔本金的还款日期；

——加权平均还款期。

# 附件 2

# 核电站出口信贷的行业谅解

# 第一章 行业谅解的范围

## 1. 适用范围

（a）本行业谅解为适用于下列合同的官方支持出口信贷作出了规定：

（1）核电站整体或部分出口，包括建设和调试核电站直接必需的全部配件、设备、原料和服务（包括相关人员培训）。

（2）已建核电站的更新，需同时满足以下两个条件：更新的总价值达到或超过8000万特别提款权，以及核电站的经济使用年限很可能因此至少延长至还款期结束。若不能满足上述任一条件，则适用于《安排》的规定。

（3）核燃料的供应与浓缩。

（4）提供核废料的管理。

（b）本行业谅解不适用于：

（1）核电站所在范围之外的、通常由买方负责的事项，特别是与土地开发、修路、乡村建设、输电线、调试厂[①]和供水设备相关的费用，以及买方所在国因官方批准程序所产生的费用（例如：土地许可、施工许可、燃料装运许可等）。

（2）核电站所在范围之外的变电站、变压器和输电线。

---

① 调试厂与核电站的买方一致，且合同的签订与该核电站初始调试厂相关，则对于初始调试厂适用的条款不得比对核电站适用的条款更为宽松。

（3）为核电站停运而提供的官方支持出口信贷。

## 第二章　出口信贷和约束性援助的规定

### 2. 最长还款期

（a）本行业谅解第 1 条（a）款第（1）点和第（2）点包括的货物和服务的最长还款期一律为 18 年。

（b）首批燃料装卸的最长还款期为自抵运日起 4 年；对随后核燃料再装卸的最长还款期为自抵运日起 2 年。

（c）核废料处理的最长还款期为 2 年。

（d）浓缩活动与核废料管理的最长还款期为 5 年。

### 3. 本金的偿还和利息的支付

（a）加入国出口信贷本金的偿还和利息的支付应采取以下方式中的一种：

（1）等额分期偿还本金。

（2）等额分期偿还本金和利息总额。

（b）本金的偿还和利息的支付不应低于每 6 个月一次，且首次本金的偿还和利息的支付应不迟于信用起始日后的 6 个月。

（c）在特殊且有正当理由的情况下，本行业谅解中第 1 条（a）款第（1）点和第（2）点提到的货物和服务的官方出口信贷支持，可不执行上述（a）和（b）款的规定。如债务人的资金状况与还款表规定的每半年等额还款计划在时间上不一致，则可适用于其他还款条件，但应满足以下标准：

（1）最长还款期应为 15 年。

（2）6 个月内单笔或多笔本金偿还数额不得超过信贷本金总额的 25%。

（3）应至少每 12 个月偿还一次本金。第一次偿还时间应不迟于信用起始日后的 12 个月；在信用起始日之后的 12 个月内，本金的偿还金额不低于总额的 2%。

（4）应至少每 12 个月支付一次利息。第一次支付时间应不迟于信用起始日后的 6 个月。

（5）还款期的加权平均期限最长不得超过 9 年。

（d）信用起始日之后的到期利息不得资本化。

## 4. 商业参考利率的确定

根据本行业谅解提供的官方融资支持，其适用的商业参考利率可根据下表的基准利率和浮动利率进行计算：

| 还款期（年） | 新建核电站① | | 所有其他合同② | |
|---|---|---|---|---|
| | 基准利率（政府债券） | 溢价（基点） | 基准利率（政府债券） | 溢价（基点） |
| <11 年 | 《安排》第 20 条规定的相关商业参考利率 | | | |
| 11～12 年 | 7 年 | 100 | 7 年 | 100 |
| 13 年 | 8 年 | 120 | 7 年 | 120 |
| 14 年 | 9 年 | 120 | 8 年 | 120 |
| 15 年 | 9 年 | 120 | 8 年 | 120 |
| 16 年 | 10 年 | 125 | 9 年 | 120 |
| 17 年 | 10 年 | 130 | 9 年 | 120 |
| 18 年 | 10 年 | 130 | 10 年 | 120 |

① 第 1 条（a）款第（1）点所提到的。
② 第 1 条（a）款第（2）～（4）点所提到的。

### 5. 可用货币

适用于官方融资支持的可用货币为：能够完全自由兑换，并可获得根据本行业谅解第 4 条以及《安排》第 20 条（还款期小于 11 年）规定的、用以计算最低利率的相关商业参考利率数据。

### 6. 对核燃料及相关服务的官方支持

在不影响本行业谅解第 7 条规定的原则下，加入国不应免费提供核燃料或服务。

### 7. 援助

加入国不应提供援助支持。

## 第三章 程序

### 8. 先期通知

（a）若加入国打算按照本行业谅解的条款提供融资支持，则应根据《安排》第 48 条的规定，在作出任何承诺前至少 10 个公历日通知其他加入国。

（b）若通知国打算提供融资支持的还款期超过 15 年和/或符合上述第 3 条（c）款的规定，且若其他任何加入国在最初的 10 个公历日内要求对此进行讨论，该加入国应再等待 10 个公历日。

（c）加入国应将讨论后的最终决定告知其他所有加入国，以增加相关审议经验。

# 第四章　审议

## 9. 未来的工作

加入国同意审查下列事项：

（a）最低浮动利率的体系。

（b）对当地费用进行官方支持的最大金额。

## 10. 审议和监督

加入国应定期审议行业谅解中的条款，最晚应不迟于 2017 年底。

# 附件3

# 民用航空器出口信贷的行业谅解

## 第一部分　一般条款

### 1. 目的

（a）本行业谅解的目的是，针对出售和租赁航空器以及下述第4条（a）款列出的其他出口的货物和服务，提供一个可预测的、持续的、透明的官方支持出口信贷使用框架。本行业谅解将寻求为此类出口信贷提供公平竞争的平台，以鼓励出口商开展竞争的基础是所出口货物和服务的质量和价格，而不是所获得的最优惠的官方支持融资条件。

（b）本行业谅解规定了可提供的最优惠的官方支持出口信贷条件。

（c）本行业谅解的目的是在所有市场上建立平衡：

（1）使不同加入国之间的竞争性融资条件平等；

（2）在选择相互竞争的下述第4条（a）款列出的货物和服务时，中立化加入国之间的官方支持，以及

（3）避免本行业谅解加入国与其他任何融资来源之间的竞争扭曲。

（d）本行业谅解的加入国承认，本行业谅解中所包含的条款仅限于实现本行业谅解的目的，而不影响《安排》的其他规定的执行及完善。

### 2. 地位

本行业谅解是其加入国之间达成的一项“君子协定”，也是

《安排》的附件3。本行业谅解作为2007年7月生效的原行业谅解的延续，是《安排》的一个完整组成部分。

### 3. 加入国

目前，本行业谅解的加入国有：澳大利亚、巴西、加拿大、欧盟、日本、韩国、新西兰、挪威、瑞士和美国。任何非加入国都可根据附录1中列出的程序成为加入国。

### 4. 适用范围

(a) 本行业谅解适用于所有由政府或代表政府为还款期为2年或2年以上的出口提供的官方支持，这些出口包括：

(1) 新造民用航空器及其内置引擎，包括买方提供的设备。

(2) 二手的、改建的、翻新的民用航空器及其内置引擎，包括上述各种情况下买方提供的设备。

(3) 备用引擎。

(4) 民用航空器及其引擎的零部件。

(5) 与民用航空器及其引擎相关的维修和服务合同。

(6) 民用航空器的改造、大修和翻新。

(7) 引擎设备。

(b) 官方支持的具体形式可包括：

(1) 出口信贷担保或保险（纯保险）。

(2) 官方融资支持：

——直接信贷/融资和再融资，或

——利率支持。

（3）上述形式的任意组合。

（c）本行业谅解不适用于下列的官方支持：

（1）新造或已用的军用航空器及相关的如上述第4条（a）款列出的货物和服务的出口，包括用于军事目的的出口。

（2）新造或已用的飞行模拟器。

## 5. 非加入国可获得的信息

加入国应在互惠的基础上，与答复其他加入国的询问一样，答复与其在官方支持的融资条件上有竞争关系的非加入国的询问。

## 6. 援助支持

加入国不应提供援助支持，除非是出于人道主义目的，且须通过共同谅解程序。

## 7. 避免或最小化损失的措施

如果是在合同生效后（当出口信贷协议和附属文件皆已生效）采取的措施，且其意图仅在于避免或最小化可能导致拒付或索赔事件所造成的损失，《安排》并不禁止出口信贷机构或融资机构接受比《安排》规定更宽松的融资条款。加入国应在其与买方/借款人达成一致后的20个工作日内，将修改过的融资条款告知其他所有加入国及经合组织秘书处。该通知应采用附录4中列出的格式进行报告，内容应包括与新融资条款有关的所有信息和动机。

# 第二部分　新造航空器

## 第一章　范围

### 8. 新造航空器

（a）本行业谅解中的新造航空器是指：

（1）由制造商拥有的，尚未以运载乘客和/或货物为目的而交付或使用过的航空器，包括买方提供的设备以及内置引擎，以及

（2）备用引擎或根据下列第 20 条（a）款规定作为原始航空器订单一部分的其他备件，也被视为新造航空器。

（b）除上述（a）款规定外，加入国还可按照适用于新造航空器的条款为一些交易提供支持，这些交易须满足如下条件：加入国给予先期通知，由于官方支持的条款延迟生效导致临时融资安排已经到位，且该延迟不应长于 18 个月。在这种情况下，还款期和最终还款日应与航空器的出售或租赁从其最初交付之日就获得了官方支持的情况相同。

## 第二章　融资条款

出口信贷的条款包括本章列出的所有条款，且应被视做一个共同的整体。

### 9. 可用货币

官方融资支持可选择的货币有欧元、日元、英镑、美元，以

及其他可完全自由兑换的货币，且可获得在计算附录3列出的最低利率时针对这些货币的所需数据。

## 10. 预付款及官方支持的最大限度

（a）对于买方/借款人风险分类属于第1类的交易（按照附录2表1划分），加入国应：

（1）在信用起始日起算当日或之前要求支付最少为航空器净价格20%的预付款。

（2）所提供的官方支持不超过航空器净价格的80%。

（b）对于买方/借款人风险分类属于第2类～第8类的交易（按照附录2表1划分），加入国应：

（1）在信用起始日起算当日或之前要求支付最少为航空器净价格15%的预付款。

（2）所提供的官方支持不超过航空器净价格的85%。

（c）适用上述第8条（b）款的加入国，应根据从信用起始日起算的分期付款的本金数额来减少官方支持的最大额度，以保证提款时的余额与自交付之日起就提供官方支持出口信贷的金额相同。在这种情况下，加入国应在航空器交付之前收到官方支持的申请。

## 11. 最低保费费率

（a）提供官方支持的加入国，对于官方支持的信贷金额，应按不低于附录2列出的最低保费费率收取保费。

（b）在必要情况下，加入国可使用已达成一致的费率转换模型，在根据官方支持余额计算的、按年收取的风险溢价率和根据最初官方支持金额计算的、需一次性趸缴保费的费率之间进行转换。

## 12. 最长还款期

（a）所有新造航空器的最长还款期均为12年。

（b）在特殊情况下，若有先期通知，最长还款期可延长至15年。在这种情况下，应在根据附录2计算出的最低保费费率基础上加收35%的附加费。

（c）不得通过与商业贷款人以同等比例共享担保权益而为官方支持出口信贷延长最长还款期。

## 13. 本金的偿还及利息的支付

（a）加入国应按照下列（1）或（2）列明的方式进行本金的偿还和利息的支付。

（1）等额分期偿还本金和应付利息总额

——分期偿还不少于每3个月一次，且首次偿还应不迟于信用起始日后的3个月。

——或者，若加入国已先期通知，分期偿还可每6个月一次，且首次偿还应不迟于信用起始日后的6个月。在这种情况下，应在根据附录2计算出的最低保费费率基础上加收15%的附加费。

——在采用浮动利率的交易中，本金的摊还应涵盖整个还款期，且按不超过提款日前5个工作日的浮动利率或掉期利率来计算。

（2）等额分期偿还本金并递减偿还应付利息：

——分期偿还不少于每3个月一次，且首次偿还应不迟于信用起始日后的3个月。

——或者，若加入国已先期通知，分期偿还可每6个月一次，且首次偿还应不迟于信用起始日后的6个月。在这种情况下，应在根据附录2计算出的最低保费费率基础上加收15%的附加费。

（b）尽管上述（a）款有规定，在加入国先期通知的情况下，偿还的本金可以是在某一特定日期最终偿还的所有余额。在这种情况下，最终还款前的本金偿还将按照上述（a）款的规定进行，且摊还期间不应长于官方支持的货物或服务所允许的最长还款期。

（c）尽管上述（a）款有规定，本金的偿还可按照不比提供给债务人条件优惠的条款进行。

（d）信用起始日之后的到期利息不应资本化。

## 14. 最低利率

（a）加入国的提供官方融资支持应适用附录3规定的最低浮动利率或最低固定利率。

（b）对于净价格至少在3500万美元以上的喷气式飞行器，以商业参考利率（CIRR）为基准的官方融资支持只能在特殊情况下予以提供。如加入国拟提供此类支持，应在作出最终承诺前至少20个公历日通知其他所有加入国，并要明确借款人。

（c）利率不包括根据上述第11条列出的保费以及下列第16条列出的费用。

## 15. 利率支持

提供利率支持的加入国应遵循本行业谅解的融资条款，并要求作为其中一方涉及该利率支持交易的任何银行或任何其他金融机构，按照与本行业谅解融资条款所有方面相一致的条款参与交易。

## 16. 费用

（a）根据保费持有期的限制，以纯保险形式提供官方支持的加入国，应在保费持有期间按照未提取部分的官方支持总额收取保费持有费，具体如下：

（1）持有期的最初六个月：每年 0 个基点。

（2）持有期的第二个六个月：每年 12.5 个基点。

（3）持有期的第三个以及最后一个六个月：每年 25 个基点。

（b）以直接信贷/融资方式提供官方支持的加入国应收取如下费用：

（1）安排费：每次提款时，在应付金额的基础上收取 25 个基点的费用。

（2）承诺及保费持有费：在保费持有期内，对于应提取的官方支持出口信贷的未提取部分，每年收取 20 个基点的费用，该笔费用可后付。

（3）管理费：每年对于官方支持总额的余额收取 5 个基点的费用，该笔费用可后付。或者，加入国可选择依照上述第 11 条（b）款的规定，在每次提款时将基于应提款额度计算出来的费用作为预付费进行支付。

## 17. 共同融资

尽管上述第 14 条和第 16 条有规定，但在包括直接信贷和纯保险官方支持（其中纯保险占官方支持总金额的比例至少为35%）的共同融资中，提供直接信贷的加入国应适用与提供纯保险的金融机构相同的融资条款和费用，以保证纯保险提供方与直接贷款方的全部成本均等。在这种情况下，提供此类支持的加入国应以附录4中列出的报告形式，报告其所提供支持的融资条款及相应费用。

# 第三部分　二手航空器、备用引擎、零部件、维修和服务合同

## 第一章　范围

### 18. 二手航空器以及其他产品和服务

本部分的行业谅解适用于二手航空器、备用引擎、零部件、改造、大修、翻新，以及与新造或二手航空器及引擎设备相关的维修和服务合同。

## 第二章　融资条款

除最长还款期之外，其他所有融资条款都应根据本行业谅解第二部分中列出的条款执行。

### 19. 二手航空器的出售

（a）根据下列（b）款，二手航空器的最长还款期应根据航空器的机龄确定，具体方式如表1所示：

表 1

| 机龄（自最初制造之日算起）/年 | 资产抵押或主权交易的最长还款期/年 | 非资产抵押或非主权交易的最长还款期/年 |
|---|---|---|
| 1 | 10 | 8.5 |
| 2 | 9 | 7.5 |
| 3 | 8 | 6.5 |
| 4 | 7 | 6 |
| 5 ~ 8 | 6 | 5.5 |
| >8 | 5 | 5 |

（b）若交易符合附录 2 第 19 条的所有要求，且对于此后可能予以官方支持的改造不是按照下列第 21 条（a）款提供的，则改造航空器的最长还款期应根据自改造之日起的期限以及航空器的机龄确定，具体方式如表 2 所示：

表 2　　资产抵押改造航空器的最长还款期（年）

| 自改造之日起的期限/年 | 机龄（自最初制造之日算起） | | | | | |
|---|---|---|---|---|---|---|
| | 1 | 2 | 3 | 4 | 5 ~ 8 | >8 |
| 0（新改造） | 10 | 9 | 8 | 8 | 8 | 8 |
| 1 | 10 | 9 | 8 | 7 | 7 | 7 |
| 2 | — | 9 | 8 | 7 | 6 | 6 |
| ≥3 | — | — | 8 | 7 | 6 | 5 |

## 20. 备用引擎和零部件

（a）当购买或预订拟安装于新造航空器上的引擎时，为备用引擎提供的官方支持应与航空器适用同样的条件。

（b）当购买新航空器时，为零部件提供的官方支持可与为航空器提供官方支持条件一致，即不超过航空器及内置引擎净价格的 5%；下述（d）款则应适用于为零部件提供的官方支持超过

5%的部分。

（c）当备用引擎不是与航空器一同采购时，最长还款期应为8年。对于单价等于或大于1000万美元的备用引擎，且交易满足附录2第19条的规定，则还款期可为10年。

（d）当其他零部件不是与航空器一同采购时，最长还款期为：

（1）合同金额等于或大于500万美元的，为5年。

（2）合同金额低于500万美元的，为2年。

## 21. 改造/大修/翻新的合同

（a）如果改造交易符合以下条件：

（1）价值等于或大于500万美元，且

——符合附录2第19条的所有要求，加入国可提供还款期最长不超过8年的官方支持。

——不符合附录2第19条的所有要求，加入国可提供还款期最长不超过5年的官方支持。

（2）价值小于500万美元，加入国可提供还款期最长不超过2年的官方支持。

（b）如果属于大修或翻新的交易，加入国可提供官方支持的还款期不超过：

（1）5年，如果合同金额等于或大于500万美元；

（2）2年，如果合同金额小于500万美元。

### 22. 维修和服务合同

加入国可为此类合同提供还款期不超过 3 年的官方支持。

### 23. 引擎工具箱

加入国可为此类合同提供还款期不超过 5 年的官方支持。

# 第四部分　透明程序

所有的交流都应在每个加入国的指定联络点之间，通过即时通讯的方式进行，比如经合组织的在线信息系统（OLIS）。除非另有一致意见，对于本行业谅解项下的所有信息交换，所有加入国都应保密。

## 第一节　信息需求

### 24. 官方支持的信息

（a）最终承诺日后的一个月内，加入国应向其他所有加入国提交附录 4 所要求的信息，并抄送秘书处。

（b）为按附录 3 第 8 条（b）款建立溢价基准，附录 3 第 8 条（c）和（d）款列出的关于纯保险溢价的信息应在每月结束后的 5 天内提交秘书处。

## 第二节　信息交换

### 25. 信息请求

（a）加入国可询问另一加入国，关于对本行业谅解涵盖的航空器出售或租赁所提供的官方支持出口信贷的使用情况信息。

（b）收到官方支持申请的加入国可告知询问国其愿意提供支持的最优惠信贷条件。

（c）收到询问的加入国应在 7 个公历日内予以回复并告知其尽可能详细的互惠信息。回复应包含其最有可能提供的支持条件。如有必要，应尽快给出完整的回复。

（d）所有询问和回复的副本都应提供给秘书处。

## 26. 当面磋商

（a）在竞争环境下，加入国可要求与另一个或多个加入国开展当面磋商。

（b）任何加入国都应在 10 个工作日内同意该类请求。

（c）磋商应在 10 个工作日结束后尽快召开。

（d）加入国主席国应与秘书处共同协调任何可能的后续行动。秘书处应尽快向加入国公布磋商结果。

## 27. 特别磋商

（a）加入国（发起国）有合理的证据相信另一加入国（回应国）提供的融资条款比本行业谅解涵盖的官方支持更为宽松，则发起国应告知秘书处；秘书处应立即将该信息告知回应国。

（b）在收到秘书处告知的 5 个工作日内，回应国应澄清其提供官方支持的融资条款。

（c）在回应国澄清后，发起国可要求秘书处在 5 个工作日内组织与回应国的特别磋商，讨论相关问题。

（d）回应国应等待特别磋商的结果（该结果应在磋商当日决定）之后再继续开展交易。

## 第三节　共同谅解

### 28. 共同谅解的程序与格式

（a）共同谅解的提议只能向秘书处提出。在线信息系统（OLIS）不显示提议发起人的身份，但秘书处可向有需要的加入国口头披露发起者身份。秘书处应对此类要求进行登记。

（b）共同谅解的提议应注明日期，并遵循以下格式：

（1）编号，后面注明“共同谅解”。

（2）进口国和买方/借款人名称。

（3）尽量精确的交易名称或描述，以便清楚地识别该交易。

（4）拟提供最宽松支持条款的共同谅解申请。

（5）已知竞标者的国籍和名称。

（6）已知竞标截止日期及标书号码。

（7）其他相关信息，包括共同谅解提议的原因和对特殊情况的描述。

### 29. 对共同谅解提议的答复

（a）应在20个公历日内作出答复，但鼓励加入国尽快回应。

（b）答复可被接受、拒绝，或提出附加信息请求，或提出修改共同谅解提议，或发起另一个替代的共同谅解提议。

（c）保持沉默或表示其无立场的加入国将被视为接受共同谅解提议。

## 30. 对共同谅解的接受

（a）20个公历日后，秘书处将向所有加入国通报共同谅解提议的状态。如不是所有加入国都接受该提议，但又没有加入国表示反对，则该提议将再延长公示8个公历日。

（b）上述延长期结束后，没有明确表示反对该提议的加入国将被视为接受该提议。然而，任何一个加入国，包括发起国，都可对一个或多个加入国明确接受的共同谅解提议提出有条件的接受。

（c）如果一个加入国不接受共同谅解其中的一项或多项内容，即暗示其接受共同谅解中其他所有内容。

## 31. 对共同谅解的异议

（a）如果发起国和提出修改或替代意见的加入国不能在上述第30条规定中延长的8个公历日内就共同谅解达成一致，则这一期限可在双方均同意的情况下继续延长。秘书处应把该延期通知所有加入国。

（b）如果一项共同谅解提议没有被接受，则可考虑运用上述第28～30条规定的程序。在这种情况下，加入国不受其最初决定的限制。

## 32. 共同谅解的生效日

秘书处应通知所有加入国共同谅解将生效或已被否决；达成一致的共同谅解将在该通报的3个公历日后生效。

### 33. 共同谅解的有效期

（a）除非另有约定，一项共同谅解一旦达成，将自生效日起持续两年有效，除非秘书处得到该谅解已无价值且所有加入国同意该观点的通知。

（b）若某加入国在原到期日前14个公历日内寻求延长共同谅解的有效期，在其他加入国无异议的前提下，该共同谅解的有效期将延长两年；后续的再延期也可通过相同的程序予以确定。

（c）秘书处应通过维护在线信息系统上的“有效共同谅解状态”清单，监督共同谅解的状态并据此通知有关加入国。相应地，秘书处要按季度发布在下一季度将要到期的共同谅解清单。

（d）对于生产竞争性航空器的非加入国提出的申请，秘书处应使其能够使用有效的共同谅解。

## 第四节　匹配

### 34. 匹配

（a）考虑到加入国的国际义务，加入国可与非加入国提供的官方支持在融资条款上保持匹配。

（b）在与非加入国提供的官方支持条件不一致情况下的匹配问题：

（1）匹配国应尽可能地努力去核实这些条款。

（2）匹配国应在其作出任何承诺的至少10个公历日之前，向秘书处及所有加入国通报其所做努力的性质和结果，以及拟提供支持的条款。

（3）如果一个存在竞争关系的加入国在前述的10个公历日内请求发起一次讨论，匹配国应在针对该条款作出任何承诺之前，再等待10个公历日。

（c）如果匹配国修改或撤回其此前已告知拟提供支持的条款，匹配国应立即通知其他所有加入国。

# 第五部分　监督与审议

## 35. 监督

（a）秘书处应监督本行业谅解的执行情况，并按年向加入国进行通报。

（b）符合第39条（a）款的每一笔交易都应按照第24条（a）款以及附录4的规定进行报告。

（c）符合第39条（b）款的每一笔交易都应按照第24条（a）款以及附录4的规定进行报告。此外：

（1）报告国应指出该笔交易与过渡清单之间的关联。

（2）应每半年对过渡清单进行一次监督；秘书处应与每一个加入国进行会谈，以达到以下目的：

——监督过渡清单上已交付的公司订单数量。

——更新下一年过渡清单上交易交付的时间表。

——识别过渡清单上因任何原因尚未或不得交付给清单上所列买方的订单。任何一笔此类订单都应从过渡清单上删除，且不得以任何方式重新配送给其他任何买方。

## 36. 审议

加入国应根据如下（a）款及（b）款的原则，随时对本行业谅解的程序与条款进行审议：

（a）加入国应以如下方式审议本行业谅解：

（1）自本行业谅解生效后第四个公历年开始，对其进行定期审议，每次审议前秘书处应提前三个月给予先期通知。

（2）应审议磋商后某加入国的要求，且在秘书处已提前三个月予以通知的情况下，提出审议的加入国应就本次审议的理由、目标以及磋商摘要提供书面材料。

（3）最低保费费率和最低利率的更新方式在附录 2 和附录 3 中分别列出。

（4）第 16 条列出的费用也应作为审议的一部分。

（b）对于上述（a）款第 1 点的审议，应考虑到以下内容：

（1）对本行业谅解第 1 条列出的目的，成员国已达成的程度；以及加入国可能希望进一步讨论的其他任何事项。

（2）考虑到上述（b）款第 1 点的基本要素，对本行业谅解的任何修正都是合理的。

（c）鉴于审议过程的重要性，为确保本行业谅解的条款能够继续满足加入国的需要，依据下述第 40 条的规定，每一个加入国都有权退出本行业谅解。

### 37. 未来工作

应考虑以下情况：

（a）检查加入国在信用起始日之前提供官方支持的做法。

（b）适用于间接贷款的条款。

（c）第19条规定的针对出售前经过显著翻新的二手航空器的最长还款期限的延展。

（d）第21条规定的针对较大金额合同的最长还款期限的延展。

（e）适用于“翻新（第21条）”和“服务（第22条）”的条款。

（f）《开普敦公约》的资格程序。

（g）“有权益的加入国”的定义。

## 第六部分 最终条款

### 38. 生效

本行业谅解的生效日期是2011年2月1日。

### 39. 过渡安排

尽管前述第38条有规定，但加入国仍可在以下情况下提供官方支持：

（a）当以下条件满足时，加入国可根据2007年7月1日生效的航空器行业谅解（“2007ASU”）所规定的条款提供官方支持：

（1）货物和服务的商务合同签署日期应不迟于2010年12月31日。

（2）2007ASU规定的第1类航空器的货物和服务应在2012年12月31日前完成实物交付，第2类、第3类航空器的货物和服务应在2013年12月31日前完成实物交付。

（3）对于每一项已通告的最终承诺，每年应收取20个基点的承担费：对于2007ASU规定的第1类航空器，该费用从最终承诺日和2011年1月31日之间的较早者算起；对于2007ASU规定的第2类、第3类航空器，该费用从最终承诺日期和2011年6月30日之间的较早者算起，直到航空器已交付。该笔承担费应替代2007ASU第17条（a）款和（b）款第2点中规定的费用；并应在收取最低保费后，另行收取。

（b）当以下情况满足时，加入国可在本行业谅解生效日前提供官方支持：

（1）货物和服务的商务合同签署日期应不迟于2010年12月31日。

（2）此类官方支持仅限于每个加入国交付69架2007ASU规定的第1类航空器和92架2007ASU规定的第2类航空器。

（3）为从本款规定的条款中获益，前述（b）款第2点中提到的航空器应登记在清单上（以下简称过渡清单），该清单应由加入国在本行业谅解生效前通报给秘书处。过渡清单应包括：

——航空器型号和数量

——暂定交付日期

——买方身份

——适用的规则框架（不论是2007ASU以前运用的航空器行业谅解还是2007ASU）

（4）前述第（1）（2）（4）条的信息应与所有加入国共享，第（3）条有关的信息由且仅由秘书处和主席国管理。

（5）对于过渡清单上的每架航空器：

——如果官方支持遵循的是比2007ASU以前普遍采用的航空器谅解，则应从最终承诺日或2011年3月31日的较早者起，每年收取35个基点的承担费，直到交付航空器。另外，还要预收不低于3%的最低保费。

——如果官方支持遵循的是2007ASU，则应从最终承诺日或2011年6月30日的较早者起，每年收取20个基点的承担费，直到航空器交付。

——上述两款列出的承担费应替代2007ASU中第17条（a）款和（b）款第2点中列出的费用；并应在最低保费之外另行收取。

（6）加入国可根据在2007ASU以前普遍采用的航空器谅解条款，为2010年10月31日当日或此前的航空器交易提供官方支持的出口信贷；交易合同不应迟于2007年4月30日达成，且不迟于2007年6月30日通知秘书处。

（c）本条款的执行应按照第35条（b）款和（c）款予以监督。

## 40. 退出

加入国可通过即时沟通（如OLIS系统）书面通知秘书处退出

本行业谅解。退出将在秘书处收到通知后的六个月后生效。退出不会影响在退出生效日之前达成协议的独立交易。

## 附录1 航空器行业谅解的加入国

1. 加入国鼓励正在发展民用航空器生产能力的非加入国加入本行业谅解。在这种背景下，加入国将邀请非加入国就加入本行业谅解的条件进行对话。

2. 秘书处将确保向有兴趣加入本行业谅解的非加入国提供关于如何成为正式加入国条款的全部信息。

3. 随后，非加入国将受加入国邀请参加与本行业谅解相关的活动并以观察员的身份参加相关会议。此类邀请的最长期限为两年，并可再做一次为期两年的延期。在此期间，非加入国将受邀提供其本国出口信贷体系，尤其是与民用航空器出口相关的审议报告。

4. 上述期限结束时，非加入国应表明其是否希望成为本行业谅解的加入国并遵守相关规定。一旦确认，非加入国则应每年承担本行业谅解执行所产生的费用。

5. 在根据本附录第4条作出确认的30个工作日后，有兴趣的非加入国将被视为加入国。

## 附录2 最低保费费率

本附录规定了计算针对本行业谅解项下交易所提供的官方支持的费率厘定的程序。第一节规定了风险分类的步骤，第二节规定了对新造和二手航空器收取的最低保费费率，第三节规定了对备用引擎、零部件、改造/大修/翻新、维修和服务合同，以及引擎工具箱收取的最低保费费率。

## 第一节 风险分类程序

1. 加入国就买方/借款人的风险分类清单（以下简称清单）达成一致，该风险分类通过信用评级机构所使用的一般评级模型来反映买方/借款人的优先无担保信用评级情况。

2. 风险分类由加入国提名的专家针对本附录表 1 列出的风险种类作出。

3. 根据本附录第 15 条规定，该清单在交易的各个阶段都具有约束力（如发起及交付阶段）。

### I 风险分类清单的建立

4. 清单应在本行业谅解生效前建立并得到加入国的同意；清单由秘书处保管，且在保密的前提下对加入国开放。

5. 应请求，秘书处可在保密的前提下告知生产航空器的非加入国某买方/借款人的风险分类；在这种情况下，秘书处应将该请求通告所有加入国。非加入国可在任何时候向秘书处提出增加清单内容的申请；提出申请的非加入国将被视为有权益的加入国参加风险分类的讨论。

### II 风险分类清单的更新

6. 根据本附录第 15 条的规定，当加入国表示拟应用不同于清单上的风险分类，或要求不在清单[①②]上的买方/借款人的风险分类信息时，清单可进行临时更新。

7. 在使用替代或新的风险分类之前，任一加入国应向秘书处发出对风险分类清单进行更新的请求。秘书处将在 2 个工作日内发送该请求至所有加入国传阅，并隐去申请国的身份信息。

8. 有权益的加入国可在 10[③] 个工作日内同意或对清单修改提出异议；未在限定时间内作出回应的，将被视为同意该项请求。如在 10 个工作日到期时仍未提出任何异议，则清单中的修改请求将被视为通过。秘书处将相应地调整清单并在 5 个工作日内通过 OLIS 系统予以发布；修改后的清单将在发布之日起生效。

## Ⅲ　异议的解决

9. 当对所提议的风险分类存在异议时，有权益的加入国应在异议通知发出后的 10 个工作日内，在技术层面尽最大努力达成一致。加入国应使用所有有助于消除异议的方法，必要时秘书处可提供支持（例如电话会议、当面磋商）。如有权益的加入国在 10 个工作日内达成一致，则应将结果告知秘书处；秘书处将相应地更新清单并在接下来的 5 个工作日内通过 OLIS 系统予以发布。修改后的清单将在发布之日起生效。

10. 如技术层面未在 10 个工作日内就异议达成一致，加入国应在 5 个工作日内决定拟应用的适合的风险分类。

---

① 当所提议的买方/借款人风险评级超过东道国的主权风险评级时，应提供解释说明。

② 对于出口合同金额低于 500 万美元的交易，加入国不愿遵循本附录第 6 ~ 8 条规定的风险分类程序时，其买方/借款人应适用风险分类“8”，并根据本行业谅解第 24 条（a）款的规定通报该交易。

③ 对于出口合同金额低于 500 万美元的交易，期限为 5 个工作日。

11. 如最终未能达成一致，加入国可求助于信用评级机构来决定买方/借款人的风险分类。在这种情况下，加入国的主席国应在10个工作日内代表加入国与买方/借款人进行沟通。沟通内容包括加入国同意的用于风险评级咨询的参考条款。最终的风险分类将在清单中登记，并自秘书处通过OLIS系统发布时起具有约束力，以确保在5个工作日内完成分风险分类更新程序。

12. 除非另有约定，该类向信用评级机构求助所产生的费用应由有利益的买方/借款人承担。

13. 在本附录第9条~第11条列出的程序内，正在实行的风险分类（清单上所列明的）仍然适用。

## Ⅳ 分类的有效期

14. 有效的风险分类是指秘书处保管的、在清单上有登记的、正在实行的风险分类。有关保费费率的任何指示与承诺只能在此基础上作出。

15. 为助加入国就保费费率作出指示和最终承诺，自秘书处在清单上登记之日起，风险分类的有效期最长为12个月。在加入国作出承诺或最终承诺，且已收取了保费持有费时，某特定交易中的风险分类有效期可延展至18个月。在12个月的有效期内，当买方/借款人的风险状况发生实质变化（如信用评级机构作出评级调整）时，风险分类可作出相应调整。

16. 除非加入国有更新需求，秘书处应在相关风险分类到期前的至少20个工作日内，将其从拟更新的清单上移除。秘书处应在2个工作日内将更新需求发送加入国传阅，并隐去申请国的身份信息，且本附录第9条~第11条列明的程序在此适用。

### V　买方/借款人的风险分类请求

17. 如在发起初期，买方/借款人要求对其本身的风险分类进行指示，且其分类还不在清单上，则该买方/借款人应自费从信用评级机构处了解其分类情况。该风险分类不应列入清单，只作为加入国进行内部风险评估的基础。

## 第二节　新造和二手航空器的最低保费费率

### I　最低保费费率的建立

18. 本附录的第 19 条 ~ 第 58 条列出了买方/借款人（或与买方/借款人为不同实体的，但为交易还款主要来源的一方）风险分类相应的最低保费费率。

19. 当以下条件都满足时，加入国可以最低保费费率或高于最低保费费率的水平提供官方支持：

（a）交易有资产抵押且满足以下所有标准的：

（1）第一优先抵押权是以航空器或引擎为基础，或与之相关的。

（2）在租赁结构中，权益让渡和/或第一优先抵押权与租金支付相关的。

（3）在可适用的法律框架下，应尽可能地在由相同各方合法拥有且从中受益的所有航空器和引擎间提供交叉违约和交叉担保。

（b）交易结构中应至少安排如表 1 所示的风险缓释措施：

表1　风险缓释措施

| ASU 风险分类 | 风险评级 | 风险缓释措施 | |
|---|---|---|---|
| | | 总计 | 采取至少“A”类措施的个数 |
| 1 | AAA 至 BBB - | 0 | 0 |
| 2 | BB + 和 BB | 0 | 0 |
| 3 | BB - | 1 | 1 |
| 4 | B + | 2 | 1 |
| 5 | B | 2 | 1 |
| 6 | B - | 3 | 2 |
| 7 | CCC | 4 | 3 |
| 8 | CC 至 C | 4 | 3 |

20. 为达到本附录第19条的目的：

（a）加入国可从以下风险缓释措施中进行选择：

“A”类风险缓释措施：

（1）减少预付款比例：即根据本行业谅解第10条（a）及（b）款所列，若对预付款比例的要求减少5个百分点（因此对应买方风险评级调增）等于一项“A”类风险缓释措施。在这种情况下，加入国以任何形式提供的官方支持不得超过扣减预付款之后的金额。

（2）直线摊销：等额分期偿还本金等于一项风险缓释措施。

（3）减少还款期限：还款期不超过10年等于一项风险缓释措施。

“B”类风险缓释措施：

（1）保证金：每笔数额等同于一季度本息还款总额的保证金

等于一项风险缓释措施。保证金的形式可以是现金或备用信用证。

（2）租金预付：租金应在每个还款日前一个季度内交付，且租金数额等同于一季度本息还款的总额。

（3）还款储备在形式和数额上反映了市场的最佳实践。

（b）在先期通知的情况下，对可适用的最低保费费率加收15%的附加费可代替上述一项“A”类风险缓释措施。

21. 根据本行业谅解第11条规定，适用的最低保费费率由最低风险基准率（RBR）组成，同时应根据下述第22条~第34条，加收反映市场情况的附加费（MRS）。

22. 本行业谅解生效的RBR是指：

**表2　　风险基准率**

| ASU风险分类 | 溢价（基点） | 预付比例（%） |
|---|---|---|
| 1 | 89 | 4.98 |
| 2 | 98 | 5.49 |
| 3 | 116 | 6.52 |
| 4 | 133 | 7.49 |
| 5 | 151 | 8.53 |
| 6 | 168 | 9.51 |
| 7 | 185 | 10.50 |
| 8 | 194 | 11.03 |

23. RBR应在“穆迪年度既定违约损失率”（LGD）4年动态平均值的基础上每年进行重置。重置所使用的适当LGD是基于第一留置权的高级抵押银行贷款，并应依表3进行计算：

**表3**

| LGD 映射 | |
|---|---|
| 4 年动态平均 | 参考 LGD |
| ≥45% | 25% |
| ≥35%且<45% | 23% |
| ≥30%且<35% | 21% |
| <30% | 19% |

24. RBR 调整因子由以下决定：

参考 LGD/19% = RBR 调整因子

25. 上述表2列明的 RBR 乘以 RBR 调整因子，以决定重置的 RBR。

26. 第一次重置程序应在2012年第一季度开展，重置后的 RBR 将在2012年4月15日生效。

27. 后续重置得出的 RBR 结果将在次年4月15日生效。一旦每年重置的 RBR 被确定，秘书处应立即将适用的费率通知所有加入国并使其可公开获取。

28. 对于每一类风险分类，MRS 应根据以下公式计算：

$$MRS = B \times [(0.5 \times MCS) - RBR]$$

其中：

——B 是下述表4中列明的每一类风险分类对应的融合系数，其变化范围是0.35~0.7。

——MCS 是指“穆迪信用溢价中间值”（MCS）的90天动态平均值，其平均寿命为7年。

29. 当风险分类包含多于一种风险评级时，溢价应取平均值。在风险分类属于第 1 类风险时，应使用 BBB - 的评级。

30. MSC 溢价在计算资产抵押时应扣减 50%。MSC 扣减的溢价应根据表 4 列明的 35% ~70% 的融合因子进行调整，其适用于 MCS 扣减溢价和 RBR 之间的差异。若融合后的溢价为负值，则不应做扣减。

表 4　　融合因子

| 风险评级 | ASU 风险分类 | 融合因子（%） |
| --- | --- | --- |
| AAA | 1 | 70 |
| AA | 1 | 70 |
| A | 1 | 70 |
| BBB + | 1 | 70 |
| BBB | 1 | 70 |
| BBB - | 1 | 70 |
| BB + | 2 | 65 |
| BB | 2 | 65 |
| BB - | 3 | 50 |
| B + | 4 | 45 |
| B | 5 | 40 |
| B - | 6 | 35 |
| CCC | 7 | 35 |
| CC | 8 | 35 |
| C | 8 | 35 |

31. MRS 应按季度进行如下更新：

——第一次更新应在 2011 年第一季度，MCS 结果应在 2011 年 4 月 15 日生效；但是，截至 2012 年 4 月 15 日，属于第 1 类风险分类所适用的 MRS 更新结果只有在 MRS 出现增加的情况下才能生效。

——后续的更新应在2011年的第二、第三、第四季度进行，MCS结果应相应在2011年7月15日、2011年10月15日、2012年1月15日生效。

——后续每一次更新，秘书处应立即通知加入国适用的MRS和最低费率，同时保证这些数据在生效前即可被公开获取。

32. 仅MRS为正值且超过25个基点时方可适用。

33. 由MRS更新引起的最低保费费率增加不能超过前一季度最低保费费率的10%。最低保费费率（由考虑增加的RBR和MRS后得出）不能超过RBR的100%。

34-1. 最低保费费率的决定：

——使用下列公式：

净MPR = MPR ×（1 + RTAS）×（1 + RFAS）×（1 + RMRS）×（1 - CTCD）×（1 + NABS）- CICD

其中：

- RTAS代表本行业谅解第12条（b）款列出的还款期限调整附加费。

- RFAS代表本行业谅解第13条（a）款第1点和第2点列出的还款频率调整附加费。

- RMRS代表本附录第20条（b）款列出的风险缓释措施替代附加费。

- CTCD代表本附录第36条列出的《开普敦公约》扣减

比例。

• NABS代表本附录2第55条（a）款第4点、第55条（b）款、第57条（b）款列出的、可适用的无资产抵押附加费。

• CICD代表本附录第54条（a）款列出的有条件保险承保扣减比例。

——保费可预付也可在整个贷款期间支付，以每年用基点表示的溢价，或任何预付费率与溢价相结合的形式为准。预付费率和溢价应使用费率转换模型（PCM）计算，以使某项既定交易的应付保费不论是预付费，还是溢价，抑或是两者的结合，都有相同的保费净现值（NPV）。对于在承保前条款就达成一致或已经确定的交易，且加权平均期限是有扣减的，则可以预付费率（以PCM计算）收取保费，且应收保费与溢价的应付净现值相符。

34-2. 表5列出了自本行业谅解最初生效日（2011年2月1日）起适用的最低保费费率：

**表5　最低保费费率**

**（还款期为12年且有资产抵押的交易）**

| 风险种类 | 风险分类 | 最低保费费率 | |
|---|---|---|---|
| | | 年溢价（基点） | 预付比例（%） |
| 1 | AAA至BBB- | 137 | 7.72 |
| 2 | BB+及BB | 184 | 10.44 |
| 3 | BB- | 194 | 11.03 |
| 4 | B+ | 208 | 11.85 |
| 5 | B | 234 | 13.38 |
| 6 | B- | 236 | 13.50 |
| 7 | CCC | 252 | 14.45 |
| 8 | CC至C | 257 | 14.74 |

## Ⅱ. 最低费率调减

35. 根据本附录第36条规定，如满足下列条件，基于上述I部分建立的最低保费费率可予以下调：

（a）资产抵押型交易与《开普敦公约》中关于航空器设备若干事项指定的航空器相关，

（b）在项目提款时，航空器运营方（从提供官方支持的加入国角度看，或者是借款人/买方或出租人，且交易结构中提供担保）所在国家列于符合降低最低费率资格的国家名单中（以下简称开普敦名单）之上，且位于符合本附录第38条资格的国家领土单位内，以及

（c）交易与根据《开普敦公约》和《航空器议定书》已在国际登记处注册的航空器相关。

36. 在上述I部分建立的最低保费费率的下调幅度不能超过可适用最低保费费率的10%。

37. 列入开普敦名单的国家需满足下列条件：

（a）是《开普敦公约》的缔约国；

（b）已作出本附录的附件I中列出的资格声明；以及

（c）已执行《开普敦公约》，包括已按照要求在其法规中作出资格声明，确保将以适当方式对《开普敦公约》的承诺体现在国家法律中。

38. 为满足本附录第35条的规定，领土单位应指：

（a）属于《开普敦公约》延展范围内的领土单位；

（b）本附录的附件 I 中列明的资格声明相关的领土单位；以及

（c）已执行《开普敦公约》，包括已按照要求在其法规中作出资格声明，确保将以适当方式对《开普敦公约》的承诺体现在国家法律中。

39. 在本行业谅解生效前，加入国需向秘书处提交最初达成一致的开普敦名单。该名单应根据本附录第 40 条 ~ 第 52 条进行更新。

40. 任何为航空器提供官方支持的加入国或非加入国都可向秘书处提出向开普敦名单中增加国家的建议。涉及这些被建议国家的信息应包括：

（a）涉及该国交存《开普敦公约》批准书的日期或批准书留存方提供的加入证明等所有相关信息；

（b）被建议增加列入开普敦名单中的国家所做声明的副本；

（c）涉及《开普敦公约》和资格声明生效日期的所有相关信息；

（d）就被建议增列入开普敦名单的国家在执行《开普敦公约》中（包括在其法规中的资格声明）所采取步骤的分析，以确保将《开普敦公约》的承诺适当地体现在其本国法律中；以及

（e）依据本附录的附件 II 的格式填写的调查问卷（即“开普敦公约问卷”或 CTC 问卷），且需经至少一家有资格的律师事务所就被建议增列入开普敦名单中的国家的相关司法权限提供法律意见。完备的 CTC 问卷应明确：

（1）相关律所的名称和办公地址；

（2）律所的相关经验，包括在立法和宪法领域、与执行国际条约有关的从业经验，以及任何向政府部门或私营部门就执行和履行《开普敦公约》提供法律意见，或被建议增列入开普敦名单中的国家履行债权人权利的特别经验；

（3）如被建议国家增列入开普敦名单①，该律所是否参与或有意参与因降低最低保费费率而可能获利的交易；

（4）CTC 问卷完成填写的日期。

41. 秘书处应在 5 个工作日内通过 OLIS 系统对包含该建议的信息进行传阅。

42. 任何为航空器提供官方支持的加入国或非加入国如认为某国所采取的行为与《开普敦公约》不符，或没有采取公约要求的措施，可向秘书处提出建议从开普敦名单中移除该国。为实现该目的，该加入国或非加入国应提交从开普敦名单中移除某国的正式建议，充分描述建议移除某国的背景原因，比如该国所采取的与《开普敦公约》承诺不符的行为，或未能维持或执行《开普敦公约》所要求的法规。提出移除某国建议的加入国或非加入国应提交所有可获得的支持性文件，秘书处将在 5 个工作日内通过 OLIS 系统将包含该建议的信息进行传阅。

43. 任何为航空器提供官方支持的加入国或非加入国均可建议让此前被移除的国家重回开普敦名单，前提是该国此后采取了改正措施或事项。同时，还应一并提交描述该国被移除出名单的背景情况以及为支持重回名单而采取的后续改正措施的建议报告。秘书处将在 5 个工作日内通过 OLIS 系统将包含该建议的信息进行传阅。

---

① 还应包括与任何参与活动相关的信息（但尊重保密义务）。

44. 加入国可根据本附录第 40 条 ~ 第 43 条，在建议提交后 20 个工作日内（第 1 阶段），对该建议提出同意或反对意见。

45. 如第 1 阶段期满，无加入国对此提出异议，则视为该建议被全体加入国接受。秘书处将据此修改开普敦名单，并在 5 个工作日内通过 OLIS 系统予以公布。修改后的开普敦名单在公布当日生效。

46. 如加入国对该建议提出异议，提出异议的加入国则应在第 1 阶段内就其立场提交书面解释。待经合组织秘书处将书面解释发送给所有加入国后，加入国应在 10 个工作日内（第 2 阶段）竭力达成一致。

47. 加入国将告知秘书处讨论结果。如各方在第 2 阶段内达成一致，秘书处将视需要相应修改开普敦名单，并在之后 5 个工作日内通过 OLIS 系统予以公布。修改后的开普敦名单在公布当日生效。

48. 如各方在第 2 阶段内未能达成一致，本行业谅解加入国的主席国（以下简称主席国）将在第 2 阶段结束后 20 个工作日内（第 3 阶段）竭力促成各方达成共识。如第 3 阶段满后仍未达成共识，将通过下述程序形成最终决定：

（a）主席国将就提议更新的开普敦名单作出书面推荐。该推荐应反映至少是为航空器出口提供官方支持的加入国公开表达观点中的多数意见。如无法形成多数意见，主席国将只基于加入国已经表达的观点作出推荐，并以书面形式列出推荐的基础，包括在无资格情况下，未能满足的资格条件。

（b）主席国在推荐中不能透露任何加入国在本附录第 40 条 ~ 第 49 条所列明程序中表达的观点或立场，以及

（c）加入国应接受主席国所提出的推荐。

49. 在依据第40条提交建议后，如加入国或主席国判定一国不具备增列入开普敦名单的资格，提出建议的加入国或非加入国可再次提交建议，要求其他加入国重新考虑该国资格。提出建议的加入国或非加入国应就此前作出不具备资格判定的依据作出解释。提出建议的加入国或非加入国也应获得并提供一份更新版的CTC问卷。新建议应符合第44～50条所列出的程序。

50. 如需根据本附录第48条规定的程序对名单中的合格国家作出任何调整，秘书处将在调整后的5个工作日内通过OLIS系统发布更新后开普敦名单的信息。修改后的开普敦名单在公布当日生效。

51. 航空器交易提款开始后发生的涉及开普敦名单中国家的增加、减少或重新增加，不应影响该交易所确定的最低保费费率。

52. 在本附录第40条～第50条规定的程序下，加入国不应透露任何关于已表达观点或立场的信息。

53. 加入国应对本附录第40条～第52条规定的执行进行监督，并在2012年上半年进行一次审议，此后将逐年或在任一加入国提出要求时进行审议。

54. 对于适用的最低保费费率可做如下调整：

（a）对于以有条件保险形式给予官方支持的交易，对适用的最低保费费率可给予5个基点（按年溢价）或0.29%（预付）的折价。

（b）最低保费费率应适用于承保的本金。

## Ⅲ. 无资产抵押交易

55. 除本附录第19条（a）款的规定，加入国还可为无资产抵押的交易提供官方支持的出口信贷，但需满足下述条件：

（a）针对非主权交易：

（1）接受官方支持的最高出口合同价值不超过1500万美元，

（2）最长还款期应为10年，

（3）接受融资支持的资产中不涉及第三方担保利益，以及

（4）应在根据上述Ⅰ部分确定的最低保费费率基础上，加收最低30%的附加费。

（b）针对主权交易，或有不可撤消和无条件主权担保支持的交易，应在根据上述Ⅰ部分确定的最低保费费率基础上，依据表6加收最低附加费。

**表6**

| 风险种类 | 附加费率（%） |
|---|---|
| 1 | 0 |
| 2 | 0 |
| 3 | 0 |
| 4 | 10 |
| 5 | 15 |
| 6 | 15 |
| 7 | 25 |
| 8 | 25 |

56. 本附录第35～51条不适用于依据本附录第55条提供的官

方支持出口信贷。

## 第三节 本行业谅解第三部分所涉二手航空器以外其他货物和服务的最低保费费率

57. 为本行业谅解第三部分所涉二手航空器以外其他货物和服务交易提供官方支持时，适用的最低保费费率如下：

（a）对于有资产抵押的交易，最低保费费率应等于根据上述I部分确定的可适用的最低溢价，且若是纯保险，应使用转换模型和适当的期限转为预付费。

（b）对于非资产抵押的交易，最低保费费率应在根据上述I部分确定的可适用的最低溢价基础上加收30%的附加费，且若是纯保险，应使用转换模型和适当的期限转为预付费。

58. 本附录第35条~第54条应适用于为本行业谅解第三部分所涉二手航空器以外的其他货物和服务交易提供的官方支持。

### 附件I：资格声明

1. 就附录2第2节而言，“资格声明”及本行业谅解中所涉及的其他声明，均指《开普敦公约》中的缔约方：

（a）已对本附件第2条作出的声明，以及

（b）未对本附件第3条作出的声明。

2. 本附件第1条（a）款所指的声明为：

（a）无力偿付：当事国声明对各类无力偿付程序将适用《航空器议定书》第11条的方案A，且根据第11条第3款方案的等待期应不超过60个公历日。

（b）注销：当事国声明将适用《航空器议定书》第13条。

（c）法律选择：当事国声明将适用《航空器议定书》第8条。

以及至少做到以下两项之一（鼓励都适用）：

（d）实施救济的方法：当事国根据《公约》第54条第2款声明，依据任何《公约》中未作出需向法院申请规定的条款，该国可在未经法院允许的情况下对债权人提供任何救济（此处，推荐在“法院允许”前加入“不需采取法律行动”的措辞，但对此措辞不做硬性要求）。

（e）及时救济：当事国声明将适用《航空器议定书》第10条项下全部规定（鼓励适用其中第5项子条款，但不做硬性要求），且为达到《航空器议定书》第10条第2款的时限要求，对完成救济的工作日亦作出了具体规定如下：

（1）《公约》第13条第1款中（a）（b）和（c）点中所指的救济（包括航空器标的物及其价值的保全；航空器标的物的占有、控制或监管；以及航空器标的物的冻结），不超过10个公历日；

（2）《公约》第13条第1款中（d）和（e）中所指的救济（包括航空器标的物的租赁或管理；航空器设备让渡后销售或使用所取得的收入），不超过30个公历日。

3. 本附件第1条（b）款所指的声明如下：

（a）减免的最终裁决：当事国不可脱离《公约》第13条或第43条单依据《公约》第55条作出声明；前提是，若当事国依据本附件第2条（d）款作出声明，根据《公约》第55条作出的声明不影响《开普敦公约》相关规定的执行。

(b)《罗马公约》：当事国不可脱离《航空器议定书》第24条单依据《航空器议定书》第32条作出声明。

(c) 租赁救济：当事国不应根据《公约》第54条第(1)款就不允许将租赁作为救济的方式作出声明。

4. 根据《航空器议定书》第11条，对于欧盟的成员国，如果修改本国法律以反映《航空器议定书》第11条方案A的条款(最长等待期为60个公历日)，成员国应被视为作出了本附件中第2条(a)款要求的资格声明。如果欧盟或相关成员国法律与本附件所列条款实质相近，则应被视为作出了满足本附件第2条(c)款和(e)款要求的资格声明。根据本附件第2条(c)款，欧盟的法律(欧盟委员会关于合同权责适用法第593/2008的规定)应与《航空器议定书》第8条实质相似。

## 附件Ⅱ：《开普敦公约》调查问卷

### Ⅰ. 基本信息

请提供以下信息：

1. 完成本问卷的律师事务所的名称及详细地址。

2. 律所的相关经验，包括在立法和宪法领域、与执行国际条约有关的从业经验，以及任何向政府部门或私营部门就执行和履行《开普敦公约》提供法律意见，或被建议增列入开普敦名单中的国家履行债权人权利的特别经验。

3. 如被建议国家增列入开普敦名单，该律所是否参与或有意参与因降低最低保费费率而可能获利的交易①。

4. 本问卷完成填写的日期。

II. 问题

1. 资格声明

1.1 当事国②是否都依据《民用航空器出口信贷行业谅解》(ASU) 的附录2中附件1的要求作出了资格声明（每一次都作出了吗)？特别是，对于第2条（d）款“实施救济的方法”以及第2条（e）款的“及时救济”，请详述一项或全部已作出的声明。

1.2 请描述已作声明与问题1.1所提出的要求有何区别。

1.3 请确认当事国未作出ASU附件1第3条至附录2所列出的任何声明。

2. 批准

1.1 当事国是否已经批准、接受、允许或加入《开普敦公约》及《航空器议定书》(“《公约》”)？请陈述批准或加入的日期并简述当事国批准或加入《公约》的过程。

1.2《公约》和资格声明是否在当事国全部领土范围内不需进一步的实施立法或通过法规，而直接具有法律效力？

1.3 如果是，请简述《公约》与《资格声明》产生法律效力

---

① 还应包括与任何参与活动相关的信息（在尊重保密义务的前提下)。

② 本问卷中的“当事国”是指被提议加入《民用航空器出口信贷行业谅解》附录2第2节中开普敦名单的国家。因此，问卷中问题的作答应适用航空器运营方（或附录2第35条（b）款中列出的相关实体）所在国特定“领土单位”内的法律，且此处“国家法”应理解为相关的当地法律。

的程序。

3. 国家和地方法律的效用

1.1 如果适用，请描述和列出当事国就《公约》与每份资格声明制定的实施法律及规章。

1.2《公约》与资格声明转变成国家法[①]后是否有悖或优先于该国任何与之冲突的法律、规章、命令、司法判例或规章操作？如果是，请详述[②]；如果不是，请提供详情。

1.3《公约》与资格声明在实际执行中是否存在任何偏差？如果存在，请描述[③]。

4. 法院及行政决定

1.1 请详述任何可能导致法院、当局以及行政机构未能全力执行《公约》与资格声明或使其失效的事件，包括司法的、监管的或行政的行为。[④⑤]

---

① 本问卷中的“国家法”是指当事国所有的国内立法，包括但不限于宪法及其修正案，任何联邦的、州的以及地区的法律或规章。

② 例如，(i) 当事国X的宪法或其他相似的法律框架服从于公约，或 (ii) 当事国X需要进行立法，该法律被明确规定要服从于《开普敦公约》和/或替代其他法律；(iii)《开普敦公约》及其实施立法 (a) 比其他法律更具体（特别法替代普通法），和/或 (b) 比其他法律更晚实行（后法优先于前法），结果形成 (a) 和/或 (b) 的情况比其他法律效力更高。

③ 例如，是否存在某些原因，使得《公约》中赋予债权人的权利与救济，包括《资格声明》规定的，(a) 被视作无效，或 (b) 本身不成立而导致无法在当事国被有效实施？

④ 例如，本问题中的行政措施可指当事国无法执行或使用让《公约》与资格声明生效的程序或资源。或者当事国无法在其登记国采取合适的程序记录不可撤销的注销登记和出口请求许可书。

⑤ 请在分析中阐述与债权人（包括官方出口信用机构）权利相关的案例或决定。

1.2 据所了解的情况，是否有任何债权人根据《公约》采取了任何法律的或行政的强制行动？如果有，请详述并阐明其是否成功。

1.3 据所了解的情况，自批准/实施以来，是否有当事国法院违反《公约》或资格声明拒绝执行债务人或担保人的偿贷义务？

1.4 据所了解的情况，是否存在一些其他的情况，使法院及行政机构依照《公约》与资格声明采取行动时受到了影响？如果是，请详述。

## 附录3　最低利率

根据附录2 中的规定，官方融资支持不应全部或部分抵消或补偿对还款违约风险所收取的适当的保费费率。

### 1. 最低浮动利率

(a) 最低浮动利率应为，由英国银行家协会（BBA）发布的，与官方支持出口信贷利息支付频率相符的货币和到期日的欧洲银行间同业拆借利率（EURIBOR）、银行券参考利率（BBSY）以及伦敦银行间同业拆借利率（LIBOR），或是参考加拿大同业拆息利率（CDOR）加上根据本附录第8 条计算出的基准利差的值。

(b) 浮动利率的建立机制应根据如下还款方式进行相应变化：

(1) 在等额分期偿还本金和支付利息的情况下，应根据相关的货币情况和付款频率，将贷款提款日前两个工作日相关有效的EURIBOR/BBSY/LIBOR/CDOR 视为固定利率，用于计算整个还款计划。本金和第一笔利息的支付计划应固定不变。第二笔利息及此后利息的支付应根据最初设立的尚未偿还的本金余额，以上一支付日前两个工作日相关有效的 EURIBOR/BBSY/LIBOR/CDOR

进行计算。

（2）在等额分期偿还本金的情况下，应根据相关的货币情况和付款频率，以贷款提款日前两个工作日内相关有效的EURIBOR/BBSY/LIBOR/CDOR来计算尚未偿还本金余额的剩余利息。

（c）在对浮动利率贷款提供官方融资支持的情况下，若满足以下条件，买方/借款人可选择将浮动利率转换为固定利率：

（1）只能转换成掉期利率；

（2）只有在被提出要求的情况下才能进行一次转换，且应根据本谅解第24条规定以最初提交秘书处的报告格式进行报告。

## 2. 最低固定利率

最低固定利率应为以下之一：

（a）与官方支持出口信贷相关货币的掉期利率，其在到期时应等于可获取的贷款加权平均期限前后最相近两年的利率。利率应在每个提款日前两个工作日设定。或，

（b）根据本附录第3条~第7条规定建立的商业参考利率（CIRR）。

选择以上任何一种利率，都应附加依照本附录第8条（f）款的规定计算得出的溢价基准。

## 3. 商业参考利率的确定

（a）商业参考利率应针对本行业谅解第9条规定的每一种可用货币进行设定，并根据在以下三种基准利率收益率之一的基础上固定上浮120个基点来计算：

（1）还款期为9年及以下的5年期政府债券收益率，

（2）还款期为9年以上12年（含）以下的7年期政府债券收益率，或

（3）还款期为12年以上15年（含）以下的9年期政府债券收益率。

（b）商业参考利率应在每月根据前一个月的数据进行计算，并在每月结束后5日内通知秘书处。秘书处应随即通知加入国适用的利率并公布相关信息。商业参考利率应于每月的第15日开始生效。

（c）加入国或非加入国可要求针对某非加入国的货币来确定商业参考利率。在与该非加入国协商中，根据本行业谅解第28条~第33条列出的共同谅解程序，加入国或秘书处可代表该非加入国提出建立适用该国货币的商业参考利率的建议。

## 4. 商业参考利率的有效期

（a）商业参考利率的适用期：应用于某笔交易的商业参考利率有效期，自其确定之日（出口合同签署日期或据此开始的适用日期）起到签署信贷协议之日不应超过6个月。若此时限内未签署信贷协议，且商业参考利率针对另外6个月进行了重设，则新商业参考利率应为重设之日的利率。

（b）信贷协议签署后，商业参考利率应适用于期限不超过6个月的提款期。在首次为期6个月的提款期结束后，应重新设定下一个6个月的商业参考利率；新商业参考利率应为下一个6个月中第一天的利率且不得低于最初设定的商业参考利率（之后每6个月的提款期均重复此程序）。

## 5. 最低利率的应用

根据信贷协议条款，借款人不允许选择将官方支持的浮动利率融资转换为预先选择的商业参考利率融资，也不允许在预先选择的商业参考利率和整个贷款期限内任一利息支付日的短期市场利率之间进行转换。

## 6. 固定利率贷款的提前还款

依照本附录第2条中规定，对固定利率贷款的全部或部分自愿提前偿还，或当贷款协议中应用的商业参考利率修改为浮动利率或掉期利率时，借款人应向提供官方融资支持的机构赔付由此产生的全部费用与损失，包括政府机构替换因提前还款而受影响的固定利率现金流所产生的成本。

## 7. 利率的即时变化

每月之中，当市场的发展变化要求对商业参考利率的修改进行通知时，修改后的利率应在秘书处收到此修改通知10个工作日后开始实行。

## 8. 溢价基准

（a）以三个月LIBOR为基础的溢价基准应每月根据（b）款，使用依照（c）款通知秘书处的数据进行计算，并从每月的第15日起生效。一旦计算得出后，秘书处应将溢价基准通知加入国并公布相关信息。

（b）以三个月LIBOR为基础的溢价基准应等于，在以下两种情况中，不低于三个月LIBOR溢价中值的平均值：（i）为浮动利率交易收取的三个月LIBOR；（ii）对于固定利率交易或资本市场发债，三个月LIBOR可通过将固定利率掉期为等价水平的浮动利率获得。上述任意一种情况下，相关加入国提交的月度基准报告中包括的溢价应是（a）款规定的生效日前三个完整公历月的溢价。使用溢价基准计算的交易或发布应满足以下条件：

（1）以美元计价的100%无条件担保交易；及

（2）为价值等于或大于3500万美元（或等值的其他货币）的航空器提供的官方支持。

（c）加入国应在知晓溢价时进行报告，且该溢价将在相应加入国的溢价基准报告中保留三个完整的公历月。对于单笔交易中包含多个报价的情况，无需将后来的报价进行事后通知。

（d）加入国应在长期贷款的溢价确立时对交易情况予以通知。对于银行的交易（包括PEFCO），溢价确立之日应为下列情况中的较早者：（i）加入国发布最终承诺之日；（ii）最终承诺后确立溢价之日；（iii）提款；以及（iv）提款后确立长期贷款溢价之日。若采用相同溢价基准、在同一银行进行数笔提款的情况下，则应在第一架航空器交易时进行通知。对于资本市场提供融资支持的贷款，溢价确立之日应为长期贷款利率确定之日，通常为相关债券发行日。若采用相同溢价基准，对同一债券进行数笔提款的情况下，则应在第一架航空器交易时进行通知。

（e）以三个月LIBOR为基础的溢价基准应适用于浮动利率的交易并应在最终承诺时予以确定。

（f）对于固定利率交易，溢价基准应通过将以三个月LIBOR为基础的溢价基准掉期为在最终承诺日可适用固定利率（如本附录第2条所规定）的价差这一方式，在最终承诺日予以确定。

（g）加入国应对溢价基准进行监督，并根据任一加入国的要求对溢价基准的机制进行审议。

## 附录4 报告形式

### (a) 基本信息

1. 通知国

2. 通知日期

3. 通知政府部门/机构的名称

4. 编号

### (b) 买方/借款人/担保人信息

5. 买方的名称及国别

6. 借款人的名称及国别

7. 担保人的名称及国别

8. 买方/借款人/担保人的性质，例如，主权、私营银行、其他私人主体

9. 买方/借款人/担保人的风险分类

### (c) 融资条款

10. 官方支持的形式，例如，纯保险、官方融资支持

11. 如提供了官方融资支持，是直接信贷/再融资/利率支持

12. 描述支持的交易，包括制造商、航空器模型以及航空器数量；阐明该交易是否遵循本谅解第39条（a）款或（b）款所列的过渡安排。

13. 最终承诺日期

14. 贷款的币种

15. 贷款的数额，以百万美元为单位：

| 种类 | 贷款数额 |
|---|---|
| I | 0 ~ 200 |
| II | 200 ~ 400 |
| III | 400 ~ 600 |
| IV | 600 ~ 900 |
| V | 900 ~ 1200 |
| VI | 1200 ~ 1500 |
| VII | 1500 ~ 2000 * |

* 超过 20 亿美元的数值以 3 亿美元的倍数表示。

16. 官方支持的比例

17. 还款期限

18. 还款方式和频率——包括适当的加权平均期限

19. 信用起始日和首次偿还本金之间的时间间隔

20. 利率：

——适用的最低利率

——适用的溢价基准

21. 总保费的收取：

——预付费用（占贷款额的比例）或

——溢价（每年高于适用利率的基点）

——如适当，请单独提供附录2第20条（b）款所述的15%的附加费

22. 直接信贷/融资情况下费用的收取：

——安排/结构费

——承诺/保费持有费

——管理费

23. 保费持有期

24. 纯保险情况下的保费持有费

25. 交易安排条件：适用的风险缓释措施/附加保费

26. 如适当，请阐明《开普敦公约》对适用保费费率的影响

## 附录5　定义表

总成本等价：在直接信贷项下，按照贷款总额的一定比例收取的保费费率净现值、利率成本和费用之和，与在纯保险项下，按照被保险贷款额度的一定比例收取的保费费率净现值、利率成本和费用之和相等。

资产抵押：符合附录2第19条（a）款所列条件的交易。

买方/借款人：包括（但不限于）如航空公司与租赁公司的商业实体，以及主权实体（或，如是不同的实体，则为交易还款的主要来源）。

买方提供设备：根据制造商销售契约中列明的要求，在交付前或交付时由买方提供的以及在生产/翻新过程中装入机舱的设备。

开普敦公约：指《移动设备国际利益公约》和《移动设备国际利益公约关于航空器设备特定问题的议定书》。

承诺：以任何形式向接受国、买方、借款人、出口商或金融机构发出的声明，表示提供官方支持的意愿或意向，包括但不限于资格审核合格函件、营销函件等。

共同谅解：加入国之间达成的谅解，同意对特定交易或在特定情况下，适用特殊的官方支持融资条款。对于其所涉及的特定交易或特殊情况，共同谅解的效力高于本行业谅解的效力。

有条件保险：针对特定风险项下的支付违约情况，在特定等待期之后向受益人提供赔付的官方支持；在等待期之内受益人无权获得加入国的支付款项。有条件保险项下的支付款项应符合原始凭证和交易的效力和除外责任要求。

改造：对一架航空器的设计类型作出主要变动，让其变成另一种类型的航空器（包括客用航空器改造成为水平轰炸机、货用航空器、搜救航空器、侦察航空器以及商业航空器），上述改造应符合负责民用航空管理当局的证明。

国别风险分类：经合组织网站上公布的《官方支持出口信贷的安排》中适用于加入国的国别风险分类。

信用评级机构：任一家国际知名信用评级机构或其他任何加入国可接受的信用评级机构。

引擎工具箱：通过技术引进，用以提高可靠性、耐用性和/或机翼性能的一套零部件。

出口信贷：一种保险、担保或融资安排，可使外国买方在一段时期内延付对所进口商品和/或服务的款项；出口信贷可以出口商提供延付的卖方信贷形式，或买方信贷形式，即由出口方的银行或其他金融机构借款给买方（或其银行）。

最终承诺：加入国根据互惠协议或单方行为承诺的、准确和全面的融资条款。

公司合同：制造商与收到航空器或引擎的一方，如买方之间，或在售后回租安排下与租期至少 5 年的承租人之间，达成的协议且明确了约束性承诺（不包括与彼时未行使选项的相关承诺）；若不履行该承诺将承担法律责任。

有权益的加入国：（1）为在其领土范围内制造的全部或部分机体及航空器引擎提供官方支持的；（2）具有实质性商业利益或与相关买方/借款人有往来经历的；或（3）被制造商/出口商要求向买方/借款人提供官方支持的加入国。

利率支持：政府或受政府委托或代表政府的机构与银行或其他金融机构之间达成的安排，允许银行或其他金融机构以等于或高于相关最低固定利率的固定利率提供的出口融资。

大修/翻新：对客用或货用航空器进行重新构造或升级的操作。

净价格：制造商或供应商在考虑了所有价格折扣及其他现金贷款金额后的开票价格，减去所有其他信贷金额或者任何相关的或可公平分摊的折让价格。该价格由每架航空器和引擎的制造商或服务的提供商在一份具有约束力的说明中列明（仅当根据购买协议的形式提及引擎时才需要提供关于引擎的说明），且由官方支持提供方要求的相关文件进行支持以确定净价格。所有进口税款（如增值税）均不包含在净价格里。

新造航空器：见本行业谅解的第 8 条（a）款。

非资产抵押交易：不符合附录 2 第 19 条（a）款所列条件的交易。

非主权交易：不符合附录 2 第 49 条（b）款所列条件的交易。

保费持有期：根据附录 2 第 35 条（b）款，一笔交易的保费费率保持不变的一段时间；该段时间从最终承诺日期算起不超过 18 个月。

保费费率转换模型：为达到本行业谅解的目的，加入国之间达成的并可获得的模型。该模型用于将预付保费转化为溢价或将溢价转为预付保费，其使用的利率与贴现率为 4.6%；加入国应定期对此进行审议。

先期通知：在发布任何承诺之前至少提前 10 个公历日发出的通知，通知内容应按照附录 4 要求的形式进行报告。

纯保险：由政府或代表政府通过出口信用担保或保险的形式提供的官方支持，即不是官方融资支持。

还款期：自信用起始日起，至合同约定的最后一笔本金偿还日止的期间。

主权交易：符合附录 2 中第 55 条（b）款所描述的交易。

信用起始日：对于航空器的销售，包括直升机、备用引擎和零部件，最近的信用起始日是买方占有实物的实际日期或加权平均日。对于服务，最近的信用起始日是向客户提交发票或客户接受服务之日。

掉期利率：以浮动利率交换固定利率（由提供方给出）得到的一项与半年期利率相等的固定利率；该利率由任意独立的市场指数提供方（如德励、彭博、路透等或其他类似机构）在贷款提款日前两天的纽约时间上午11点发布。

加权平均期限：贷款项下清偿一半的本金所需要的时间。计算方法是，将每笔本金到期还款日与信用起始日之间的时间间隔，考虑该笔本金所占加权比重后，相加得出总和（以年为单位）。

# 附件4

# 可再生能源、气候变化减缓和水资源项目出口信贷的行业谅解

本行业谅解旨在为国际倡议中包括的、有助于减缓气候变化的，涉及可再生能源、温室气体减排、高能效以及水资源项目等特定行业的项目提供充分的融资条件。本行业谅解为《安排》的补充，加入国均同意其融资条款，其实施目的与《安排》目的保持一致。

## 第一章 行业谅解的范围

### 1. 附录I中可再生能源行业项目的适用范围

（a）本行业谅解为用于附录I所列行业合同的官方支持出口信贷规定了适用的融资条款，适用合同包括：

（1）可再生能源电厂整体或部分出口，包括建设和调试这些设备直接必需的全部配件、设备、材料和服务（包括相关人员培训）。

（2）已建可再生能源电厂的更新应满足相关电厂的经济使用年限很可能因此至少延长至还款期结束的条件。若此条件不能满足，则适用于《安排》的规定。

（b）本行业谅解不适用于电厂所在范围之外的、通常由买方负责的事项，特别是与发电厂不直接相关的供水设备，与土地开发、修路、乡村建设、输电线和户外配电装置相关的费用，以及买方所在国因官方批准程序所产生的费用（例如土地许可、施工许可等），但下述情况除外：

（1）在户外配电装置的买方与可再生能源电厂的买方一致，且合同的达成与该电厂初始户外配电装置有关的情况下，初始户外配电装置的条款不得优于可再生能源电厂的条款。

（2）对于可再生能源电厂所在范围以外的最低电压阈值为60千

伏的变电站、变压器以及输电线的条款不得比电厂的条款更为宽松。

## 2. 附录 II 中气候变化减缓行业项目的适用范围

（a）本行业谅解为附录 II 所列行业合同的官方支持出口信贷规定了适用的融资条款。根据本行业谅解第 11 条的审议规定，适用的行业清单及其相应用于定义项目资格的技术中立原则，可随发展而进行调整。

（b）这些合同应涉及项目整体或部分出口，包括建设和调试一项可识别项目直接必需的全部配件、设备、材料和服务（包括相关人员培训），并符合以下要求：

（1）项目的碳排放量为较低至零或达到二氧化碳当量要求，并/或带来高能效。

（2）项目应至少达到附录 II 所列的性能标准。

（3）融资条件仅在项目遇到具体融资困难时才可放宽，并应根据项目具体的融资需求和所处的市场条件进行调整。

## 3. 附录 III 中适应性项目的适用范围

（a）本行业谅解为符合附录 III 所列标准的项目合同的官方支持出口信贷规定了融资条款。

（b）这些合同应涉及项目整体或部分的出口，包括建设和调试一项可识别项目直接必需的全部配件、设备、材料和服务（包括相关人员培训），并符合以下要求：

（1）符合附录 III 中所列的条件；

（2）融资条件仅在项目遇到具体融资困难时才可放宽，并应根据项目具体的融资需求和所处的市场条件进行调整。

（c）本行业谅解适用于对已有项目的更新升级，适应项目的因素应满足经济使用年限很可能因此至少延长至还款期结束的条件。若此条件不能满足，则适用于《安排》的规定。

### 4. 水资源项目的适用范围

本行业谅解为涉及用水供给和废水处理设施相关项目的整体或部分出口合同的官方支持出口信贷规定了适用的融资条款，适用项目包括：

（a）城市饮用水供给（包括向居民及小商户供水）的基础设施，即为获得饮用水的纯化设施和供水网络（包括防漏控制设施）。

（b）废水收集和处理设施，即收集和处理居民生活和工业废水及污水，包括水的再利用和再循环过程，以及直接与这些活动相关的淤泥处理。

（c）已建相关设施的更新应满足相关设施的经济使用年限很可能因此至少延长至还款期结束的条件。若此条件不能满足，则适用于《安排》的规定。

## 第二章　出口信贷的条件

### 5. 最长还款期

（a）对附录Ⅰ中所列行业的合同，以及本行业谅解第 4 条定义的水资源项目，其官方支持的出口信贷最长还款期为 18 年。

（b）按照附录Ⅱ所列项目分类，对其中合同金额不低于 1000 万特别提款权合同提供的官方支持出口信贷，最长还款期为：

（1）对于A类项目的合同：18年。

（2）对于B类和C类项目的合同：15年。

（c）按照附录Ⅱ所列项目分类，对其中合同金额小于1000万特别提款权合同提供的官方支持出口信贷，最长还款期为：

（1）对于《安排》第11条规定的第I类国家，最长还款期为5年；在按照本行业谅解第10条规定进行先期通知的情况下，还款期可延长至8.5年。

（2）对于第II类国家，最长还款期为10年。

（3）尽管上述（1）和（2）条规定，对于《安排》第13条规定的非核电站项目，最长还款期为12年。

（d）对符合附录Ⅲ标准的且合同金额超过1000万特别提款权的项目提供的官方支持出口信贷，最长还款期限为15年。

## 6. 本金的偿还和利息的支付

（a）加入国出口信贷本金的偿还和利息的支付应采取以下方式中的一种：

（1）等额分期偿还本金。

（2）等额分期偿还本金和利息总额。

（b）本金的偿还和利息的支付不应低于每6个月一次，且首次本金的偿还和利息的支付不迟于信用起始日后的6个月。

（c）在特殊且有正当理由的情况下，官方支持可不执行上述（a）和（b）的规定。如债务人的资金状况与还款表规定的每半年等额还款计划在时间上不一致，则可适用于其他还款条件，但应满足以下标准：

（1）6 个月内单笔或多笔本金偿还数额不得超过信贷本金总额的 25%。

（2）应至少每 12 个月偿还一次本金。第一次偿还时间应不迟于信用起始日后的 18 个月；在信用起始日之后的 18 个月内，本金的偿还金额不低于总额的 2%。

（3）应至少每 12 个月支付一次利息。第一次支付时间应不迟于信用起始日后的 6 个月。

（4）还款期的加权平均期限最长不得超过最长期限的 60%。

（d）信用起始日之后的到期利息不得资本化。

## 7. 最低利率

加入国为固定利率贷款提供的官方融资支持，应适用下表规定的最低利率：

| 还款期/年 | 标准最低利率 | | 用于长建设期项目的最低利率，即<br>——新的大型水电站项目<br>——附录 2 分类 A 的项目<br>——附录 3 适应性项目 | |
|---|---|---|---|---|
| | 政府债券（年） | 溢价（基点） | 政府债券（年） | 溢价（基点） |
| <11 | 《安排》第 20 条规定的相关商业参考利率 | | | |
| 11 ~ 12 | 7 | 100 | 7 | 100 |
| 13 | 7 | 120 | 8 | 120 |
| 14 | 8 | 120 | 9 | 120 |
| 15 | 8 | 120 | 9 | 120 |
| 16 | 9 | 120 | 10 | 125 |
| 17 | 9 | 120 | 10 | 130 |
| 18 | 10 | 120 | 10 | 130 |

### 8. 可用货币

适用于官方融资支持的可用货币为：能够完全自由兑换，并且可获得根据本行业谅解第7条以及《安排》第20条（还款期小于11年）规定的、用以计算最低利率的相关商业参考利率数据。

### 9. 当地费用

（a）对于合同金额不低于1000万特别提款权的官方支持出口信贷，对于当地费用的官方支持不应超过合同总价值的30%。

（b）对于合同金额小于1000万特别提款权的官方支持出口信贷：

（1）对于附录Ⅰ所列行业，对于当地费用的官方支持不应超过出口合同金额的45%。

（2）对于附录Ⅱ所列行业以及本行业谅解中第4条定义的水资源项目，对于当地费用的官方支持不应超过出口合同金额的30%。

（c）若对于当地费用的官方支持超过合同总金额的15%，则应根据本行业谅解第10条规定进行先期通知，并明确接受官方支持的当地费用的性质。

## 第三章 程序

### 10. 先期通知

（a）若加入国打算按照本行业谅解的条款提供融资支持，应根据以下规定，在作出任何承诺前至少10个公历日通知其他加入国：

（1）当该融资支持根据本行业谅解的第1、2或4条扩展时，参照《安排》第48条；

（2）当该融资支持根据本行业谅解的第3条扩展时，参照《安排》第47条；

（b）对本行业谅解附录Ⅱ所列项目，先期通知应包括项目的详细描述，以证明该项目符合本行业谅解第2条（b）款规定的支持标准。

（c）对于遵循本行业谅解附录III的支持项目，先期通知应包括：

（1）对项目的详细描述，以证明该项目符合本行业谅解第3条（b）款规定的支持标准；以及

（2）附录III所要求的，由独立第三方出具的审议结果。

（d）尽管有上述（a）款第1点的规定，若通知国打算提供还款期超过15年的融资支持和/或符合上述第6条（c）款的情况，根据《安排》第47条，通知国应在作出任何承诺前至少10个公历日进行先期通知。

（e）加入国应将讨论后的最终决定告知所有其他加入国，以增加相关审议经验。

## 第四章　监督和审议

### 11. 未来的工作

加入国同意审议下列事项：

（a）期限调整风险保费。

（b）低排放/高能效化石燃料电厂（包括碳捕获和封存预留定义）的条件。

（c）零耗能建筑。

（d）智能电网。

（e）燃料电池项目。

## 12. 监督和审议

（a）秘书处应每年报告一次本行业谅解的执行情况。

（b）加入国应在2017年年底前完成对本行业谅解的适用范围及其他条款的定期审议。

（c）应定期审议附录Ⅱ的内容，包括应加入国要求评估项目分类和/或类型是否应增加或去除，或者标准是否应进行调整。新项目分类和/或类型的建议需满足本行业谅解第2条（b）款规定的标准，并按照附录4中的方法处理。

（d）加入国应在2018年6月30日前对本行业谅解附录III的内容进行审议，以对与适应项目、市场条件以及通知过程中产生的经验有关的国际倡议进行评估，以决定相关定义、项目标准，融资条款是否应保留或进行修改。

（e）2018年12月31日后，除非加入国一致同意，否则附录III相关的融资条款应终止。

## 附录Ⅰ：可再生能源行业

下列可再生能源领域可适用本行业谅解规定的融资条款，只要其影响根据《2012 年关于官方支持出口信贷和环境的共同方法及社会尽职调查①的建议》（由 OECD 出口信贷和信贷担保工作组〈ECG〉成员进行修改并经 OECD 委员会批准）得到解决。

（a）风能②

（b）地热能

（c）潮汐和潮汐流能

（d）波浪能

（e）渗透能

（f）太阳光电能

（g）太阳光热能

（h）海洋热能

（i）生物能：所有可持续使用的垃圾沼气、污水处理厂沼气、生物沼气能源或来自生物燃料能源设施的燃料。“生物燃料”意为从农业（包括植物和动物）、林业和相关行业的产品、废物和残留物获得的可生物降解的部分，以及工业和城市废物中可生物降解的部分。

（j）水能

---

① 2012 年的建议同样适用于不采用上述融资条款的项目。

② 对于风力涡轮机组装中使用的自升式钻井平台，最长还款期为 12 年。

（k）可再生能源项目中的能源效率

## 附录Ⅱ：气候变化减缓行业

| 项目分类 | 定义 | 基本原理 | 适用标准 | 还款期 |
|---|---|---|---|---|
| A 类项目：碳捕获与封存 | | | | |
| 类型 1：采用碳捕获与封存技术的化石燃料电厂 | 为实现环境安全和永久性封存二氧化碳的目的，而将二氧化碳从化石燃料发电产生的排放物中分离并传输到封存装置的过程。 | 在燃烧化石燃料能源条件下实现低碳排放。 | 向大气排放的碳浓度应达到小于或等于 350 公吨/百万度的标准①；<br>或所有项目中，碳捕获和封存率应将工厂的碳排放量减少 65% 或以上；<br>或对申请出口信贷支持的设备，对其排放的二氧化碳捕获率应至少达到 85%；85% 是指在常用操作条件下的标准。 | 18 年 |
| 类型 2：其他碳捕获与封存项目 | 为实现环境安全和永久性封存二氧化碳的目的，而将二氧化碳从工业或能源发电产生的排放物中分离并传输到封存装置的过程。 | 显著减少碳的排放量。 | 所有项目中，碳捕获和封存率应将工业或能源发电产生的碳排放量减少 65% 或以上；<br>或对申请官方出口信贷的设备，对其排放的二氧化碳捕获率应至少达到 85%；85% 是指在常用操作条件下的标准。 | 18 年 |

① 在燃烧天然气的情况下，向大气排放的碳浓度应显著降低。

续表

| 项目分类 | 定义 | 基本原理 | 适用标准 | 还款期 |
| --- | --- | --- | --- | --- |
| B 类项目：化石燃料的替代 | | | | |
| 类型 1：废物能源 | 通过对混合固体废物进行热处理（包括气化）而产生能源的项目。 | 抵消通过使用传统能源排放的温室气体，并且减少从废物中产生的温室气体，如甲烷。 | 在蒸汽循环的情况下，锅炉（或蒸汽发生器）的能量转换率至少为净热效率①的 75%。<br>在气化过程中，气化率至少为净热效率的 65%。② | 15 年 |
| 类型 2：混合发电厂 | 从可再生能源也从化石燃料产生电能的发电厂。 | 为满足工厂运行的需要，在可再生能源产生的能量不可用或不足够时，工厂将使用化石燃料发电。化石燃料支持了可再生能源在混合能源工厂的应用，因此，与传统化石燃料厂相比，混合能源厂大大降低了碳的排放量。 | 模型 1：<br>两类独立的发电能源：可再生能源和化石燃料。<br>项目的设计应保证每年输出的能量至少有 50% 来自可再生能源。<br>模型 2：<br>混合可再生能源和化石燃料作为单独的发电能源。项目的设计应保证每年输出的能量至少有 75% 来自可再生能源。 | 15 年 |

① 锅炉（或蒸汽发生器）能源转化率 =（蒸汽产出的净热量/燃料产生的热量或热值［LHV］）（×100%）

② 气化率 =（燃料产生的每公斤气体的热值/平均一公斤燃料产生的净热值（LHV））（×100%）

续表

| 项目分类 | 定义 | 基本原理 | 适用标准 | 还款期 |
|---|---|---|---|---|
| C 类项目：能源效率 | | | | |
| 类型 1：热电混合项目 | 在单一的集成系统里同时产生多种能源（电能、机械能、热能）。<br>热电厂的输出应包括为商业或住宅提供的电能或机械能以及热能。 | 在传统热电厂中，约有不超过三分之二的用于发电的初始能量因热耗而浪费。因此，混合热电形式成为一项可有效减少温室气体排放的选择。此外，蒸汽冷凝电厂（规模为几千瓦到 1000 兆瓦）生产中使用的热机和燃料（包括生物能和太阳热能）可以产生混合热电①。 | 净热效率占总能效的比例至少为 75%。② | 15 年 |

① 政府间气候变化专门委员会（IPCC）第四次评估报告：气候变化2007http：//www. ipcc. ch/publicatinos_ and_ data/ar4/wh3/en/ch4s4 - 3 - 5. html.

② 热电混合系统的总系统效率（$\eta_0$）是可利用的净电力输出（$W_E$）和可利用的净热能输出（$\Sigma Q_{TH}$）之和，再除以总燃料输入（$Q_{FUEL}$），即，$\eta_0 = \frac{W_E + \sum Q_{TH}}{Q_{FUEL}}$。

续表

| 项目分类 | 定义 | 基本原理 | 适用标准 | 还款期 |
|---|---|---|---|---|
| 类型 2：区域制热和/或冷却 | 用于从能量生产基地到使用终端传送和分配热能的网络。 | 通过减少管道和转换损失、提高余热的再利用等方式，改善通过修建管道传输蒸汽和/或热水热能效的区域热能能效。区域冷却是一种可显著减少二氧化碳排放、空气污染和提高能源安全（比如通过取代个体空气调节设施）的综合技术。 | 区域管道的热导系数应至少小于欧洲标准 EN253：2009 热导系数的 80%（该数据随标准的变化而更新）。 | 15 年 |

## 附录Ⅲ：气候变化适应性项目的适用标准

满足以下条件的项目可以适用本行业谅解的融资条款：

（a）气候变化适应性是项目的主要目标，在项目计划以及支持性文件中对此有明确的说明和解释，该目标亦为项目设计的基础。

（b）项目的计划书应包含对项目以及有关气候变化风险的识别和分析，并且说明针对上述风险的解决办法和技术。

（c）项目应接受来自第三方的独立审议，该审议可以为项目计划的一部分或单独执行，并且可以在例如有关当局网站等的公开渠道获得。该审议应评估特定的有关气候变化的风险，并且说明针对上述风险的解决办法和技术。

（d）项目的使用期限应超过 15 年。

## 附录Ⅳ：决定适用本行业谅解第 2 条行业的方法

当建议在本行业谅解附录Ⅱ中增加项目分类或类型时，加入国应提供关于该项目分类或类型的详细描述以及该项目如何能符合本行业谅解第 2 条（b）款所列标准的信息；这些信息应包括：

（a）针对项目分类或类型对气候变化减缓的直接贡献的评估，包括以碳排放量或二氧化碳当量和/或高能效的测量数据为基础，采用传统和正在使用的新技术，对行业项目性能进行比较。上述比较应基于定量的测量方法，比如对生产每个单位的碳排放量减少情况进行测定。

（b）针对所建议的项目分类或类型的技术和性能标准的描述，包括任何与现有最佳可行技术（BAT）有关的信息；如适合，描述中应包含在现有最佳可行技术的基础上，该新技术应如何进一步改进等信息。

（c）针对所建议的项目分类或类型遇到融资障碍的描述，包括任何融资需求和市场条件，以及在本行业谅解中列明的能用于继续开展项目的条款。

## 附录Ⅴ：定义表

最佳可行技术：按照欧盟第 96/61/EC（第 2.1 条）指令，“最佳可行技术”应指在发展过程中最有效和先进的技术阶段；其操作方法指出了特定技术在计算排放限值以阻止或减少排放量和对环境影响等方面技术的适用性和不可用性：

(a)“技术”应既包括采用的技术，还包括装置的设计、建造、维护、运营和拆除方法。

(b)“可行”技术应指已经开发的且相关行业可使用的，在经济和技术上切实可行，考虑了成本和收益情况，并合理易得的技术；这些技术可由成员国使用或研发。

(c)“最佳”应指在为达到更好的环境保护而采用的最有效的方式。

温室气体：温室气体包括二氧化碳、甲烷、一氧化二氮、氢氟碳化物、全氟碳化物和六氟化硫。

大型水电项目：按照国际大坝委员会（ICOLD）的定义，大型水坝是指高度为 15 米或从地基起算高于 15 米的水坝。水坝高度在 5 ~ 15 米，水库容积超过 300 万立方米的水坝也被归为大型水坝。

# 附件5

# 铁路出口信贷的行业谅解

本行业谅解的加入国同意，本行业谅解的融资条款作为《安排》的补充之一，应按照《安排》规定的目的予以实施。

## 第一章　行业谅解的范围

### 1. 适用范围

本行业谅解列出了运营铁路所需的基础设施资产合同相关的官方支持出口信贷所适用的融资条款。铁路基础设施资产包括铁路控制（如信号及其他铁路信息技术）、电气化、轨道、机车车辆，以及其他相关工程作业等项目。

## 第二章　出口信贷的规定

### 2. 最长还款期

（a）对于本行业谅解适用范围内的官方支持的出口信贷项目，最长还款期规定如下：

（1）第I类国家（《安排》第11条所定义）的项目：12年。

（2）第II类国家（《安排》第11条所定义）的项目：14年。

（b）适用上述（a）款规定的最长还款期，应符合以下条件：

（1）交易合同金额超过1000万特别提款权；以及

（2）还款期不超过融资铁路基础设施资产的可使用年限；以及

（3）对于第I类国家的项目，还应符合以下标准：

——有不受官方出口信贷支持的私人金融机构参与银团贷款：

i）整个贷款期间，加入国属于贷款份额较小的一方，且按同等比例行使权利；

ii）加入国提供的官方出口信贷支持成分不超过银团贷款的50%。

——任何官方支持的保费费率不得压低私人市场融资价格，并且与参加银团贷款的其他私人金融机构的报价相当。

（c）加入国可根据《安排》第58～63条，通过共同谅解的方式，要求放弃适用以上（b）款第3点的规定。在此情况下，提出共同谅解提议的加入国，不论是在共同谅解还是在通知后的每笔单独交易中，都应提供对该支持的详细解释，包括定价的具体数据，以及要求弃用上述（b）款第3点规定的合理原因。

### 3. 本金与利息的偿还

本金和利息的偿还应遵循《安排》第14条的规定，但该条（d）款第4条中所指的最长加权平均还款期应为：

（a）对于第I类国家的项目，6.25年；

（b）对于第II类国家的项目，7.25年。

### 4. 最低固定利率

加入国为固定利率贷款提供的官方融资支持，应适用最低利率，具体如下：

（a）对于还款期为12年及12年以下的项目，最低利率是根据《安排》第20条规定所确定的相应商业参考利率。

（b）对于还款期超过12年的项目，无论何种币种，最低利率是根据《安排》第20条规定所确定的相应商业参考利率基础上，再上浮20个基点。

## 第三章 程序

### 5. 先期通知

（a）加入国如有意向为第I类国家的项目提供支持，应根据《安排》第47条，至少在其作出任何承诺之前10个公历日，发出先期通知。通知应包括有关官方支持的全面解释，以及具体的定价数据。

（b）若加入国打算为以下两种情况的交易提供支持，则应根据《安排》第48条，在作出任何承诺前至少10个公历日进行先期通知：

（1）第II类国家的交易；或

（2）依照本行业谅解第2条（c）款所列共同谅解提供支持的交易。此类先期通知应符合共同谅解的要求，并可能和相应的共同谅解的批准程序同时进行。

### 6. 共同谅解的有效期

尽管《安排》第63条（a）款对《共同谅解》的有效期作出了规定，但所有已达成的《共同谅解》都将于2018年12月31日终止，除非加入国根据本行业谅解第7条（d）款一致同意延长本行业谅解的有效期。

# 第四章　监督和审议

## 7. 监督和审议

（a）秘书处应每年报告本行业谅解的执行情况。

（b）遵循下列（c）款规定，自 2017 年 12 月 31 日起，除非加入国另有约定，本行业谅解第 2 条第（b）段第 3 款（ii）项所规定的不超过银团贷款 50% 的占比要求，将变更为占比不超过 35%。

（c）加入国应在 2017 年 6 月 30 日之前，对本行业谅解进行审议，评估市场条件以及其他因素，以决定相关条款是否应继续执行或予以修改。

（d）自 2017 年 12 月 31 日起，除非加入国另有约定，本行业谅解的条款效力终止。

# 附件6

# 适用于项目融资交易的条款

# 第一章 一般规定

## 1. 适用范围

（a）本附件规定了加入国可对符合附录1所列标准的项目融资交易提供官方支持的条款。

（b）本附件未作规定之处，仍应适用《安排》的条款。

# 第二章 融资条款[①]

## 2. 最长还款期

最长还款期为14年。

## 3. 本金偿还和利息支付

出口信贷的本金可以采取不等额的方式分期偿还，本金和利息的分期支付间隔可以超过半年，只要满足以下条件：

（a）6个月内单笔或多笔本金偿还数额不超过信贷本金总额

---

① （a）第2条和第3条（d）款中规定的融资条款应适用最终承诺作出在2015年12月31日及在此之前的交易。

（b）2015年12月31日之后，第2条和第3条（d）款中规定的融资条款不再适用，除非加入国另有约定。

（c）若上述融资条款不再适用，则第2条和第3条（d）款的规定替换如下：

第2条——最长还款期一律为14年，除非，加入国为高收入OECD国家的项目提供的官方出口信贷支持占项目银团贷款份额的35%以上，则最长还款期为10年。

第3条（d）款——还款期的加权平均期限不得超过7.25年，除非，加入国为高收入OECD国家的项目提供的官方出口信贷支持占项目银团贷款份额的35%以上，则还款期的加权平均期限不得超过5.25年。

的25%。

（b）首笔本金偿还时间不晚于信用起始日之后的24个月，在信用起始日之后的24个月内，本金偿还额不低于信贷本金总额的2%。

（c）应至少每12个月支付一次利息，首笔利息支付时间不晚于信用起始日之后的6个月。

（d）加权平均还款期不超过7.25年。

（e）加入国应根据本附件第5条给予先期通知。

### 4. 最低固定利率

若加入国为固定利率贷款提供官方融资支持：

（a）对于还款期在12年及12年以下的项目，加入国应适用根据《安排》第20条规定所确定的相应商业参考利率（CIRRs）。

（b）对于还款期在12年以上的项目，无论何种币种，应在CIRR的基础上上浮20个基点。

## 第三章　程序

### 5. 项目融资交易的先期通知

加入国应至少在作出任何承诺之前10个公历日，向所有加入国通知其将根据本附件条款提供官方支持的意向。通知应按照《安排》附件5的规定发出。若任何加入国在此期间要求通知国就支持条款给予解释，通知国须再等10个公历日才能作出承诺。

# 附录1 项目融资交易的标准条件

## 1. 基本标准

交易应符合以下标准：

（a）贷款人对一个特殊的经济实体提供融资，并同意将该经济实体的现金流和收入作为偿还贷款的来源，以该经济实体的资产作为还款担保。

（b）贷款人为一个（在法律上和经济上）独立的项目公司，如特殊目的公司，在能够产生收益的投资项目中的相关出口贸易提供融资。

（c）在项目各参与方之间有适当的风险分担，如私人股东或有良好信誉的公共股东、出口商、贷款人、产品/服务的协议购买人，也包括股本的充足性。

（d）项目在整个还款期间产生的现金流足以支付运营成本并偿还外来资金形成的债务。

（e）可以从项目收益中优先扣除运营成本并偿还债务。

（f）非主权买方/借款人，且未获得主权还款担保（政府出具的履约担保除外，如购销安排）。

（g）项目收益/资产上设定资产抵押，如权益转让、抵押、收入账户质押。

（h）在项目完成之后，对项目的私人行业股东/发起人无追索权或仅具有限追索权。

## 2. 高收入 OECD 国家中项目融资交易的额外标准

交易应符合以下标准:

(a) 有不受官方出口信贷支持的私人金融机构参与银团贷款:

(1) 整个贷款期间，加入国属于贷款份额较小的一方，且按同等比例行使权利;

(2) 加入国提供的官方出口信贷支持成分不超过银团贷款的50%。

(b) 任何官方支持的保费费率不得压低私人市场融资价格，并且与参加银团贷款的其他私人金融机构的报价相当。

# 附件 7

## 通知中应提供的信息

下述第 1 小节列出的信息在所有根据《安排》（包括其附件）作出的通知中均应提供。此外，在适当情况下，第 2 小节列出的与特定类型通知相关的信息也应提供。

## I. 所有通知中均应提供的信息

（a）基本信息

1. 通知国

2. 通知日期

3. 通知政府部门/通知机构的名称

4. 编号

5. 原始通知或对以前通知修改（包括有关的修改编号）

6. 国际货币基金贷款项目编号（如果相关）

7. 信贷额度编号（如果相关）

8. 作出通知所依据的《安排》的相关规定

9. 受匹配的通知编号（如果相关）

10. 对受匹配的支持方式的描述（如果相关）

11. 目的国

（b）买方/借款人/担保人信息

12. 买方国别

13. 买方名称

14. 买方地址

15. 买方性质

16. 借款人国别（如不同于买方）

17. 借款人名称（如不同于买方）

18. 借款人地址（如不同于买方）

19. 借款人性质（如不同于买方）

20. 担保人国别（如相关）

21. 担保人名称（如相关）

22. 担保人地址（如相关）

23. 担保人性质（如相关）

（c）出口货物和/或服务与项目的信息

24. 对出口货物和/或服务的描述

25. 对项目的描述（如果相关）

26. 项目地址（如果相关）

27. 投标截止日（如果相关）

28. 信贷额度到期日（如果相关）

29. 对于所支持的合同金额，无论是实际金额（对所有的信贷额度和项目融资交易或任何自愿基础上的个别交易）还是根据下列衡量标准（单位：百万特别提款权）确定的金额：

| 类别 | 自 | 至 |
|---|---|---|
| I： | 0 | 1 |
| II： | 1 | 2 |
| III： | 2 | 3 |
| IV： | 3 | 5 |
| V： | 5 | 7 |
| VI： | 7 | 10 |
| VII： | 10 | 20 |
| VIII： | 20 | 40 |
| IX： | 40 | 80 |
| X： | 80 | 120 |
| XI： | 120 | 160 |
| XII： | 160 | 200 |
| XIII： | 200 | 240 |
| XIV： | 240 | 280 |
| XV： | 280 | * |

* 指代的数额中超过 2.8 亿的特别提款权，以 4000 万特别提款权的倍数表示，例如 4.1 亿特别提款权应表示为类别 XV +3。

30. 合同币种

（d）官方出口信贷支持的融资条款

31. 信贷金额：所有的信贷额度和项目融资交易或任何自愿基础上个别交易的实际金额，或根据特别提款权衡量标准确定的金额

32. 信贷币种

33. 预付款（占所支持合同总金额的比例）

34. 当地费用（占所支持合同总金额的比例）

35. 信用起始日和对应适用的第10条有关规定的引用

36. 还款期长度

37. 基础利率

38. 利率或溢价

## II. 在适当情况下，与特定条款相关的通知中应提供的额外信息

（a）《安排》第14条（d）款第5点

1. 还款方式

2. 还款频率

3. 信用起始日和第一次本金偿还日之间的时间间隔

4. 信用起始日前利息资本化的金额

5. 还款期的加权平均值

6. 根据第14条（a）款到（c）款就不提供支持的原因作出解释

（b）《安排》第24条、第27条、第30条和第31条

1. 债务人的国别风险分类

2. 债务人的买方风险分类

3. 提款期长度

4. 对政治（国别）风险的覆盖比例

5. 对商业（买方）风险的覆盖比例

6. 承保特质（即低于标准、标准或高于标准）

7. 基于没有第三方担保的根据债务人国别风险分类确定的最低保费费率，涉及多边/地区性机构以及降低风险和/或买方信用增进

8. 适用的最低保费费率（MPR）

9. 实际收取的保费费率（以本金的比例表示）

（c）《安排》第24条（c）款第3点

1. 所应用的基准（见附件9）

（d）《安排》第24条（e）款第1点

1. 担保人的国别风险分类

2. 担保人的买方风险分类

3. 确认符合附件10所列的全部标准

4. 担保所覆盖所有金额（即本金和利率）的比例（即全部或部分金额）

5. 说明担保人和债务人之间是否存在任何财务关系

6. 如担保人和债务人之间存在关系：

——关系形式（如母—子公司、子—母公司、共同所有）

——确认担保人在法律上和财务上的独立性以及可以履行债

务人的还款义务

——确认担保人不会受债务人所在国事件、法规或主权干预的影响

(e)《安排》第 27 条（e）款

1. 债务人的买方风险分类

2. 公认的信用评级机构（CRA）外币评级

3. 买方风险分类优于公认的信用评级机构（CRA）评级的合理性

(f)《安排》第 30 条

1. 所使用的国别风险降低技术

2. 确认符合附件 7 所列全部标准

3. 对于技术 1，使用技术后得到可适用的国别风险分类

4. 对于技术 2：

——使用的当地货币

——应用的当地货币融资（LCF）的金额

(g)《安排》第 31 条

1. 适用的买方信用增进方法（BRCEs）

2. 用于每一信用增进的信用增进因子（CEF）

3. 拟应用的总信用增进因子（CEF）

（h）《安排》第49条、第50条

1. 约束性援助的形式（即发展性援助、或预混信贷、或相关融资）

2. 根据第40条规定计算的约束性和部分非约束性援助融资的总体优惠水平

3. 用来计算优惠水平的差别贴现率（DDR）

4. 在计算优惠水平时对现金偿还的处理方法

5. 对信贷额度使用的限制

（i）附件1第5条（e）款

1. 提供：

——首次支付利息的日期，若晚于信用起始日开始后的6个月

——支付利息的频率，若低于每6个月一次

（j）附件2第8条

1. 增加对出口合同的描述，即新核电站、已有核电站更新、核燃料供应以及浓缩或管理核废料设施。

2. 本金偿还以及利息支付应根据：附件2第3条（a）款第1点、第3条（a）款第2点或第3条（c）款。

3. 依照附件2第3条（c）款提供的官方支持项目，请提供：

——还款方式

——还款频率

——信用起始日和第一次本金偿还日之间的时间间隔

——信用起始日前利息资本化的金额

——还款期的加权平均值

——根据附件 2 第 3 条（a）和（b）款就不提供支持的原因作出解释

4. 依照附件 2 第 4 条适用的最低利率。

（k）附件 4 第 10 条

1. 增加对以下项目的描述：

——新可再生能源和水资源项目，或对已建可再生能源和水资源项目的更新，包括附件 4 附录 1 所列特殊行业，或

——若是水电站项目，不论是否为新的大型水电项目（如附件 4 附录 4 所确定的）或

——对于附件 4 附录 2 所列项目，证明项目如何符合附件 4 第 2 条（b）款所述的支持标准。

——对于附件 4 附录 3 所列项目：

（1）证明项目如何分别符合附件 4 第 3 条（b）款或（c）款所述支持标准的详细描述，以及

（2）可获得附件 4 附录 3 中要求的由独立第三方出具的审议结果。

2. 本金的偿还以及利息的支付按照附件 4 第 6 条（a）款第 1

点、第6条（a）款第2点或第6条（c）款执行。

3. 按照附件4第6条（c）款提供的官方支持项目，请提供：

——还款方式

——还款频率

——信用起始日和第一次本金偿还日之间的时间间隔

——信用起始日前利息资本化的金额

——还款期的加权平均值

——根据附件4第6条（a）和（b）款就不提供支持的原因作出解释。

4. 按照附件4第7条适用的最低利率。

(l) 附件5第5条

1. 对于官方支持有关条款的全面解释，包括：

——解释提供铁路基础设施项目相关条款的原因

——还款期是否超过已接受融资的铁路基础设施的使用年限

2. 对于I类国家的交易：

——项目总债务，包括官方和私人贷款人

——对私人贷款机构所负的债务总额

——加入国提供的债务比例

——确认在加入国和不享受官方出口信贷支持的私人金融机

构参加同一银团贷款的情况下，（i）整个贷款期间，加入国是贷款份额较小的一方并按同等比例行使权利；（ii）加入国提供的官方出口信贷支持成分不超过银团贷款的50%。

——具体的定价数据，用以说明官方支持的保费费率不削减可获得的私人市场融资，并且与其他加入贷款银团的私人金融机构收取的相应费率是同等的。

（m）附件6第5条

1. 解释为何提供项目融资的有关条款

2. 交钥匙工程的合同金额，分包合约所占比重等

3. 详尽的项目介绍

4. 信用起始日前提供的覆盖类型

5. 信用起始日前对政治风险的覆盖比例

6. 信用起始日前对商业风险的覆盖比例

7. 信用起始日后提供的覆盖比例

8. 信用起始日后对政治风险的覆盖比例

9. 信用起始日后对商业风险的覆盖比例

10. 建设期长度（如适用）

11. 提款期长度

12. 还款期加权平均值

13. 还款方式

14. 还款频率

15. 信用起始日和第一次本金偿还日之间的时间间隔

16. 截至信贷期中点本金偿还的比例

17. 信用起始日前利息资本化的金额

18. 出口信用机构（ECA）收到其他费用，如承诺费（可选，除了买方在高收入经合组织国家的交易情况以外）

19. 保费费率（可选，除了项目在高收入经合组织国家的交易情况以外）

20. 确认（必要的时候进行解释）交易具有以下特点：

——贷款人对一个特殊的经济实体提供融资，并同意将该经济实体的现金流和收入作为偿还贷款的来源，以该经济实体的资产作为还款担保。

——贷款人为一个（在法律上和经济上）独立的项目公司，如特殊目的公司，在能够产生收益的投资项目中的相关出口贸易提供融资。

——在项目各参与方之间有适当的风险分担，如私人股东或有良好信誉的公共股东、出口商、贷款人、产品/服务的协议购买人，也包括股本的充足性。

——项目在整个还款期间产生的现金流足以支付运营成本并偿还外来资金形成的债务。

——可以从项目收益中优先扣除运营成本并偿还债务。

——非主权买方/借款人，且未获得主权还款担保（政府出具的履约担保除外，如购销安排）。

——项目收益/资产上设定资产抵押，如权益转让、抵押、收入账户质押。

——在项目完成之后，对项目的私人行业股东/发起人无追索权或仅具有限追索权。

（n）附件6第5条，针对高收入OECD国家的项目

1. 项目的总债务，包括官方和私人借款人

2. 对私人贷款机构所负的债务总额

3. 加入国提供的债务所占比例

4. 确认：

——在加入国和不享受官方出口信贷支持的私人金融机构参加同一银团贷款的情况下，整个贷款期间，加入国是贷款份额较小的一方并按同等比例行使权利。

——在上述（m）款第19条项下报告的保费费率并不削减可获得的私人市场融资，并且与其他加入贷款银团的私人金融机构收取的相应费率是同等的。

# 附件8

# 最低保费费率的计算

**最低保费费率（MPR）公式**

如债务人/担保人所在国别是 1 ~ 7 类国家时，计算出口信贷适用的 MPR 公式为：

$$MPR = \{[(a_i \times HOR + b_i) \times \max(PCC, PCP)/0.95] \times (1 - LCF) + [c_{in} \times PCC/0.95 \times HOR \times (1 - CEF)]\} \times QPF_i \times PCF_i \times BTSF$$

其中：

——$a_i$是 $i$（$i=1 \sim 7$）类国家适用的国别风险分类系数

——$c_{in}$是适用的 $n$ 类买方（$n$ = SOV +，SOV/CCO，CC1 ~ CC5）在 $i$ 类国别风险国家的买方风险系数

——$b_i$是国别风险分类常量

——*HOR* 为风险期

——*PCC* 为商业（买方）风险承保比例

——*PCP* 为政治（国家）风险承保比例

——*CEF* 为信用增进因子

——$QPF_i$为 $i$（$i=1 \sim 7$）类国别风险中的产品质量因子

——*PCF* 为 $i$（$i=1 \sim 7$）类国别风险中的承保比例因子

——*BTSF* 为优于主权信用因子

——*LCF* 为当地货币因子

## 适用的国别风险分类

适用的国别风险分类根据《安排》第24条（e）款决定，系数 $a_i$ 和 $b_i$ 的值从下表得到：

| | 1 | 2 | 3 | 4 | 5 | 6 | 7 |
|---|---|---|---|---|---|---|---|
| a | 0.090 | 0.200 | 0.350 | 0.550 | 0.740 | 0.900 | 1.100 |
| b | 0.350 | 0.350 | 0.350 | 0.350 | 0.750 | 1.200 | 1.800 |

## 适用的买方风险评级选择

可适用的买方风险评级在下表中列明，结合国别和买方风险评级，表中列明了CC1～CC5的买方评级分类以及对应信用评级机构的买方评级分类。对于每一项用于辅助计算债务人（和担保人）分类的买方评级（SOV+至CC5）的定性描述在附件11中列明。

| 国别风险分类 | | | | | | |
|---|---|---|---|---|---|---|
| 1 | 2 | 3 | 4 | 5 | 6 | 7 |
| SOV+ | SOV+ | SOV+ | SOV+ | SOV+ | SOV+ | SOV+ |
| SOV/CC0 | SOV/CC0 | SOV/CC0 | SOV/CC0 | SOV/CC0 | SOV/CC0 | SOV/CC0 |
| CC1<br>AAA至<br>AA- | CC1<br>A+至<br>A- | CC1<br>BBB+至<br>BBB- | CC1<br>BB+至<br>BB | CC1<br>BB- | CC1<br>B+ | CC1<br>B |
| CC2<br>A+至<br>A- | CC2<br>BBB+至<br>BBB- | CC2<br>BB+至<br>BB | CC2<br>BB- | CC2<br>B+ | CC2<br>B | CC2<br>B-或<br>更低 |
| CC3<br>BBB+<br>至BBB- | CC3<br>BB+<br>至BB | CC3<br>BB- | CC3<br>B+ | CC3<br>B | CC3<br>B-或<br>更低 | |

续表

| 1 | 2 | 3 | 4 | 5 | 6 | 7 |
|---|---|---|---|---|---|---|
| CC4<br>BB+<br>至BB | CC4<br>BB- | CC4<br>B+ | CC4<br>B | CC4<br>B-或<br>更低 | | |
| CC5<br>BB-或<br>更低 | CC5<br>B+或<br>更低 | CC5<br>B或<br>更低 | CC5<br>B-或<br>更低 | | | |

对于特定的买方风险评级，其系数 $c_{in}$ 可从下表中得到：

| 买方风险评级 | 国别风险分类 | | | | | | |
|---|---|---|---|---|---|---|---|
| | 1 | 2 | 3 | 4 | 5 | 6 | 7 |
| SOV+ | 0.000 | 0.000 | 0.000 | 0.000 | 0.000 | 0.000 | 0.000 |
| SOV/CC0 | 0.000 | 0.000 | 0.000 | 0.000 | 0.000 | 0.000 | 0.000 |
| CC1 | 0.110 | 0.120 | 0.110 | 0.100 | 0.100 | 0.100 | 0.125 |
| CC2 | 0.200 | 0.212 | 0.223 | 0.234 | 0.246 | 0.258 | 0.271 |
| CC3 | 0.270 | 0.320 | 0.320 | 0.350 | 0.380 | 0.480 | n/a |
| CC4 | 0.405 | 0.459 | 0.495 | 0.540 | 0.621 | n/a | n/a |
| CC5 | 0.630 | 0.675 | 0.720 | 0.810 | n/a | n/a | n/a |

**风险期（HOR）**

风险期（HOR）可按下列公式计算：

标准还款安排（即每半年等额偿还本金）

HOR =（提款期长度 ×0.5）+ 还款期长度

非标准还款安排

HOR =（提款期 ×0.5）+［加权平均还款期长度 −0.25）×0.5］

上述公式中，时间的单位为年。

**商业（买方）风险承保比例（PCC）和政治（国家）风险承保比例（PCP）**

承保比例（PCC 和 PCP）在公式中均表示为小数（即，95%表示为 0.95）。

**买方信用增进**

对于没有采用增信手段的项目，信用增进因子（CEF）的值为 0。对于采用增信手段的项目的 CEF 值，按附件 7 要求，需满足《安排》第 31 条（c）款的条件，且不超过 0.35。

**产品质量因子（QPF）**

QPF 从下表中得到：

| 产品质量 | 国家风险分类 | | | | | | |
|---|---|---|---|---|---|---|---|
| | 1 | 2 | 3 | 4 | 5 | 6 | 7 |
| 低于标准 | 0.9965 | 0.9935 | 0.9850 | 0.9825 | 0.9825 | 0.9800 | 0.9800 |
| 标准 | 1.0000 | 1.0000 | 1.0000 | 1.0000 | 1.0000 | 1.0000 | 1.0000 |
| 高于标准 | 1.0035 | 1.0065 | 1.0150 | 1.0175 | 1.0175 | 1.0200 | 1.0200 |

**承保比例因子（PCF）**

PCF 按照以下方法计算：

在 Max（PCC，PCP）≤0.95 的情况下，PCF = 1

在 Max（PCC，PCP）>0.95 的情况下，

PCF = 1 + （（Max（PCC，PCF）－0.95）/0.05）×承保比例系数

承保比例系数如下表所示：

| 承保比例系数 | 国家风险分类 | | | | | | |
|---|---|---|---|---|---|---|---|
| | 1 | 2 | 3 | 4 | 5 | 6 | 7 |
| | 0.00000 | 0.00337 | 0.00489 | 0.01639 | 0.03657 | 0.05878 | 0.08598 |

**优于主权信用因子（BTSF）**

当债务人被列为优于主权（SOV +）的买方风险评级时，BTSF = 0.9，否则，BTSF = 1。

**当地货币因子（LCF）**

对于采用当地货币降低国别风险的交易，LCF 不超过 0.2；对于其他情况，LCF 为 0。

# 附件9

# 对于涉及第0类国家交易的市场基准

**出口信贷未覆盖的部分或银团贷款中非出口信用机构（ECA）承保的部分**

私人银行/机构对出口信贷中未覆盖部分（或银团贷款中非ECA承保的部分）要求的价格，可能与ECA承保的部分最为匹配。对于未承保的比例或部分的定价，仅适用于商业融资条款的情形（例如：IFI融资的部分将不适用）。

**特定的公司债券**

公司债券可以反映特定的信用风险，但应注意匹配ECA合同的特点，如期限、计价货币以及增信手段。若使用一级市场公司债券（即发行时明确收益率）或二级市场公司债券（即在合适的收益率曲线——通常选用相应的货币互换收益率曲线之上，期权价值调整了风险溢价），债务人的上述债券应优先适用。若无法获得上述信息，应适用同类借款人与同类交易的一级或二级市场公司债券。

**特定的信用违约互换**

信用违约互换（CDS）是针对违约风险的一种保障形式。CDS溢价是CDS买方按照名义本金的比例，按期支付的费用，通常以基点计量。CDS买方通过在整个互换存续期（或直到信用事件发生）内向卖方支付费用，以购买保险的形式有效规避了违约风险。债务人的CDS曲线应优先适用，若无法获得上述信息，应适用同类借款人与同类交易的CDS曲线。

**指数化信用违约互换**

指数化信用违约互换是一个行业（或其中一部分、一个地理区域）中已注册的 CDS 的集合。因此，指数化信用违约互换的溢价综合反映了该指数跟踪的某一特定市场板块的信用风险。当无法获得特定 CDS 或特定 CDS 市场缺乏流动性时，指数化信用违约互换的相关度最高。

**贷款基准**

分为一级市场贷款基准（即贷款发行时的定价）或二级市场贷款基准（即目前从其他金融机构购买该贷款的金融机构所预期的贷款收益率）。对于一级市场贷款基准，所有的费用都应已知，从而计算出整体的收益率情况。若使用贷款基准，债务人的贷款基准应优先适用，若无法获得上述信息，应适用同类借款人与同类交易的贷款基准。

**基准市场曲线**

基准市场曲线反映了一个行业整体或买方群体的信用风险情况。当对于某一特定买方的信息不足时，该市场信息或具有相关性。通常来讲，信息的质量取决于其所在市场的流动性。在任何情况下，应寻找与 ECA 合同特点（例如：日期、信用评级、期限、计价货币等）最匹配的市场工具。

**融资资源的加权平均成本（WACFR）**

WACFR 可能通过买方的财务报告计算得出。但在使用此方法时应格外小心，确保一家企业的融资资源加权平均成本可以反映其已获融资的真实情况。

# 附件 10

# 关于适用第三国还款担保以及多边或区域性机构分类的标准和条件

**目的**

本附件对《安排》第 24 条（e）款中所述的适用第三国还款担保以及经分类的多边或区域性机构还款担保，应遵循的标准和条件作出了规定。本附件还规定了关于《安排》第 28 条所述的多边或区域性机构的评估和分类的标准。

**适用**

情况 1：全额担保

当位于买方/借款人所在国之外的实体对可能出险的全部金额（本金和利息）提供担保时，可适用的国别风险分类可以是担保人所在国的国别风险分类，可适用的买方风险分类可以是担保人所属的买方风险分类，但应满足下列标准：

——担保覆盖整个信贷期。

——担保是不可撤销、无条件和见索即付。

——担保具有法律效力，并在担保人所在国管辖权内具有执行权。

——担保人有信誉偿还被担保的债务额。

——担保人应遵守其所在国有关货币监管与汇兑的法规。

当经分类的多边或区域性机构作为担保人时，应满足以下标准：

——担保覆盖整个信贷期。

——担保是不可撤销、无条件和见索即付。

——担保人对全额贷款承担法律上的担保义务。

——直接向债权人还款。

如果担保人是被担保实体的子公司/母公司，加入国应根据个案确定：（1）鉴于子公司/母公司之间的关系以及子公司对母公司承担的法律义务的程度，该子公司/母公司是否在法律和财务上独立并具有履行还款义务的能力；（2）子公司/母公司是否会受到当地事件/法规或主权干涉的影响；（3）在发生违约时，总公司/母公司是否会认为自己应承担还款责任。

情况2：有限额度担保

当位于买方/借款人所在国之外的实体对可能出险的金额（本金和利息）提供有限额度担保时，对于被担保的这部分信贷，可适用的国别风险分类可以是担保人所在国家的国别风险分类，可适用的买方风险分类可以是担保人所属的买方风险分类，但同样应满足情况1所列的各项标准。

对于未被担保部分，仍应适用债务人所在国的国别风险分类和债务人所属的买方风险分类。

多边或区域性机构的风险分类

若多边或区域性机构基本上不受其所在国家的货币监管和汇兑法规管制，则该机构适用于风险等级分类。应在个案基础上，根据每个机构的特点进行风险评估，并结合考虑以下因素，将这些机构划分为国别风险0至7等级。

——该机构在法律上和财务上的独立性；

——该机构的全部资产享有国有化或征收豁免权；

——该机构有权自由汇兑资金；

——该机构不受驻在国政府的干预；

——该机构免予税负；以及

——该机构的所有成员国均有义务向机构补充资金，使其能够履行义务。

评估还应考虑在机构所在国或债务人所在国发生国别信用风险违约时的历史还款记录；以及在评估过程中应予考虑的任何其他因素。

多边和区域性机构的风险分类表是开放性的，一个加入国可以要求根据上述考虑因素对某一指定机构进行审议。多边和区域性机构的分类应向所有加入国公开。

# 附件 11

## 买方风险分类的定性描述

**优于主权（SOV +）**

这属于特殊情况下的分类。该风险分类的实体拥有极好的信用记录，即使在主权债务危机期间或主权违约的情况下，仍能履行其还款义务。国际信用评级机构定期发布报告，列出评级超过主权外币评级的公司及相应实体。除非通过主权风险评估方法（Sovereign Risk Assessment Methodology）确定的主权风险显著高于国别风险，通常加入国可推荐其认为评级优于主权评级的实体。如要获得优于所在国主权评级的分类，一个实体应同时具备以下多个特点，甚至通常具备以下绝大多数特点或类似特点：

——信用记录极好；

——与其负债相比，拥有充足的外汇收入；

——跨国公司，在境外设有分支机构或经营跨国业务，尤其是在高评级国家的境内拥有分支机构或跨国业务，具有很强的运营能力和创造现金流的能力；

——该实体拥有国外所有者或战略合作伙伴，在没有正式担保情况下，成为可依赖的财务支持的来源；

——该实体有享受国家优惠政策待遇的记录，包括汇兑限制豁免、外汇收入上缴豁免以及税收优惠；

——高评级的国际银行对该实体承诺信用额度，尤其是没有重大不利变动（MAC）条款约束的信用额度。MAC 条款使银行有权在主权危机或其他风险事件发生时，撤回已承诺的贷款额度；

——该实体拥有离岸资产，尤其是流动性资产，通常表现为出口商可以获取或持有一定海外现金流用于偿还债务。

通常情况下，SOV + 买方风险分类不适用于：

——公有实体或公共设施、国家部委等次主权实体、地方政府等；

——在主权国家管辖权内经营的金融机构；

——主要以本国货币向本国内市场销售产品的实体。

**主权（SOV）**

主权债务人/担保人是明确地经法律授权、代表主权国家承担债务偿还义务的实体，通常是一国的财政部或中央银行①。主权风险的特征是：

——债务人/担保人经法律授权，代表主权国家承担债务偿还义务，完全代表主权国家的信誉和信用；

——在主权风险重组的情况下，债务被纳入重组范围，且主权国家通过重组继承获得该债务，承担偿还债务的义务。

**等同主权（CC0）：极好的信用质量**

“等同主权”分类包括两种类型的债务人/担保人：

——公共实体，尽职调查显示，在追偿前景和违约风险方面，该买方实际受到主权国家的信誉、信用/支持，或者主权国家为其提供流动性和偿付支持的可能性很高。等同主权的非主权公共实体也包括政府拥有的某个行业中垄断性或近乎垄断性的公司（如

① 最通常地，这成为中央银行或财政部承担的风险。若为中央政府体系内，除财政部以外的实体，则应通过尽职调查来确认该实体是否完全代表该主权的信任和信用。

电力、石油、天然气）。

——企业实体，在违约风险和追偿前景方面，拥有极好的信用记录，风险近似于主权国家。这类企业实体可能是，主权国家为其提供流动性和偿付支持可能性很高的大型蓝筹公司或非常重要的银行。

极好的信用质量表明还款风险可忽略，还款能力很强，不易受到可预知事件的影响。这类信用质量的实体，通常同时具备以下全部或几个业务与财务方面的特征：

——创造现金流和收入的能力介于极强与很强之间；

——流动性水平介于极好与很好之间；

——杠杆率介于极低与很低之间；

——经营状况介于极好与很好之间，且可证明管理能力很强。

该实体的另一特点是，很好地对外披露财务及所有权状况，除非该实体获得其母公司（或主权）支持的可能性很高，且后者的风险分类等于或优于该实体。

基于债务人/担保人所在国的风险分类，有认证资格的信用评级机构可能会对风险分类为 CC0 的债务人/担保人，作出介于 AAA（第 1 类国家）和 B（第 7 类国家）之间的评级。

**很好的信用质量（CC1）**

还款风险被认为是低或很低。债务人/担保人的还款能力很强，且不易受到可预知事件的影响。这类债务人/担保人受到外部环境和经济形势变化的负面影响有限或非常有限。这类信用质量的实体，通常同时具备以下全部或几个业务与财务方面的特征：

——创造现金流和收入的能力介于很强与强之间；

——流动性水平介于很好与好之间；

——杠杆率介于很低与低之间；

——经营状况很好，且可证明管理能力很强。

该实体的另一特点是，很好地对外披露财务及所有权状况，除非该实体获得其母公司（或主权）支持的可能性很高，且后者的风险分类等于或优于该实体。

基于债务人/担保人所在国的风险分类，有认证资格的信用评级机构可能会对风险分类为 CC1 的债务人/担保人，作出介于 AAA（第 1 类国家）和 B（第 7 类国家）之间的评级。

**介于好与较好之间的信用质量，高于平均水平（CC2）**

还款风险被认为是低。债务人/担保人的还款能力强或较强，且不易受到可预知事件的影响。这类债务人/担保人受到外部环境和经济形势变化的负面影响有限。这类信用质量的实体，通常同时具备以下全部或几个业务与财务方面的特征：

——创造现金流和收入的能力介于强与较强之间；

——流动性水平介于好与较好之间；

——杠杆率介于低与较低之间；

——经营状况较好，且可证明管理能力较强。

该实体的另一特点是，很好地对外披露财务及所有权状况，除非该实体获得其母公司（或主权）支持的可能性很高，且后者的风险分类等于或优于该实体。

基于债务人/担保人所在国的风险分类，有认证资格的信用评级机构可能会对风险分类为 CC2 的债务人/担保人，作出介于 A +（第 1 类国家）和 B – 或以下（第 7 类国家）之间的评级。

**一般的信用质量，平均水平（CC3）**

还款风险被认为是一般或较低。债务人/担保人的还款能力一般或较强，当面临重大持续不稳定因素，或不利的商业、金融或经济形势，信用风险可能上升，可能无法按期偿还债务。但是，可能找到其他可替代的商业或财务解决办法，以继续履行偿债义务。这类信用质量的实体，通常同时具备以下全部或几个业务与财务方面的特征：

——创造现金流和收入的能力介于较强与一般之间；

——流动性水平介于较好与一般之间；

——杠杆率介于较低与一般之间；

——经营状况一般，且可证明管理能力一般。

该实体的另一特点是，很好地对外披露财务及所有权状况，除非该实体获得其母公司（或主权）支持的可能性很高，且后者的风险分类等于或优于该实体。

基于债务人/担保人所在国的风险分类，有认证资格的信用评级机构可能会对风险分类为 CC3 的债务人/担保人，作出介于 BBB +（第 1 类国家）和 B – 及以下（第 6 类国家）之间的评级。

**较弱的信用质量，低于平均水平（CC4）**

还款风险被认为是较高。债务人/担保人的还款能力一般或较弱，当面临重大持续不稳定因素，或不利的商业、金融或经济形势，信用风险可能上升，可能无法按期偿还债务。但是，可能找到其他可替代的商业或财务解决办法，以继续履行偿债义务。这类信用质量的实体，通常同时具备以下全部或几个业务与财务方面的特征：

——创造现金流和收入的能力介于一般与较弱之间；

——流动性水平介于一般与较低之间；

——杠杆率介于一般与较高之间；

——经营状况较差，且可证明管理能力较差。

该实体的另一特点是，很好地对外披露财务及所有权状况，除非该实体获得其母公司（或主权）支持的可能性很高，且后者的风险分类等于或优于该实体。

基于债务人/担保人所在国的风险分类，有认证资格的信用评级机构可能会对风险分类为 CC4 的债务人/担保人，作出介于 BB+（第 1 类国家）和 B-及以下（第 5 类国家）之间的评级。

**弱的信用质量（CC5）**

还款风险被认为是高或很高。债务人/担保人的还款能力较弱或弱，尽管当前有还款能力，但安全边际有限。由于债务人/担保人的还款能力有赖于可持续的、有利的商业和经济环境，不利的经济、商业、金融环境很有可能影响其支付能力或支付意愿，导致还款风险上升。这类信用质量的实体，通常同时具备以下全部或几个业务与财务方面的特征：

——创造现金流和收入的能力介于较弱与弱之间；

——流动性水平介于较低与低之间；

——杠杆率介于较高与高之间；

——经营状况差，证明管理能力的记录有限或无记录。

该实体的另一特点是，很好地对外披露财务及所有权状况，除非该实体获得其母公司（或主权）支持的可能性很高，且后者的风险分类等于或优于该实体。

基于债务人/担保人所在国的风险分类，有认证资格的信用评级机构可能会对风险分类为 CC5 的债务人/担保人，作出介于 BB－（第 1 类国家）和 B－及以下（第 4 类国家）之间的评级。

# 附件 12

# 关于适用国别风险降低技术和买方信用增进的标准和条件

**目的**

本附件对《安排》第30条（a）款所述的国别风险降低技术和第31条（a）款所述的买方信用增进的运用作出详述，包括有关标准、条件和特殊情况，以及对MPR的影响。

**国别风险降低技术**

## 1. 离岸未来现金流结构与离岸监管账户结合使用

定义：

一方当事人出具的一份书面文件，例如契约、声明或信托安排，签章并交付给第三方（即非文件当事方），待到特定条件满足，由该第三方交付给另一当事方并开始生效。如果在考虑所列附加因素的基础上满足了下列标准，国别风险降低技术可以降低或消除汇款风险，尤其是对高风险国别分类。

标准：

——监管账户与一个赚取外汇项目相关联，且监管账户的流入资金是由该项目本身和/或其他离岸出口应收账款产生。

——监管账户离岸建立，即：位于项目所在国之外，其所在地的汇款风险及其他国别风险应是十分有限的（即在一个高收入OECD国家或高收入欧元区国家）。

——监管账户应开立在一流银行，该银行不得直接或间接受控于债务人利益或债务人所在国。

——账户的资金来源应通过长期的或其他合适的合同来保证。

——进入监管账户的债务人收入来源总和（即：由项目本身产生和/或其他来源产生）应是硬通货币，且可合理地被认为足以偿还整个贷款期内的债务。这些收入应来自于一个或多个信誉良好的外国客户，这类外国客户所在国应为相对项目所在国风险状况更好的国家（即通常为高收入 OECD 国家或高收入欧元区国家）。

——债务人不可撤销地指示外国客户直接向监管账户支付（即：付款不通过一个受债务人控制的账户，也不经过债务人所在国）。

——留存在监管账户中的资金应至少相当于 6 个月内的偿债额度。如项目融资采用灵活的还款条件，则账户中应至少留存相当于 6 个月偿债额度的金额。此金额可随时根据偿债情况变动。

——债务人不能随意支配监管账户（即：只能在贷款清偿完毕后支配）。

——在整个信贷期内，贷款人作为直接受益人，对账户内的资金享有权益。

——监管账户的开立，应获得所有当地的及任何其他有关当局的必要的法律授权。

——在贷款期内，监管账户与合约安排不能是有条件的，和/或可撤销的，和/或有限的。

需要考虑的其他因素：

如何适用上述技术，还取决于个案情况，并考虑以下因素：

——国家、债务人（即：公共或私营）、行业、所涉及商品或服务的弱点（包括它们在整个信贷期内的可获得性）、采购方；

——法律结构，例如：机制是否有效免受债务人或其所在国的影响；

——技术实施过程中受到政府干预、续期或收回的影响程度；

——账户是否与项目其他相关风险相互隔离；

——可能流入账户的资金金额，以及确保持续流入资金的机制；

——有关巴黎俱乐部（Paris Club）的情况（例如：可能的债务豁免）；

——除汇兑风险以外的其他可能的国家风险影响；

——是否与账户所在国风险相隔离；

——与采购方订立的合同，包括性质与期限；以及

——与贷款总额相关的全球预期外汇收入。

对 MPR 的影响

适用国别风险降低技术，可使交易适用的国别风险分类上升一个级别，但第 I 类国别风险的交易除外。

## 2. 当地货币融资

定义：

如果合同和融资以当地货币计量，而非硬通货币，以及在当地融资，可以规避或降低汇兑风险。以当地货币计量的主要还款义务，原则上不会因发生前两项国别信用风险而受到影响。

标准：

——ECA 的责任和赔款，或者直接对贷款人的还款全部以当地货币计量/支付。

——ECA 通常不承担汇兑风险。

——通常情况下，无须将当地货币存款兑换成硬通货币。

——借款人使用其本国货币在本国偿还贷款，属于有效、合法地清偿债务。

——若借款人的收入为当地货币，其不会受到不利汇率波动的影响。

——借款人所在国的汇兑法规不应对借款人以当地货币还款的义务产生任何影响。

需要考虑的其他因素：

该技术可有选择性地适用于健康经济环境下课自由兑换和汇款的货币。若在加入国的 ECA 确认赔偿责任之后，当地币变得“不可转移”或“不可兑换”，ECA 应以其本国货币履行赔偿义务（而由直接贷款人承担这种风险）。

对 MPR 的影响

适用该风险降低技术，可使 MPR 的国别信用风险部分得到不超过 20% 的折扣（即当地币因素（LCF）的值不高于 0.2）。

**买方信用增进方法**

下表列出了可以适用的买方信用增进方法的定义，以及通过 MPR 公式代入买方信用增进因子（CEF）算出的对可适用的 MPR 产生的最大影响。

| 信用增进方法 | 定义 | 最大的CEF |
|---|---|---|
| 合同收益或应收账款的转让 | 当借款人与一家实力雄厚的采购方订立了合同，不论是离岸交易或是国内交易，在法律上具有执行力的合同权益转让，可享有执行借款人合同权益的权利，和/或在贷款发生违约后，代替借款人在主要合同项下作出决策。在一个交易中，与第三方的直接协议（在矿产或能源交易中与当地政府代理有直接协议），可使贷款人在交易遇到征收或合同违约事件时，有渠道向政府寻求救济和补偿。<br>一个处在艰难市场环境或行业的公司，可能对那些处于更稳定环境中的一家或多家公司进行产品销售，并持有对后者的应收账款。这些应收账款通常以硬通货计量，但可能不是任何一项具体合同关系的标的。应收账款转让相当于在借款人的账户上设定了资产抵押，使贷款人在借款人的现金流中享有一定优先受偿权。 | 0.10 |
| 资产抵押 | 控制一项财产，通过：（1）在可移动、具有价值的财产上设定按揭抵押；（2）财产本身具有整体价值。<br>资产抵押应考虑可重复获得的物品，例如火车机车、医疗设备或建筑设备。当衡量抵押物的价值时，ECA应考虑资产抵押在法律上的追偿难度。换言之，若资产抵押能得到健全法律体制的保护，抵押权益更有价值；若对抵押物的追偿力存有疑问，抵押权益也因此受到削弱。抵押物的准确价值由市场决定。由于抵押物可被移动至另一管辖区域，这里所指的“市场”比本地市场的范畴更宽泛，注意：如适用资产抵押作为买方信用增进手段，通常都在交易所在国境内持有资产抵押。 | 0.25 |

续表

| 信用增进方法 | 定义 | 最大的 CEF |
| --- | --- | --- |
| 固定资产抵押 | 固定资产抵押的典型是无法随意移动或拆除的设备组成部分，例如涡轮机或集成生产线上的生产机械。固定资产抵押的意图和价值在于，使 ECA 在贷款违约时能够得到损失补偿，从而基于杠杆效应提供融资。固定资产抵押的价值随经济、法律、市场和其他因素的变化而波动。 | 0.15 |
| 监管账户 | 监管账户是为保障贷款人利益、由不受买方/债务人控制或不与买方/债务人有共同利益的第三方持有的偿债账户或其他形式的现金应收账款账户。监管资金必须预先存入或提前予以监管。监管账户的价值基本可达到现金账户账面价值的 100%。监管账户对现金的控制力更强，确保资金在被随意支取之前能用于清偿债务。注意：如适用监管账户作为买方信用增进手段，通常都在交易所在国境内持有监管账户。现金担保显著降低了分期付款的违约风险。 | 监管金额占贷款额的百分比，最高不超 0.10 |

# 附件 13

## 开发性特点清单

**援助贷款项目开发性特点清单**

近年来，为确保由官方开发性援助（ODA）提供全部或部分融资支持的发展中国家项目有利于促进发展，开发援助委员会（DAC）提出了诸多项目标准，主要规定在：

1. 《开发援助委员会关于项目评估规则》，1998 年版；

2. 《开发援助委员会关于关联融资、约束性和部分约束性官方发展援助的指导规则》，1987 年版；以及

3. 《官方开发性援助的合理采购方式》，1986 年版。

**项目符合项目所在国的整体投资优先性（项目选择）**

项目是否属于项目所在国中央财政和规划当局已批准的投资和公共支出计划中的一部分？

（具体指出提及项目的政策性文件，如项目所在国的投资计划）

项目是否同时得到国际开发融资机构的融资支持？

是否有证据显示，项目曾因开发优先性较低，而被一个国际开发融资机构或开发援助委员会的其他成员考虑但被拒绝？

如果是私人行业项目，是否已通过项目所在国政府的批准？

项目是否被纳入援助国和接受国之间签署的、援助范围更广的政府间协定？

**项目筹备和评估**

项目是否已按照《开发援助委员会关于项目评估规则》（PPA）规定的一系列标准进行筹备、设计和评估？与项目评估有关的规则如下：

（a）经济方面（PPA 第 30 段至第 38 段）。

（b）技术方面（PPA 第 32 段）。

（c）财务方面（PPA 第 23 段至第 29 段）。

如果是产生收入的项目，尤其是在竞争性市场上产生收入的情况，援助性融资的优惠部分是否传导给资金的最终使用者？（PPA 第 25 段）

（a）机构评估（PPA 第 40 段至第 44 段）。

（b）社会和分配分析（PPA 第 47 段至第 57 段）。

（c）环境评估（PPA 第 55 段至第 57 段）。

**采购程序**

应采用以下哪种采购模式？（有关定义参见《官方开发性援助的合理采购方式》中有关规则）

（a）国际竞标（采购规则 3 及其附件 2：有效国际竞标的最低条件）。

（b）国内竞标（采购规则 4）。

（c）非正式竞标或议标（采购规则 5A 或 5B）。

是否需要检查供货价格和质量？（PPA 第 63 段）

# 附件 14

## 定义表

为《安排》的目的：

（a）承诺：以任何形式向接收国、买方、借款人、出口方或金融机构发出的声明，表示其提供官方支持的意愿或意向。

（b）共同谅解：加入国之间达成的谅解，同意对特定交易或在特定情况下，适用特殊的官方支持融资条款。对于共同谅解中所指的特定交易或特定情况，共同谅解中规则的效力高于《安排》中规则的效力。

（c）约束性援助的优惠水平：对于赠与，优惠水平是100%。对于贷款，优惠水平取决于名义贷款额与借款人未来偿还的贴现现值之间的差额。该差额表现为名义贷款额的一个百分比。

（d）停运：核电站的关闭或拆除。

（e）出口合同金额：出口货物和/或服务的购买者支付或代表其支付的全部金额，但不包括本表后面将要定义的当地费用；对于租赁，应扣除相当于利息的那部分租金。

（f）最终承诺：对于一项出口信用交易（可针对单笔交易或一个信贷额度），最终承诺是加入国通过互惠协议或单边行为承诺的准确和全面的融资条款。

（g）初始燃料装载：初始燃料装载应仅包括初始安装的核芯及两次后续加载，总量不超过一个核芯的三分之二。

（h）利率支持：政府与银行或其他金融机构之间达成的安排，允许银行或其他金融机构以CIRR或高于CIRR的固定利率提供出口融资。

（i）信贷额度：无论何种形式，针对一系列交易提供出口信贷的框架性安排，这些交易可能与某个特定项目相关或不相关。

(j) 当地费用：在买方所在国必需发生的购买货物或服务的费用，这些费用是为执行出口合同或为完成项目（出口合同构成项目的一部分）而发生。但在买方所在国支付给出口方代理的佣金除外。

(k) 纯保险：由政府或代表政府通过出口信用担保或保险的形式提供的官方支持，不是官方融资支持。

(l) 还款期：自本附件定义的信用起始日起，至约定的最后一笔本金偿还日止的期间。

(m) 信用起始日：

(1) 零部件（中间产品），包括相关服务：对于部件或零件，信用起始日是不晚于买方接受货物的实际日期或接受货物的加权平均日期（包括服务，若可适用）；对于服务，信用起始日是向客户提交发票之日或客户接受服务之日。

(2) 准资本性货物，包括相关服务——通常是单价相对较低，用于工业生产或者其他生产性或商业用途的机械、设备：对于准资本性货物，信用起始日是不晚于买方接受货物的实际日期或接受货物的加权平均日期，或者，在出口商有试运行义务的情况下，信用起始日是不晚于试运行之日；对于服务，信用起始日是向客户提交发票之日或客户接受服务之日。对于供货商有试运行义务的服务合同，信用起始日就不晚于试运行之日。

(3) 资本性货物和项目服务：价值高、用于工业生产或者其他生产性或商业用途的机械、设备：

——对于有独立用途的分项组成的资本性货物的销售合同，信用起始日是不晚于买方实际控制货物的日期，或买方实际控制货物的加权平均日期。

——对于用作成套设备或工厂的资本性设备的销售合同，在供货商没有试运行义务的情况下，信用起始日是不晚于买方实际控制合同项下提供的整套设备（不包括零配件）之日。

——如出口商有试运行义务，信用起始日是不晚于试运行之日。

——对于服务贸易，信用起始日是不晚于向客户提交发票之日或客户接受服务之日。对于供货商有试运行义务的服务合同，信用起始日是不晚于试运行之日。

（4）成套设备或工厂——价值高、需要使用资本性货物的成套生产性设备：

——对于用作成套设备或工厂的资本性设备的销售合同，在供货商没有试运行义务的情况下，信用起始日是不晚于买方实际控制合同项下提供的整套设备（不包括零配件）之日。

——对于承包商没有试运行义务的工程建设合同，信用起始日是不晚于工程完工之日。

——对于供货商或承包商根据合同约定有试运行义务的合同，信用起始日是不晚于完成安装或建设、初步调试以保证可投入运营之日。无论根据合同条款当时货物是否已移交给买方，也无论供货商或承包商是否还有后续义务，例如保证有效运转或培训当地人员，上述信用起始日的规定都适用。

——如果一个项目的各部分独立实施，信用起始日分别为每个单独部分的信用起始日，或各信用起始日的加权平均日期，或者，当供货商合同仅涉及项目关键部分而非整个项目时，信用起始日为整个项目的信用起始日。

——对于服务，信用起始日是不晚于向客户提交发票或客户接受服务之日。对于供货商有试运行义务的服务合同，信用起始日不晚于试运行之日。

（n）约束性援助：援助（在法律上或事实上）要求向援助国或其他指定国家采购货物和/或服务，包括贷款、赠与或优惠水平在0以上的相关融资安排。

该定义中的“约束性”适用于以下情形：

受援国和援助国之间的正式协议或任何形式的非正式谅解；或者，包括根据《安排》第34条中列出的形式，受援国、其他实质性发展中国家及加入国不能自由及全部获得的融资采购的一揽子计划，或涉及发展援助委员会或加入国认为与约束性援助等同的实际操作。

（o）非约束性援助：贷款或赠与的款项可以全部、自由地用于采购任何国家的货物或服务。

（p）加权平均还款期：贷款项下清偿一半的本金所需要的时间。计算方法是，将每笔本金到期还款日与信用起始日之间的时间间隔，考虑该笔本金所占加权比重后，相加得出总和（以年为单位）。

TAD/PG (2015)1

# ARRANGEMENT ON OFFICIALLY SUPPORTED EXPORT CREDITS

—2015 REVISION

(effective as of 15 January 2015)

# TABLE OF CONTENTS

CHAPTER I: GENERAL PROVISIONS ..... 225

1. PURPOSE ..... 225
2. STATUS ..... 225
3. PARTICIPATION ..... 225
4. INFORMATION AVAILABLE TO NON-PARTICIPANTS ..... 226
5. SCOPE OF APPLICATION ..... 226
6. SECTOR UNDERSTANDINGS ..... 227
7. PROJECT FINANCE ..... 228
8. WITHDRAWAL ..... 228
9. MONITORING ..... 228

CHAPTER II: FINANCIAL TERMS AND CONDITIONS FOR EXPORT CREDITS ..... 229

10. DOWN PAYMENT, MAXIMUM OFFICIAL SUPPORT AND LOCAL COSTS ..... 229
11. CLASSIFICATION OF COUNTRIES FOR MAXIMUM REPAYMENT TERMS ..... 230
12. MAXIMUM REPAYMENT TERMS ..... 231
13. REPAYMENT TERMS FOR NON-NUCLEAR POWER PLANTS ..... 232
14. REPAYMENT OF PRINCIPAL AND PAYMENT OF INTEREST ..... 233
15. INTEREST RATES, PREMIUM RATES AND OTHER FEES ..... 235

16. VALIDITY PERIOD FOR EXPORT CREDITS ········ 235
17. ACTION TO AVOID OR MINIMISE LOSSES ············ 236
18. MATCHING ············ 236
19. MINIMUM FIXED INTEREST RATES UNDER OFFICIAL FINANCING SUPPORT ············ 236
20. CONSTRUCTION OF CIRRs ············ 237
21. VALIDITY OF CIRRs ············ 238
22. APPLICATION OF CIRRs ············ 238
23. PREMIUM FOR CREDIT RISK ············ 239
24. MINIMUM PREMIUM RATES FOR CREDIT RISK ··· 239
25. COUNTRY RISK CLASSIFICATION ············ 243
26. SOVEREIGN RISK ASSESSMENT ············ 245
27. BUYER RISK CLASSIFICATION ············ 246
28. CLASSIFICATION OF MULTILATERAL AND REGIONAL INSTITUTIONS ············ 248
29. PERCENTAGE AND QUALITY OF OFFICIAL EXPORT CREDIT COVER ············ 248
30. COUNTRY RISK MITIGATION TECHNIQUES ········ 249
31. BUYER RISK CREDIT ENHANCEMENTS ············ 249
32. REVIEW OF THE VALIDITY OF THE MINIMUM PREMIUM RATES FOR CREDIT RISK ············ 251
CHAPTER III: PROVISIONS FOR TIED AID ············ 252
33. GENERAL PRINCIPLES ············ 252
34. FORMS OF TIED AID ············ 252
35. ASSOCIATED FINANCING ············ 253
36. COUNTRY ELIGIBILITY FOR TIED AID ············ 255
37. PROJECT ELIGIBILITY ············ 256
38. MINIMUM CONCESSIONALITY LEVEL ············ 257
39. EXEMPTIONS FROM COUNTRY OR PROJECT

ELIGIBILITY FOR TIED AID ........ 257
40. CALCULATION OF CONCESSIONALITY LEVEL OF TIED AID ........ 259
41. VALIDITY PERIOD FOR TIED AID ........ 261
42. MATCHING ........ 262
CHAPTER IV: PROCEDURES ........ 263
*SECTION 1: COMMON PROCEDURES FOR EXPORT CREDITS AND TRADE-RELATED AID* ........ 263
43. NOTIFICATIONS ........ 263
44. INFORMATION ON OFFICIAL SUPPORT ........ 263
45. PROCEDURES FOR MATCHING ........ 263
46. SPECIAL CONSULTATIONS ........ 264
*SECTION 2: PROCEDURES FOR EXPORT CREDITS* ........ 265
47. PRIOR NOTIFICATION WITH DISCUSSION ........ 265
48. PRIOR NOTIFICATION ........ 266
*SECTION 3: PROCEDURES FOR TRADE-RELATED AID* ........ 267
49. PRIOR NOTIFICATION ........ 267
50. PROMPT NOTIFICATION ........ 268
*SECTION 4: CONSULTATION PROCEDURES FORTIED AID* ........ 269
51. PURPOSE OF CONSULTATIONS ........ 269
52. SCOPE AND TIMING OF CONSULTATIONS ........ 269
53. OUTCOME OF CONSULTATIONS ........ 271
*SECTION 5: INFORMATION EXCHANGE FOR EXPORT CREDITS AND TRADERELATED AID* ........ 271
54. CONTACT POINTS ........ 271
55. SCOPE OF ENQUIRIES ........ 272
56. SCOPE OF RESPONSES ........ 272

57. FACE-TO-FACE CONSULTATIONS ······················ 273
58. PROCEDURES AND FORMAT OF COMMON LINES ······················ 273
59. RESPONSES TO COMMON LINE PROPOSALS ········· 274
60. ACCEPTANCE OF COMMON LINES ······················ 275
61. DISAGREEMENT ON COMMON LINES ················ 276
62. EFFECTIVE DATE OF COMMON LINE ················ 276
63. VALIDITY OF COMMON LINES ························ 276
*SECTION 6: OPERATIONAL PROVISIONS FOR THE COMMUNICATION OF MINIMUM INTEREST RATES (CIRRs)* ································ 277
64. COMMUNICATION OF MINIMUM INTEREST RATES ················································ 277
65. EFFECTIVE DATE FOR APPLICATION OF INTEREST RATES ·································· 277
66. IMMEDIATE CHANGES IN INTEREST RATES ········· 278
*SECTION 7: REVIEWS* ······································ 278
67. REGULAR REVIEW OF THE ARRANGEMENT ······ 278
68. REVIEW OF MINIMUM INTEREST RATES ············ 278
69. REVIEW OF MINIMUM PREMIUM RATES AND RELATED ISSUES ··································· 279
ANNEX I SECTOR UNDERSTANDING ON EXPORT CREDITS FOR SHIPS ····························· 280
ANNEX II SECTOR UNDERSTANDING ON EXPORT CREDITS FOR NUCLEAR POWER PLANTS ·········································· 286
ANNEX III SECTOR UNDERSTANDING ON EXPORT CREDITS FOR CIVIL AIRCRAFT ·············· 293
ANNEX IV SECTOR UNDERSTANDING ON EXPORT

CREDITS FOR RENEWABLE ENERGY, CLIMATE CHANGE MITIGATION AND ADAPTATION, AND WATER PROJECTS ··· 365
ANNEX V SECTOR UNDERSTANDING ON EXPORT CREDITS FOR RAIL INFRASTRUCTURE ······ 387
ANNEX VI TERMS AND CONDITIONS APPLICABLE TO PROJECT FINANCE TRANSACTIONS ········ 392
ANNEX VII INFORMATION TO BE PROVIDED FOR NOTIFICATIONS ································ 397
ANNEX VIII CALCULATION OF THE MINIMUM PREMIUM RATES ······································ 411
ANNEX IX MARKET BENCHMARKS FOR TRANSACTIONS IN CATEGORY ZERO COUNTRIES ··········· 417
ANNEX X CRITERIA AND CONDITIONS GOVERNING THE APPLICATION OF A THIRD PARYT REPAYMENT GUARANTEE AND THE CLASSIFICATION OF MULTILATERAL OR REGIONAL INSTITUTIONs ······································ 420
ANNEX XI BUYER RISK CATEGORIES QUALITATIVE DESCRIPTIONS ································ 424
ANNEX XII CRITERIA AND CONDITIONS GOVERNING THE APPLICATION OF COUNTRY RISK MITIGATION TECHNIQUES AND BUYER RISK CREDIT ENHANCEMENTS ································ 433
ANNEX XIII CHECKLIST OF DEVELOPMENTAL QUALITY ······································ 441
ANNEX XIV LIST OF DEFINITIONS ······················ 444

# 1. CHAPTER I: GENERAL PROVISIONS

## 1. PURPOSE

a) The main purpose of the Arrangement on Officially Supported Export Credits, referred to throughout this document as the Arrangement, is to provide a framework for the orderly use of officially supported export credits.

b) The Arrangement seeks to foster a level playing field for official support, as defined in Article 5 a), in order to encourage competition among exporters based on quality and price of goods and services exported rather than on the most favourable officially supported financial terms and conditions.

## 2. STATUS

The Arrangement, developed within the OECD framework, initially came into effect in April 1978 and is of indefinite duration. The Arrangement is a Gentlemen's Agreement among the Participants; it is not an OECD Act①, although it receives the administrative support of the OECD Secretariat (hereafter: "the Secretariat").

## 3. PARTICIPATION

The Participants to the Arrangement currently are: Australia,

---

① As defined in Article 5 of the OECD Convention.

Canada, the European Union, Japan, Korea, New Zealand, Norway, Switzerland and the United States. Other OECD Members and non-members may be invited to become Participants by the current Participants.

## 4. INFORMATION AVAILABLE TO NON – PARTICIPANTS

a) The Participants undertake to share information with non – Participants on notifications related to official support as set out in Article 5 a).

b) A Participant shall, on the basis of reciprocity, reply to a request from a non – Participant in a competitive situation on the financial terms and conditions offered for its official support, as it would reply to a request from a Participant.

## 5. SCOPE OF APPLICATION

The Arrangement shall apply to all official support provided by or on behalf of a government for export of goods and/or services, including financial leases, which have a repayment term of two years or more.

a) Official support may be provided in different forms:

1) Export credit guarantee or insurance (pure cover).

2) Official financing support:

– direct credit/financing and refinancing, or

– interest rate support.

3) Any combination of the above.

b) The Arrangement shall apply to tied aid; the procedures set out in Chapter IV shall also apply to trade – related untied aid.

c) The Arrangement does not apply to exports of Military Equipment and Agricultural Commodities.

d) Official support shall not be provided if there is clear evidence that the contract has been structured with a purchaser in a country which is not the final destination of the goods, primarily with the aim of obtaining more favourable repayment terms.

## 6. SECTOR UNDERSTANDINGS

a) The following Sector Understandings are part of the Arrangement:

– Ships (Annex I)

– Nuclear Power Plants (Annex II)

– Civil Aircraft (Annex III)

– Renewable Energy, Climate Change Mitigation and Adaptation, and Water Projects (Annex IV)

– Rail Infrastructure (Annex V)

b) A Participant to a Sector Understanding may apply its provisions for official support for export of goods and/or services covered by that Sector Understanding. Where a Sector Understanding does not include a corresponding provision to that of the Arrangement, a Participant to the Sector Understanding shall apply the provision of the Arrangement.

## 7. PROJECT FINANCE

a) The Participants may apply the terms and conditions set out in Annex VI to the export of goods and/or services for transactions that meet the criteria set out in Appendix 1 of Annex VI.

b) Paragraph a) above applies to the export of goods and services covered by the Sector Understanding on Export Credits for Nuclear Power Plants, the Sector Understanding on Export Credits for Renewable Energy, Climate Change Mitigation and Adaptation, and Water Projects, and the Sector Understanding on Export Credits for Railway Infrastructure.

c) Paragraph a) above does not apply to the export of goods and services covered by the Sector Understanding on Export Credits for Civil Aircraft or the Sector Understanding on Export Credits for Ships.

## 8. WITHDRAWAL

A Participant may withdraw by notifying the Secretariat in writing by means of instant communication, *e.g.* the OECD On – Line Information System (OLIS). The withdrawal takes effect 180 calendar days after receipt of the notification by the Secretariat.

## 9. MONITORING

The Secretariat shall monitor the implementation of the Arrangement.

# 2. CHAPTER II: FINANCIAL TERMS AND CONDITIONS FOR EXPORT CREDITS

Financial terms and conditions for export credits encompass all the provisions set out in this Chapter which shall be read in conjunction one with the other.

The Arrangement sets out limitations on terms and conditions that may be officially supported. The Participants recognise that more restrictive financial terms and conditions than those provided for by the Arrangement traditionally apply to certain trade or industrial sectors. The Participants shall continue to respect such customary financial terms and conditions, in particular the principle by which repayment terms do not exceed the useful life of the goods.

## 10. DOWN PAYMENT, MAXIMUM OFFICIAL SUPPORT AND LOCAL COSTS

a) The Participants shall require purchasers of goods and services which are the subject of official support to make down payments of a minimum of 15% of the export contract value at or before the starting point of credit as defined in Annex XIV. For the assessment of down payments, the export contract value may be reduced proportionally if the transaction includes goods and services from a third country which are not officially supported. Financing/insurance of 100% of the premium is permissible. Premium may or may not be included in the export contract value. Retention payments made after the starting point of credit are not regarded as down payment in this context.

b) Official support for such down payments shall only take the form of insurance or guarantee against the usual pre-credit risks.

c) Except as provided for in paragraphs b) and d), the Participants shall not provide official support in excess of 85% of the export contract value, including third country supply but excluding local costs.

d) The Participants may provide official support for local costs, provided that:

1) Official support provided for local costs shall not exceed 30% of the export contract value.

2) It shall not be provided on terms more favourable/less restrictive than those agreed for the related exports.

3) Where official support for local cost exceeds 15% of the export contract value, such official support shall be subject to prior notification, pursuant to Article 48, specifying the nature of the local costs being supported.

## 11. CLASSIFICATION OF COUNTRIES FOR MAXIMUM REPAYMENT TERMS

a) Category I countries are High Income① OECD countries. All other countries are in Category II.

---

① Defined by the World Bank on an annual basis according to *per capita* GNI.

b) The following operational criteria and procedures apply when classifying countries:

1) Classification for Arrangement purposes is determined by *per capita* GNI as calculated by the World Bank for the purposes of the World Bank classification of borrowing countries.

2) In cases where the World Bank does not have enough information to publish *per capita* GNI data, the World Bank shall be asked to estimate whether the country in question has *per capita* GNI above or below the current threshold. The country shall be classified according to the estimate unless the Participants decide to act otherwise.

3) If a country is reclassified in accordance with Article 11 a), the reclassification will take effect two weeks after the conclusions drawn from the above - mentioned data from the World Bank have been communicated to all Participants by the Secretariat.

4) In cases where the World Bank revises figures, such revisions shall be disregarded in relation to the Arrangement. Nevertheless, the classification of a country may be changed by way of a Common Line and Participants would favourably consider a change due to errors and omissions in the figures subsequently recognised in the same calendar year in which the figures were first distributed by the Secretariat.

c) A country will change category only after its World Bank category has remained unchanged for two consecutive years.

## 12. MAXIMUM REPAYMENT TERMS

Without prejudice to Article 13, the maximum repayment term varies according to the classification of the country of destination determined by the criteria in Article 11.

a) For Category I countries, the maximum repayment term is five years, with the possibility of agreeing up to eight – and – a – half years when the procedures for prior notification set out in Article 48 are followed.

b) For Category II countries, the maximum repayment term is ten years.

c) In the event of a contract involving more than one country of destination the Participants should seek to establish a Common Line in accordance with the procedures in Articles 58 to 63 to reach agreement on appropriate terms.

## 13. REPAYMENT TERMS FOR NON – NUCLEAR POWER PLANTS

a) For non – nuclear power plants, the maximum repayment term shall be 12 years. If a Participant intends to support a repayment term longer than that provided for in Article 12, the Participant shall give prior notification in accordance with the procedure in Article 48.

b) Non – nuclear power plants are complete power stations, or parts thereof, not fuelled by nuclear power; they include all components, equipment, materials and services (including the training of personnel) directly required for the construction and commissioning of such non – nuclear power stations. This does not include items for which the buyer is usually responsible, in particular costs associated with land development, roads, construction villages, power lines, and switchyard and water supply located outside the power plant site boundary, as well as costs arising in the buyer's country from official approval procedures ( *e. g.* site permits, construction permit, fuel loading permits), except:

1) in cases where the buyer of the switchyard is the same as the buyer of the power plant, the maximum repayment term for the original switchyard shall be the same as that for the non-nuclear power plant (*i. e.* 12 years); and

2) the maximum repayment term for sub – stations, transformers and transmission lines with a minimum voltage threshold of 100 kV shall be the same as that for the non – nuclear power plant.

## 14. REPAYMENT OF PRINCIPAL AND PAYMENT OF INTEREST

a) The principal sum of an export credit shall be repaid in equal instalments.

b) Principal shall be repaid and interest shall be paid no less frequently than every six months and the first instalment of principal and interest shall be made no later than six months after the starting point of credit.

c) For export credits provided in support of lease transactions, equal repayments of principal and interest combined may be applied in lieu of equal repayments of principal as set out in paragraph a).

d) On an exceptional and duly justified basis, export credits may be provided on terms other than those set out in paragraphs a) through c) above. The provision of such support shall be explained by an imbalance in the timing of the funds available to the obligor and the debt service profile available under an equal, semi – annual repayment schedule, and shall comply with the following criteria:

1) No single repayment of principal or series of principal payments within a six – month period shall exceed 25% of the principal sum of the credit.

2) Principal shall be repaid no less frequently than every 12 months. The first repayment of principal shall be made no later than 12 months after the starting point of credit and no less than 2% of the principal sum of the credit shall have been repaid 12 months after the starting point of credit.

3) Interest shall be paid no less frequently than every 12 months and the first interest payment shall be made no later than six months after the starting point of credit.

4) The maximum weighted average life of the repayment period shall not exceed:

– For transactions with sovereign buyers (or with a sovereign repayment guarantee), four-and-a-half years for transactions in Category I Countries and five-and-a-quarter years for Category II Countries.

– For transactions with non-sovereign buyers (and with no sovereign repayment guarantee), five years for Category I Countries and six years for Category II Countries.

– Notwithstanding the provisions set out in the two previous *tirets*, for transactions involving support for non-nuclear power plants according to Article 13, six-and-aquarter years.

5) The Participant shall give prior notification in accordance with Article 48 that explains the reason for not providing support according to paragraphs a) through c) above.

e) Interest due after the starting point of credit shall not be capitalised.

## 15. INTEREST RATES, PREMIUM RATES AND OTHER FEES

a) Interest excludes:

1) any payment by way of premium or other charge for insuring or guaranteeing supplier credits or financial credits;

2) any payment by way of banking fees or commissions relating to the export credit other than annual or semi-annual bank charges that are payable throughout the repayment period; and

3) withholding taxes imposed by the importing country.

b) Where official support is provided by means of direct credits/financing or refinancing, the premium either may be added to the face value of the interest rate or may be a separate charge; both components are to be specified separately to the Participants.

## 16. VALIDITY PERIOD FOR EXPORT CREDITS

Financial terms and conditions for an individual export credit or line of credit, other than the validity period for the Commercial Interest Reference Rates (CIRRs) set out in Article 21, shall not be fixed for a period exceeding six months prior to final commitment.

## 17. ACTION TO AVOID OR MINIMISE LOSSES

The Arrangement does not prevent export credit authorities or financing institutions from agreeing to less restrictive financial terms and conditions than those provided for by the Arrangement, if such action is taken after the contract award (when the export credit agreement and ancillary documents have already become effective) and is intended solely to avoid or minimise losses from events which could give rise to non – payment or claims.

## 18. MATCHING

Taking into account a Participant's international obligations and consistent with the purpose of the Arrangement, a Participant may match, according to the procedures set out in Article 45, financial terms and conditions offered by a Participant or a non – Participant. Financial terms and conditions provided in accordance with this Article are considered to be in conformity with the provisions of Chapters I, II and, when applicable, Annexes I, II, III, IV, V and VI.

## 19. MINIMUM FIXED INTEREST RATES UNDER OFFICIAL FINANCING SUPPORT

a) The Participants providing official financing support for fixed rate loans shall apply the relevant CIRRs as minimum interest rates. CIRRs are interest rates established according to the following principles:

1) CIRRs should represent final commercial lending interest rates in the domestic market of the currency concerned;

2) CIRRs should closely correspond to the rate for first class domestic borrowers;

3) CIRRs should be based on the funding cost of fixed interest rate finance;

4) CIRRs should not distort domestic competitive conditions; and

5) CIRRs should closely correspond to a rate available to first class foreign borrowers.

b) The provision of official financing support shall not offset or compensate, in part or in full, for the appropriate credit risk premium to be charged for the risk of non-repayment pursuant to the provisions of Article 23.

## 20. CONSTRUCTION OF CIRRs

a) Each Participant wishing to establish a CIRR shall initially select one of the following two base rate systems for its national currency:

1) three-year government bond yields for a repayment term of up to and including five years; five-year government bond yields for over five and up to and including eight-and-ahalf years; and seven-year government bond yields for over eight-and-ahalf years; or

2) five-year government bond yields for all maturities.

Exceptions to the base rate system shall be agreed by the Participants.

b) CIRRs shall be set at a fixed margin of 100 basis points above each Participant's base rate unless Participants have agreed otherwise.

c) Other Participants shall use the CIRR set for a particular currency should they decide to finance in that currency.

d) A Participant may change its base-rate system after giving six months' advance notice and with the counsel of the Participants.

e) A Participant or a non-Participant may request that a CIRR be established for the currency of a non-Participant. In consultation with the interested non-Participant, a Participant or the Secretariat on behalf of that non-Participant may make a proposal for the construction of the CIRR in that currency using Common Line procedures in accordance with Articles 58 to 63.

## 21. VALIDITY OF CIRRs

The interest rate applying to a transaction shall not be fixed for a period longer than 120 days. A margin of 20 basis points shall be added to the relevant CIRR if the terms and conditions of the official financing support are fixed before the contract date.

## 22. APPLICATION OF CIRRs

a) Where official financing support is provided for floating rate loans, banks and other financing institutions shall not be allowed to offer the option of the lower of either the CIRR (at time of the original contract) or the short-term market rate throughout the life of the loan.

b) In the event of a voluntary, early repayment of a loan of or any portion thereof, the borrower shall compensate the government institution providing official financing support for all costs and losses incurred as a result of such early repayment, including the cost to the government institution of replacing the part of the fixed rate cash inflow interrupted by the early repayment.

## 23. PREMIUM FOR CREDIT RISK

The Participants shall charge premium, in addition to interest charges, to cover the risk of non-repayment of export credits. The premium rates charged by the Participants shall be risk-based, shall converge and shall not be inadequate to cover long-term operating costs and losses.

## 24. MINIMUM PREMIUM RATES FOR CREDIT RISK

The Participants shall charge no less than the applicable Minimum Premium Rate (MPR) for Credit Risk.

a) The applicable MPR is determined according to the following factors:

– the applicable country risk classification;

– the time at risk (*i. e.* the Horizon of Risk or HOR);

– the selected buyer risk category of the obligor;

– the percentage of political and commercial risk cover and quality of official export credit product provided;

– any country risk mitigation technique applied; and

– any buyer risk credit enhancements that have been applied.

b) MPRs are expressed in percentages of the principal value of the credit as if premium were collected in full at the date of the first drawdown of the credit. An explanation of how to calculate the MPRs, including the mathematical formula, is provided in Annex VIII.

c) There are no MPRs for transactions involving obligors in Category 0 countries, High Income OECD Countries and High Income Euro Area Countries[1]. The premium rates charged by Participants for transactions in such countries shall be determined on a case-by-case basis. In order to ensure that the premium rates charged for transactions involving obligors in such countries do not undercut private market pricing, the Participants shall adhere to the following procedure:

– Taking into consideration the availability of market information and the characteristics of the underlying transaction, Participants shall determine the premium rate to be applied by benchmarking against one or more of the market benchmarks set forth in Annex IX, choosing the benchmark (s) deemed most appropriate for the specific transaction.

– Notwithstanding the preceding paragraph, if the relevance of the market information is limited for liquidity or other reasons, or if the transaction is small (credit value below Special Drawing Rights (SDR)

---

[1] The status of a country in terms of: (1) whether it is a High Income country (as defined by the World Bank on an annual basis according to *per capita* GNI), (2) membership in the OECD and (3) whether it is part of the Euro Area is reviewed on an annual basis. The designation of a country under Article 25 c) as a High Income OECD country or a High Income Euro Area country as well as the removal of such designation will only come into effect after the country's income classification (High Income or otherwise) has remained unchanged for two consecutive years. A change in a country's designation as a High Income OECD country or a High Income Euro Area country as well as the removal of such designation related to a change in OECD membership or being part of the Euro Area will come into effect immediately at the time of the annual review of countries' status.

10 million), the Participants shall charge no less than the MPR corresponding to the appropriate buyer risk category in Country Risk Category 1.

– On a temporary basis①, the Participants shall give prior notification according to Article 48 for any transaction with obligor/guarantor in a Category 0 country, High Income OECD Country or High Income Euro Area Country having a credit value of greater than SDR 10 million.

d) The "highest risk" countries in Category 7 shall, in principle, be subject to premium rates in excess of the MPRs established for that Category; these premium rates shall be determined by the Participant providing official support.

e) In calculating the MPR for a transaction, the applicable country risk classification shall be the classification of the obligor's country and the applicable buyer risk classification shall be the classification of the obligor②, unless:

– security in the form of an irrevocable, unconditional, on-demand, legally valid and enforceable guarantee of the total debt repayment obligation for the entire duration of the credit is provided by a third party that is creditworthy in relation to the size of the guaranteed debt. In the case of a third party guarantee, a Participant may choose to apply the country risk classification of the country in which the

---

① The requirement for prior notification set out in the third *tiret* of Article 24 c) shall be discontinued on 30 June 2015.

② The premium rates charged for transactions with a third party guarantee provided by an obligor in a High Income OECD country or a High Income Euro Area country are subject to the requirements set out in Article 24 c).

guarantor is located and the buyer risk category of the guarantor[①]; or

– a Multilateral or Regional Institution as set out in Article 28 is acting either as borrower or guarantor for the transaction, in which case the applicable Country Risk Classification and buyer risk category may be that of the specific Multilateral or Regional Institution involved.

f) The criteria and conditions relating to the application of a third party guarantee according to the situations described in the first and second *tirets* of paragraph e) above are set out in Annex X.

g) The HOR convention used in the calculation of an MPR is one-half of the disbursement period plus the entire repayment period and assumes a regular export credit repayment profile, *i. e.* repayment in equal semi-annual instalments of principal plus accrued interest beginning six months after the starting point of credit. For export credits with non-standard repayment profiles, the equivalent repayment period (expressed in terms of equal, semi-annual instalments) is calculated using the following formula: equivalent repayment period = (average weighted life of the repayment period -0. 25) / 0. 5.

h) The Participant choosing to apply an MPR associated with a third party guarantor located in a country other than that of the obligor shall give prior notification according to Article 47. The Participant choosing to apply a MPR associated with a Multilateral or Regional Institution acting as a guarantor shall give prior notification in accordance with Article 48.

---

① In the case of a third party guarantee, the applicable country risk classification and buyer risk category must be related to the same entity, *i. e.* either the obligor or the guarantor.

## 25. COUNTRY RISK CLASSIFICATION

With the exception of High Income OECD countries and High Income Euro Area countries, countries shall be classified according to the likelihood of whether they will service their external debts (*i. e.* country credit risk).

a) The five elements of country credit risk are:

– general moratorium on repayments decreed by the obligor's/guarantor's government or by that agency of a country through which repayment is effected;

– political events and/or economic difficulties arising outside the country of the notifying Participant or legislative/administrative measures taken outside the country of the notifying Participant which prevent or delay the transfer of funds paid in respect of the credit;

– legal provisions adopted in the obligor's/guarantor's country declaring repayments made in local currency to be a valid discharge of the debt, notwithstanding that, as a result of fluctuations in exchange rates, such repayments, when converted into the currency of the credit, no longer cover the amount of the debt at the date of the transfer of funds;

– any other measure ordecision of the government of a foreign country which prevents repayment under a credit; and

– cases of force majeure occurring outside the country of the notifying Participant, *i. e.* war (including civil war), expropriation, revolution, riot, civil disturbances, cyclones, floods, earthquakes, eruptions, tidal waves and nuclear accidents.

b) Countries are classified into one of eight Country Risk Categories (0-7). MPRs have been established for Categories 1 through 7, but not for Category 0, as the level of country risk is considered to be negligible for countries in this Category. The credit risk associated with transactions in Category 0 countries is predominantly related to the risk of the obligor/guarantor.

c) The classification of countries① is achieved through the Country Risk Classification Methodology, which is comprised of:

– The Country Risk Assessment Model (the Model), which produces a quantitative assessment of country credit risk which is based, for each country, on three groups of risk indicators: the payment experience of the Participants, the financial situation and the economic situation. The methodology of the Model consists of different steps including the assessment of the three groups of risk indicators, and the combination and flexible weighting of the risk indicator groups.

– The qualitative assessment of the Model results, considered country-by-country to integrate the political risk and/or other risk factors not taken into account in full or in part by the Model. If appropriate, this may lead toan adjustment to the quantitative Model assessment to reflect the final assessment of the country credit risk.

d) Country Risk Classifications shall be monitored on an on-going

---

① For administrative purposes, some countries that are eligible to be classified into one of the eight Country Risk Categories may not be classified if they do not generally receive officially supported export credits. For such non-classified countries, Participants are free to apply the country risk classification which they deem appropriate.

basis and reviewed at least annually and changes resulting from the Country Risk Classification Methodology shall be immediately communicated by the Secretariat. When a country is re-classified in a lower or higher Country Risk Category, the Participants shall, no later than five working days after the re-classification has been communicated by the Secretariat, charge premium rates at or above the MPRs associated with the new Country Risk Category.

e) The country risk classifications shall be made public by the Secretariat.

## 26. SOVEREIGN RISK ASSESSMENT

a) For all countries classified through the Country Risk Classification Methodology according to Article 25 d), the risk of the sovereign shall be assessed in order to identify, on an exceptional basis, those sovereigns:

- that are not the lowest-risk obligor in the country and;

- whose credit risk is significantly higher than country risk.

b) The identification of sovereigns meeting the criteria listed in paragraph a) above shall be undertaken according to the Sovereign Risk Assessment Methodology that has been developed and agreed by the Participants.

c) The list of sovereigns identified as meeting the criteria listed in paragraph a) above shall be monitored on an on-going basis and reviewed at least annually and changes resulting from the Sovereign Risk Assessment Methodology shall be immediately communicated by the Secretariat.

d) The list of sovereigns identified under paragraph b) above shall be made public by the Secretariat.

## 27. BUYER RISK CLASSIFICATION

Obligors and, as appropriate, guarantors in countries classified in Country Risk Categories 1-7 shall be classified into one of the buyer risk categories that have been established in relation to the country of the obligor/guarantor①. The matrix of buyer risk categories into which obligors and guarantors shall be classified is provided in Annex VIII. Qualitative descriptions of the buyer risk categories are provided in Annex XI.

a) Buyer-risk classifications shall be based on the senior unsecured credit rating of the obligor/guarantor as determined by the Participant.

b) Notwithstanding paragraph a) above, transactions supported according to the terms and conditions of Annex VI and transactions having a credit value of SDR 5 million or less may be classified on a transaction basis, *i. e.* after the application of any buyer risk credit enhancements; however, such transactions, regardless of how they are classified, are not eligible for any discounts for the application of buyer risk credit enhancements.

c) Sovereign obligors and guarantors are classified in buyer risk category SOV/CC0.

---

① Rules related to the classification of buyers should be understood to stipulate the most favourable classification that can be applied, *e. g.* a sovereign buyer may be classified in a less favourable buyer risk classification.

d) On an exceptional basis, non-sovereign obligors and guarantors may be classified in the "Better than Sovereign" (SOV +) buyer risk category① if:

– the obligor/guarantor has a foreign currency rating from an accredited credit rating agency (CRA)② that is better than the foreign currency rating (from the same CRA) of their respective sovereign, or

– the obligor/guarantor's is located in a country in which sovereign risk has been identified as being significantly higher than country risk.

e) The Participants shall give prior notification accordingto Article 48 for transactions:

– with a non-sovereign obligor/guarantor where the premium charged is below that set by Buyer Risk Category CC1, *i. e.* CC0 or SOV +;

– with a non-sovereign obligor/guarantor having a credit value of greater than SDR 5 million where a Participant assesses a buyer risk rating for a non-sovereign obligor/guarantor that is rated by an Accredited CRA, and the buyer risk rating assessed is better than the Accredited CRA rating③.

f) In the event of competition for a specific transaction, whereby the obligor/guarantor has been classified by competing Participants in

① The MPRs associated with the Better than Sovereign (SOV +) buyer risk category are 10% lower than the MPRs associated with the Sovereign (CC0) buyer risk category.

② The Secretariat shall compile and maintain a list of such accredited CRAs.

③ Where the non-sovereign borrower is rated by more than one accredited CRA, notification is only required where the buyer risk rating is more favourable than the most favourable of the CRA ratings.

different buyer risk categories, the competing Participants shall seek to arrive at a common buyer risk classification. If agreement on a common classification is not reached, the Participant (s) having classified the obligor/guarantor in a higher buyer risk classification are not prohibited from applying the lower buyer risk classification.

## 28. CLASSIFICATION OF MULTILATERAL AND REGIONAL INSTITUTIONS

Multilateral and Regional Institutions shall be classified into one of eight Country Risk Categories (0-7)① and reviewed as appropriate; such applicable classifications shall be made public by the Secretariat.

## 29. PERCENTAGE AND QUALITY OF OFFICIAL EXPORT CREDIT COVER

The MPRs are differentiated to take account of the differing quality of export credit products and percentage of cover provided by the Participants as set out in Annex VIII. The differentiation is based on the exporter's perspective (*i. e.* to neutralise the competitive effect arising from the differing qualities of product provided to the exporter/financial institution).

a) The quality of an export credit product is a function of whether the product is insurance, guarantee or direct credit/financing, and for insurance products whether cover of interest during the claims waiting period (*i. e.* the period between the due date of payment by the obligor and the date that the insurer is liable to reimburse the exporter/financial

---

① With respect to buyer risk, classified multilateral and regional institutions shall be classified in Buyer Risk Category SOV/CC0.

institution) is provided without a surcharge.

b) All existing export credit products offered by the Participants shall be classified into one of the three product categories which are:

– Below standard product, *i. e.* insurance without cover of interest during the claims waiting period and insurance with cover of interest during the claims waiting period with an appropriate premium surcharge;

– Standard product, *i. e.* insurance with cover of interest during the claims waiting period without an appropriate premium surcharge and direct credit/financing; and

– Above standard product, *i. e.* guarantees.

## 30. COUNTRY RISK MITIGATION TECHNIQUES

a) The Participants may apply the following country risk mitigation techniques, the specific application of which is set out in Annex XII:

– Offshore Future Flow Structure Combined with Offshore Escrow Account

– Local Currency Financing

b) The Participant applying an MPR reflecting the use of country risk mitigation shall give prior notification according to Article 47.

## 31. BUYER RISK CREDIT ENHANCEMENTS

a) The Participants may apply the following buyer risk credit enhancements (BRCE) which allow for the application of a Credit

Enhancement Factor (CEF) greater than 0:

– Assignment of Contract Proceeds or Receivables

– Asset Base Security

– Fixed Asset Security

– Escrow Account

b) Definitions of the BRCE and maximum CEF values are set out in Annex XII.

c) BRCEs may be used alone or in combination with the following restrictions:

– The maximum CEF that can be achieved through the use of the BRCEs is 0. 35.

– "Asset Based Security" and "Fixed Asset Security" cannot be used together in one transaction.

– In the event that applicable country risk classification has been improved through the use of "Offshore Future Flow Structure Combined with Offshore Escrow Account", no BRCEs may be applied.

d) The Participants shall give prior notification according to Article 48 for transactions with a non-sovereign obligor/guarantor having a credit of greater than SDR 5 million where BRCEs result in the application of a CEF of greater than 0.

## 32. REVIEW OF THE VALIDITY OF THE MINIMUM PREMIUM RATES FOR CREDIT RISK

a) To assess the adequacy of MPRs and to allow, if necessary, for adjustments, either upwards or downwards, Premium Feedback Tools (PFTs), shall be used in parallel to monitor and adjust the MPRs on a regular basis.

b) The PFTs shall assess the adequacy of the MPRs in terms of both the actual experience of institutions providing official export credits as well as private market information on the pricing of credit risk.

c) A comprehensive review of all aspects of the premium rules of the Arrangement shall take place no later than 31 December 2015.

# 3. CHAPTER III: PROVISIONS FOR TIED AID

## 33. GENERAL PRINCIPLES

a) The Participants have agreed to have complementary policies for export credits and tied aid. Export credit policies should be based on open competition and the free play of market forces. Tied aid policies should provide needed external resources to countries, sectors or projects with little or no access to market financing. Tied aid policies should ensure best value for money, minimise trade distortion, and contribute to developmentally effective use of these resources.

b) The tied aid provisions of the Arrangement do not apply to the aid programmes of multilateral or regional institutions.

c) These principles do not prejudge the views of the Development Assistance Committee (DAC) on the quality of tied and untied aid.

d) A Participant may request additional information relevant to the tying status of any form of aid. If there is uncertainty as to whether a certain financing practice falls within the scope of the definition of tied aid set out in Annex XIV, the donor country shall furnish evidence in support of any claim to the effect that the aid is in fact "untied" in accordance with the definition in Annex XIV.

## 34. FORMS OF TIED AID

Tied aid can take the form of:

a) Official Development Assistance (ODA) loans as defined in the "DAC Guiding Principles for Associated Financing and Tied and Partially Untied Official Development Assistance (1987)";

b) ODA grants as defined in the "DAC Guiding Principles for Associated Financing and Tied and Partially Untied Official Development Assistance (1987)"; and

c) Other Official Flows (OOF), which includes grants and loans but excludes officially supported export credits that are in conformity with the Arrangement; or

d) Any association, *e. g.* mixture, in law or in fact, within the control of the donor, the lender or the borrower involving two or more of the preceding, and/or the following financing components:

1) an export credit that is officially supported by way of direct credit/financing, refinancing, interest rate support, guarantee or insurance to which the Arrangement applies; and

2) other funds at or near market terms, or down payment from the purchaser.

## 35. ASSOCIATED FINANCING

a) Associated financing may take various forms including mixed credits, mixed financing, joint financing, parallel financing or single integrated transactions. The main characteristics are that they all feature:

– a concessional component that is linked in law or in fact to the non-concessional component;

– either a single part or all of the financing package that is, in effect, tied aid; and

– concessional funds those are available only if the linked non-concessional component is accepted by the recipient.

b) Association or linkage "in fact" is determined by such factors as:

– the existence of informal understandings between the recipient and the donor authorities;

– the intention by the donor to facilitate the acceptability of a financing package through the use of ODA;

– the effective tying of the whole financing package to procurement in the donor country;

– the tying status of ODA and the means of tendering for or contracting of each financing transaction; or

– any other practice, identified by the DAC or the Participants in which a *de facto* liaison exists between two or more financing components.

c) The following practices shall not prevent the determination of an association or linkage "in fact":

– contract splitting through the separate notification of the component parts of one contract;

– splitting of contracts financed in several stages;

– non-notification of interdependent parts of a contract; and/or

– non-notification because part of the financing package is untied.

## 36. COUNTRY ELIGIBILITY FOR TIED AID

a) There shall be no tied aid to countries whose *per capita* GNI, according to the World Bank data, is above the upper limit for lower middle income countries. The World Bank recalculates this threshold on an annual basis①. A country will be reclassified only after its World Bank category has been unchanged for two consecutive years.

b) The following operational criteria and procedures apply when classifying countries:

1) Classification for Arrangement purposes is determined by *per capita* GNI as calculated by the World Bank for the purposes of the World Bank classification of borrowing countries; this classification shall be made public by the Secretariat.

2) In cases where the World Bank does not have enough information to publish *per capita* GNI data, the World Bank shall be asked to estimate whether the country in question has *per capita* GNI above or below the current threshold. The country shall be classified according to the estimate unless the Participants decide to act otherwise.

3) If a country's eligibility for tied aid does change in accordance with paragraph a) above, the reclassification shall take effect two weeks after the conclusions drawn from the above mentioned World Bank data

---

① Based on the annual review by the World Bank of its country classification, a *per capita* Gross National Income (GNI) threshold will be used for the purpose of tied aid eligibility; such threshold is available on the OECD website (http://www.oecd.org/trade/exportcredits/classification.htm).

have been communicated to all Participants by the Secretariat. Before the effective date of reclassification, no tied aid financing for a newly eligible country may be notified; after that date, no tied aid financing for a newly promoted country may be notified, except that individual transactions covered under a prior committed credit line may be notified until the expiry of the credit line (which shall be no more than one year from the effective date).

4) In cases where the World Bank revises figures such revisions shall be disregarded in relation to the Arrangement. Nevertheless, the classification of a country may be changed by way of a Common Line, in accordance with the appropriate procedures in Articles 58 to 63, and the Participants would favourably consider a change due to errors and omissions in the figures subsequently recognised in the same calendar year as the figures that were first distributed by the Secretariat.

## 37. PROJECT ELIGIBILITY

a) Tied aid shall not be extended to public or private projects that normally should be commercially viable if financed on market or Arrangement terms.

b) The key tests for such aid eligibility are:

– whether the project is financially non-viable, *i. e.* does the project lack capacity with appropriate pricing determined on market principles, to generate cash flow sufficient to cover the project's operating costs and to service the capital employed, i. *e.* the first key test; or

– whether it is reasonable to conclude, based on communication with other Participants, that it is unlikely that the project can be financed on market or Arrangement terms, *i. e.* the second key test. In respect of projects larger than SDR 50 million special weight shall be given to the expected availability of financing at market or Arrangement terms when considering the appropriateness of such aid.

c) The key tests under paragraph b) above are intended to describe how a project should be evaluated to determine whether it should be financed with such aid or with export credits on market or Arrangement terms. Through the consultation process described in Articles 51 to 53, a body of experience is expected to develop over time that will more precisely define, for both export credit and aid agencies, *ex ante* guidance as to the line between the two categories of projects.

## 38. MINIMUM CONCESSIONALITY LEVEL

The Participants shall not provide tied aid that has a concessionality level of less than 35%, or 50% if the beneficiary country is a Least Developed Country (LDC), except for the cases set out below, which are also exempt from the notification procedures set out in Articles 49 a) and 50 a):

a) Technical assistance: tied aid where the official development aid component consists solely of technical co-operation that is less than either 3% of the total value of the transaction or SDR 1 million, whichever is lower; and

b) Small projects: capital projects of less than SDR 1 million that are funded entirely by development assistance grants.

## 39. EXEMPTIONS FROM COUNTRY OR PROJECT ELIGIBILITY FOR TIED AID

a) The provisions of Articles 36 and 37 do not apply to tied aid where the concessionality level is 80% or more except for tied aid that forms part of an associated financing package, described in Article 35.

b) The provisions of Article 37 do not apply to tied aid with a value of less than SDR 2 million except for tied aid that forms part of an associated financing package, described in Article 35.

c) Tied aid for LDCs as defined by the United Nations is not subject to the provisions of Articles 36 and 37.

d) The Participants shall give favourable consideration to an acceleration of tied aid procedures in line with the specific circumstances:

– a nuclear or major industrial accident that causes serious transfrontier pollution, where any affected Participant wishes to provide tied aid to eliminate or mitigate its effects, or

– the existence of a significant risk that such an accident may occur, where any potentially affected Participant wishes to provide tied aid to prevent its occurrence.

e) Notwithstanding Articles 36 and 37, a Participant may, exceptionally, provide support by one of the following means:

– the Common Line procedure as defined in Annex XIV and described in Articles 58 to 63; or

– the justification on aid grounds through support by a substantial body of the Participants as described in Articles 51 and 52; or

– a letter to the OECD Secretary-General, in accordance with the procedures in Article 53, which the Participants expect will be unusual and infrequent.

## 40. CALCULATION OF CONCESSIONALITY LEVEL OF TIED AID

The concessionality level of tied aid is calculated using the same method as for the grant element used by the DAC, except that:

a) The discount rate used to calculate the concessionality level of a loan in a given currency, *i. e.* the Differentiated Discount Rate (DDR), is subject to annual change on 15 January and is calculated as follows:

– The average of the CIRR + Margin

Margin (M) depends on the repayment term (R) as follows:

| R | M |
|---|---|
| less than 15 years | 0.75 |
| from 15 years up to, but not including 20 years | 1.00 |
| from 20 years up to but not including 30 years | 1.15 |
| from 30 years and above | 1.25 |

– For all currencies the average of the CIRR is calculated taking an average of the monthly CIRRs valid during the six-month period between 15 August of the previous year and 14 February of the current year. The calculated rate, including the Margin, is rounded to the nearest ten basis points. If there is more than one CIRR for the currency, the CIRR for the longest maturity as set out in Article 20 a), shall be used for this calculation.

b) The base date for the calculation of the concessionality level is the starting point of credit as set out in Annex XIV.

c) For the purpose of calculating the overall concessionality level of an associated financing package, the concessionality levels of the following credits, funds and payments are considered to be zero:

– export credits that are in conformity with the Arrangement;

– other funds at or near market rates;

– other official funds with a concessionality level of less than the minimum permitted under Article 38 except in cases of matching; and

– down payment from the purchaser.

Payments on or before the starting point of credit that are not considered down payment shall be included in the calculation of the concessionality level.

d) The discount rate in matching: in matching aid, identical matching means matching with an identical concessionality level that is recalculated with the discount rate in force at the time of matching.

e) Local costs and third country procurement shall be included in the calculation of concessionality level only if they are financed by the donor country.

f) The overall concessionality level of a package is determined by multiplying the nominal value of each component of the package by the respective concessionality level of each component, adding the results, and dividing this total by the aggregate nominal value of the components.

g) The discount rate for a given aid loan is the rate in effect at the time of notification. However, in cases of prompt notification, the discount rate is the one in effect at the time when the terms and conditions of the aid loan were fixed. A change in the discount rate during the life of a loan does not change its concessionality level.

h) If a change of currency is made before the contract is concluded, the notification shall be revised. The discount rate used to calculate the concessionality level will be the one applicable at the date of revision. A revision is not necessary if the alternative currency and all the necessary information for calculation of the concessionality level are indicated in the original notification.

i) Notwithstanding paragraph g) above, the discount rate used to calculate the concessionality level of individual transactions initiated under an aid credit line shall be the rate that was originally notified for the credit line.

## 41. VALIDITY PERIOD FOR TIED AID

a) The Participants shall not fix terms and conditions for tied aid, whether this relates to the financing of individual transactions or to an aid protocol, an aid credit line or to a similar agreement, for more than two years. In the case of an aid protocol, an aid credit line or similar agreement, the validity period shall commence at the date of its signature, to be notified in accordance with Article 50; the extension of a credit line shall be notified as if it were a new transaction with a note explaining that it is an extension and that it is renewed at terms allowed at the time of the notification of the extension. In the case of individual transactions, including those notified under an aid protocol, an aid credit line or similar agreement, the validity period shall commence at the date of notification of the commitment in accordance with Article 49 or 50, as appropriate.

b) When a country has become ineligible for 17-year World Bank Loans for the first time, the validity period of existing and new tied aid protocols and credit lines notified shall be restricted to one year after the date of the potential reclassification in accordance with procedures in Article 36 b).

c) Renewal of such protocols and credit lines is possible only on terms which are in accordance with the provisions of Articles 36 and 37 of the Arrangement following:

– the reclassification of countries; and

– a change in the provisions of the Arrangement.

In these circumstances, the existing terms and conditions can be maintained notwithstanding a change in the discount rate set out in Article 40.

## 42. MATCHING

Taking into account a Participant's international obligations and consistent with the purpose of the Arrangement, a Participant may match, according to the procedures set out in Article 45, financial terms and conditions offered by a Participant or a non-Participant.

# 4. CHAPTER IV: PROCEDURES

*SECTION 1: COMMON PROCEDURES FOR EXPORT CREDITS AND TRADE-RELATED AID*

## 43. NOTIFICATIONS

The notifications set out by the procedures in the Arrangement shall be made in accordance with, and include the information contained in Annex VII, and shall be copied to the Secretariat.

## 44. INFORMATION ON OFFICIAL SUPPORT

a) As soon as a Participant commits the official support which it has notified in accordance with the procedures in Articles 47 to 50, it shall inform all other Participants accordingly by including the notification reference number on the relevant reporting form.

b) In an exchange of information in accordance with Articles 55 to 57, a Participant shall inform the other Participants of the credit terms and conditions that it envisages supporting for a particular transaction and may request similar information from the other Participants.

## 45. PROCEDURES FOR MATCHING

a) Before matching financial terms and conditions assumed to be offered by a Participant or a non-Participant pursuant to Articles 18 and 42, a Participant shall make every reasonable effort, including as appropriate by use of the face-to-face consultations described in Article

57, to verify that these terms and conditions are officially supported and shall comply with the following:

1) The Participant shall notify all other Participants of the terms and conditions it intends to support following the same notification procedures required for the matched terms and conditions. In the case of matching a non-Participant, the matching Participant shall follow the same notification procedures that would have been required had the matched terms been offered by a Participant.

2) Notwithstanding sub-paragraph 1) above, if the applicable notification procedure would require the matching Participant to withhold its commitment beyond the final bid closing date, then the matching Participant shall give notice of its intention to match as early as possible.

3) If the initiating Participant moderates or withdraws its intention to support the notified terms and conditions, it shall immediately inform all other Participants accordingly.

b) A Participant intending to offer identical financial terms and conditions to those notified according to Articles 47 and 48 may do so once the waiting period stipulated therein has expired. This Participant shall give notification of its intention as early as possible.

## 46. SPECIAL CONSULTATIONS

a) A Participant that has reasonable grounds to believe that financial terms and conditions offered by another Participant (the initiating Participant) are more generous than those provided for in the Arrangement shall inform the Secretariat; the Secretariat shall immediately make available such information.

b) The initiating Participant shall clarify the financial terms and conditions of its offer within two working days following the issue of the information from the Secretariat.

c) Following clarification by the initiating Participant, any Participant may request that a special consultation meeting of the Participants be organised by the Secretariat within five working days to discuss the issue.

d) Pending the outcome of the special consultation meeting of the Participants, financial terms and conditions benefiting from official support shall not become effective.

*SECTION 2: PROCEDURES FOR EXPORT CREDITS*

## 47. PRIOR NOTIFICATION WITH DISCUSSION

a) A Participant shall notify all other Participants at least ten calendar days before issuing any commitment in accordance with Annex VII if:

– the applicable country risk classification and buyer risk category used to calculate the MPR is that of a third party guarantor located outside of the obligor's country [*i. e.* determined according to the first *tiret* of Article 24 e)];

– the applicable MPR has been decreased through the application of a country risk mitigation technique listed in Article 30; or

– it intends to provide support in accordance with Article 10 a) 2) or d) of Annex IV.

– it intends to provide support in accordance with Article 5 a) of

Annex V.

b) If any other Participant requests a discussion during this period, the initiating Participant shall wait an additional ten calendar days.

c) A Participant shall inform all other Participants of its final decision following a discussion to facilitate the review of the body of experience in accordance with Article 69. The Participants shall maintain records of their experience with regard to premium rates notified in accordance with paragraph a) above.

## 48. PRIOR NOTIFICATION

a) A Participant shall, in accordance with Annex VII, notify all other Participants at least ten calendar days before issuing any commitment if it intends to:

1) Provide support in accordance with Article 10 d) 3).

2) Support a repayment term of more than five years to a Category I country.

3) Provide support in accordance with Article 13 a).

4) Provide support in accordance with Article 14 d).

5) Provide support in accordance with Article 24 c) when the credit value is greater than SDR 10 million. ①

6) Apply a premium rate in accordance with the second *tiret* of

---

① The requirement for prior notification set out in the third *tiret* of Article 24 c) shall be discontinued on 31 December 2014.

Article 24 e), whereby the applicable country risk classification and buyer risk category used to calculate the MPR have been determined by the involvement as obligor or guarantor of a classified multilateral or regional institution.

7) Apply a premium rate in accordance with Article 27 e) whereby the selected buyer risk category used to calculate the MPR for a transaction:

– with a non-sovereign obligor/guarantor is lower than CC1 (*i. e.* CC0 or SOV+);

– with a non-sovereign obligor/guarantor having a credit of greater than SDR 5 million is better than the Accredited CRA rating.

8) Apply a premium rate in accordance with Article 31 a) whereby the use of buyer risk credit enhancements results in the application of a CEF of greater than 0.

9) Provide support in accordance with Article 8 a) of Annex II.

10) Provide support in accordance with Article 10 a) 1) of Annex IV.

11) Provide support in accordance with Article 5 b) of Annex V.

b) If the initiating Participant moderates or withdraws its intention to provide support for such transaction, it shall immediately inform all other Participants.

*SECTION 3: PROCEDURES FOR TRADE-RELATED AID*

## 49. PRIOR NOTIFICATION

a) A Participant shall give prior notification in accordance with

Annex VII if it intends to provide official support for:

– Trade-related untied aid with a value of SDR 2 million or more, and a concessionality level of less than 80% ;

– Trade-related untied aid with a value of less than SDR 2 million and a grant element (as defined by the DAC) of less than 50% ;

– Trade-related tied aid with a value of SDR 2 million or more and a concessionality level of less than 80% ; or

– Trade-related tied aid with a value of less than SDR 2 million and a concessionality level of less than 50% , except for the cases set out in Articles 38 a) and b).

– Tied aid in accordance with Article 39 d).

b) Prior notification shall be made at the latest 30 working days before the bid closing or commitment date, whichever is the earlier.

c) If the initiating Participant moderates or withdraws its intention to support the notified terms and conditions, it shall immediately inform all other Participants accordingly.

d) The provision of this Article shall apply to tied aid that forms part of an associated financing package, as described in Article 35.

## 50. PROMPT NOTIFICATION

a) A Participant shall promptly notify all other Participants, *i. e.* within two working days of the commitment, in accordance with Annex VII, if it provides official support for tied aid with a value of either:

– SDR 2 million or more and a concessionality level of 80% or more; or

– less than SDR 2 million and a concessionality level of 50% or more except for the cases set out in Articles 38 a) and b).

b) A Participant shall also promptly notify all other Participants when an aid protocol, credit line or similar agreement is signed.

c) Prior notification need not be given if a Participant intends to match financial terms and conditions that were subject to a prompt notification.

*SECTION 4: CONSULTATION PROCEDURES FORTIED AID*

## 51. PURPOSE OF CONSULTATIONS

a) A Participant seeking clarification about possible trade motivation for tied aid may request that a full Aid Quality Assessment (detailed in Annex XIII) be supplied.

b) Furthermore, a Participant may request consultations with other Participants, in accordance with Article 52. These include face-to-face consultations as outlined in Article 57 in order to discuss:

– first, whether an aid offer meets the requirements of Articles 36 and 37; and

– if necessary, whether an aid offer is justified even if the requirements of Articles 36 and 37 are not met.

## 52. SCOPE AND TIMING OF CONSULTATIONS

a) During consultations, a Participant may request, among other items, the following information:

– the assessment of a detailed feasibility study/project appraisal;

– whether there is a competing offer with non-concessional or aid financing;

– the expectation of the project generating or saving foreign currency;

– whether there is co-operation with multilateral organisations such as the World Bank;

– the presence of International Competitive Bidding (ICB), in particular if the donor country's supplier is the lowest evaluated bid;

– the environmental implications;

– any private sector participation; and

– the timing of the notifications (*e.g.* six months prior to bid closing or commitment date) of concessional or aid credits.

b) The consultation shall be completed and the findings on both questions in Article 51 notified by the Secretariat to all Participants at least ten working days before the bid closing date or commitment date, whichever comes first. If there is disagreement among the consulting parties, the Secretariat shall invite other Participants to express their views within five working days. It shall report these views to the notifying Participant, which should reconsider going forward if there appears to be no substantial support for an aid offer.

## 53. OUTCOME OF CONSULTATIONS

a) A donor which wishes to proceed with a project despite the lack of substantial support shall provide prior notification of its intentions to other Participants, no later than 60 calendar days after the completion of the Consultation, *i. e.* acceptance of the Chairman's conclusion. The donor shall also write a letter to the Secretary-General of the OECD outlining the results of the consultations and explaining the overriding non-trade related national interest that forces this action. The Participants expect that such an occurrence will be unusual and infrequent.

b) The donor shall immediately notify the Participants that it has sent a letter to the Secretary-General of the OECD, a copy of which shall be included with the notification. Neither the donor nor any other Participant shall make a tied aid commitment until ten working days after this notification to Participants has been issued. For projects for which competing commercial offers were identified during the consultation process, the aforementioned ten-working-day period shall be extended to 15 days.

c) The Secretariat shall monitor the progress and results of consultations.

*SECTION 5: INFORMATION EXCHANGE FOR EXPORT CREDITS AND TRADERELATED AID*

## 54. CONTACT POINTS

All communications shall be made between the designated contact points in each country by means of instant communication, *e. g.* OLIS, and shall be treated in confidence.

## 55. SCOPE OF ENQUIRIES

a) A Participant may ask another Participant about the attitude it takes with respect to a third country, an institution in a third country or a particular method of doing business.

b) A Participant which has received an application for official support may address an enquiry to another Participant, giving the most favourable credit terms and conditions that the enquiring Participant would be willing to support.

c) If an enquiry is made to more than one Participant, it shall contain a list of addressees.

d) A copy of all enquiries shall be sent to the Secretariat.

## 56. SCOPE OF RESPONSES

a) The Participant to which an enquiry is addressed shall respond within seven calendar days and provide as much information as possible. The reply shall include the best indication that the Participant can give of the decision it is likely to take. If necessary, the full reply shall follow as soon as possible. Copies shall be sent to the other addressees of the enquiry and to the Secretariat.

b) If an answer to an enquiry subsequently becomes invalid for any reason, because for example:

– an application has been made, changed or withdrawn, or

– other terms are being considered,

a reply shall be made without delay and copied to all other addressees of the enquiry and to the Secretariat.

## 57. FACE-TO-FACE CONSULTATIONS

a) A Participant shall agree within ten working days to requests for face-to-face consultations.

b) A request for face-to-face consultations shall be made available to Participants and non-Participants. The consultations shall take place as soon as possible after the expiry of the ten-working-day period.

c) The Chairman of the Participants shall co-ordinate with the Secretariat on any necessary follow-up action, *e. g.* a Common Line. The Secretariat shall promptly make available the outcome of the consultation.

## 58. PROCEDURES AND FORMAT OF COMMON LINES

a) Common Line proposals are addressed only to the Secretariat. A proposal for a Common Line shall be sent to all Participants and, where tied aid is involved, all DAC contact points by the Secretariat. The identity of the initiator is not revealed on the Common Line Register on the Bulletin Board of the OLIS. However, the Secretariat may orally reveal the identity of the initiator to a Participant or DAC member on demand. The Secretariat shall keep a record of such requests.

b) The Common Line proposal shall be dated and shall be in the following format:

– Reference number, followed by "Common Line".

– Name of the importing country and buyer.

– Name or description of the project as precise as possible to clearly identify the project.

– Terms and conditions foreseen by the initiating country.

– Common Line proposal.

– Nationality and names of known competing bidders.

– Commercial and financial bid closing date and tender number to the extent it is known.

– Other relevant information, including reasons for proposing the Common Line, availability of studies of the project and/or special circumstances.

c) A Common Line proposal put forward in accordance with Article 36 b) 4) shall be addressed to the Secretariat and copied to other Participants. The Participant making the Common Line proposal shall provide a full explanation of the reasons why it considers that the classification of a country should differ from the procedure set out in Article 36 b).

d) The Secretariat shall make publicly available the agreed Common Lines.

## 59. RESPONSES TO COMMON LINE PROPOSALS

a) Responses shall be made within 20 calendar days, although the Participants are encouraged to respond to a Common Line proposal as quickly as possible.

b) A response may be a request for additional information, acceptance, and rejection, a proposal for modification of the Common Line or an alternative Common Line proposal.

c) A Participant which advises that it has no position because it has not been approached by an exporter, or by the authorities in the recipient country in case of aid for the project, shall be deemed to have accepted the Common Line proposal.

## 60. ACCEPTANCE OF COMMON LINES

a) After a period of 20 calendar days, the Secretariat shall inform all Participants of the status of the Common Line proposal. If not all Participants have accepted the Common Line, but no Participant has rejected it, the proposal shall be left open for a further period of eight calendar days.

b) After this further period, a Participant which has not explicitly rejected the Common Line proposal shall be deemed to have accepted the Common Line. Nevertheless, a Participant, including the initiating Participant, may make its acceptance of the Common Line conditional on the explicit acceptance by one or more Participants.

c) If a Participant does not accept one or more elements of a Common Line it implicitly accepts all other elements of the Common Line. It is understood that such a partial acceptance may lead other Participants to change their attitude towards a proposed Common Line. All Participants are free to offer or match terms and conditions not covered by a Common Line.

d) A Common Line which has not been accepted may be reconsidered using the procedures in Articles 58 and 59. In these circumstances, the Participants are not bound by their original decision.

## 61. DISAGREEMENT ON COMMON LINES

If the initiating Participant and a Participant which has proposed a modification or alternative cannot agree on a Common Line within the additional eight-calendar day period, this period can be extended by their mutual consent. The Secretariat shall inform all Participants of any such extension.

## 62. EFFECTIVE DATE OF COMMON LINE

The Secretariat shall inform all Participants either that the Common Line will go into effect or that it has been rejected; the Common Line will take effect three calendar days after this announcement. The Secretariat shall make available on OLIS a permanently updated record of all Common Lines which have been agreed or are undecided.

## 63. VALIDITY OF COMMON LINES

a) A Common Line, once agreed, shall be valid for a period of two years from its effective date, unless the Secretariat is informed that it is no longer of interest, and that this is accepted by all Participants. A Common Line shall remain valid for a further two-year period if a Participant seeks an extension within 14 calendar days of the original date of expiry. Subsequent extensions may be agreed through the same procedure. A Common Line agreed in accordance with Article 36 b) 4) shall be valid until World Bank data for the following year is available.

b) The Secretariat shall monitor the status of Common Lines and shall keep the Participants informed accordingly, through the maintenance of the listing "The Status of Valid Common Lines" on OLIS. Accordingly, the Secretariat, inter alia, shall:

– Add new Common Lines when these have been accepted by the Participants.

– Update the expiry date when a Participant requests an extension.

– Delete Common Lines which have expired.

– Issue, on a quarterly basis, a list of Common Lines due to expire in the following quarter.

*SECTION 6: OPERATIONAL PROVISIONS FOR THE COMMUNICATION OF MINIMUM INTEREST RATES (CIRRs)*

## 64. COMMUNICATION OF MINIMUM INTEREST RATES

a) CIRRs for currencies that are determined according to the provisions of Article 20 shall be sent by means of instant communication at least monthly to the Secretariat for circulation to all Participants.

b) Such notification shall reach the Secretariat no later than five days after the end of each month covered by this information. The Secretariat shall then inform immediately all Participants of the applicable rates and make them publicly available.

## 65. EFFECTIVE DATE FOR APPLICATION OF INTEREST RATES

Any changes in the CIRRs shall enter into effect on the fifteenth day after the end of each month.

## 66. IMMEDIATE CHANGES IN INTEREST RATES

When market developments require the notification of an amendment to a CIRR during the course of a month, the amended rate shall be implemented ten days after notification of this amendment has been received by the Secretariat.

*SECTION 7: REVIEWS*

## 67. REGULAR REVIEW OF THE ARRANGEMENT

a) The Participants shall review regularly the functioning of the Arrangement. In the review, the Participants shall examine, inter alia, notification procedures, implementation and operation of the DDR system, rules and procedures on tied aid, questions of matching, prior commitments and possibilities of wider participation in the Arrangement.

b) This review shall be based on information of the Participants' experience and on their suggestions for improving the operation and efficacy of the Arrangement. The Participants shall take into account the objectives of the Arrangement and the prevailing economic and monetary situation. The information and suggestions that Participants wish to put forward for this review shall reach the Secretariat no later than 45 calendar days before the date of review.

## 68. REVIEW OF MINIMUM INTEREST RATES

a) The Participants shall periodically review the system for setting

CIRRs in order to ensure that the notified rates reflect current market conditions and meet the aims underlying the establishment of the rates in operation. Such reviews shall also cover the margin to be added when these rates are applied.

b) A Participant may submit to the Chairman of the Participants a substantiated request for an extraordinary review in case this Participant considers that the CIRR for one or more than one currency no longer reflect current market conditions.

## 69. REVIEW OF MINIMUM PREMIUM RATES AND RELATED ISSUES

The Participants shall regularly monitor and review all aspects of the premium rules and procedures. This shall include:

a) The Country Risk Classification and Sovereign Risk Assessment Methodologies to review their validity in the light of experience;

b) The level of the MPRs to ensure that they remain an accurate measure of credit risk, taking into account both the actual experience of institutions providing official export credits as well as private market information on the pricing of credit risk;

c) The differentiations in the MPRs which take account of the differing quality of export credit products and percentage of cover provided; and

d) The body of experience related to the use of country risk mitigation and buyer risk credit enhancements and the continued validity and appropriateness of their specific impact on the MPRs.

# ANNEX I: SECTOR UNDERSTANDING ON EXPORT CREDITS FOR SHIPS

## CHAPTER I: SCOPE OF THE SECTOR UNDERSTANDING

### 1. PARTICIPATION

The Participants to the Sector Understanding are: Australia, the European Union, Japan, Korea, New Zealand and Norway.

### 2. SCOPE OF APPLICATION

This Sector Understanding, which complements the Arrangement, sets out specific guidelines for officially supported export credits relating to export contracts of:

a) Any new sea-going vessel of 100 gt and above used for the transportation of goods or persons, or for the performance of a specialised service (for example, fishing vessels, fish factory ships, ice breakers and as dredgers, that present in a permanent way by their means of propulsion and direction (steering) all the characteristics of self-navigability in the high sea), tugs of 365 kw and over and to unfinished shells of ships that are afloat and mobile. The Sector Understanding does not cover military vessels. Floating docks and mobile offshore units are not covered by the Sector Understanding, but should problems arise in connection with export credits for such structures, the Participants to the Sector Understanding (hereinafter the "Participants"), after consideration of substantiated requests by any Participant, may decide that they shall be covered.

b) Any conversion of a ship. Ship conversion means any conversion of sea-going vessels of more than 1 000 gt on condition that conversion operations entail radical alterations to the cargo plan, the hull or the propulsion system.

c) 1) Although hovercraft-type vessels are not included in the Sector Understanding, Participants are allowed to grant export credits for hovercraft vessels on equivalent conditions to those prevailing in the Sector Understanding. They commit themselves to apply this possibility moderately and not to grant such credit conditions to hovercraft vessels in cases where it is established that no competition is offered under the conditions of the Sector Understanding.

2) In the Sector Understanding, the term "hovercraft" is defined as follows: an amphibious vehicle of at least 100 tons designed to be supported wholly by air expelled from the vehicle forming a plenum contained within a flexible skirt around the periphery of the vehicle and the ground or water surface beneath the vehicle, and capable of being propelled and controlled by airscrews or ducted air from fans or similar devices.

3) It is understood that the granting of export credits at conditions equivalent to those prevailing in this Sector Understanding should be limited to those hovercraft vessels used on maritime routes and non-land routes, except for reaching terminal facilities standing at a maximum

distance of one kilometre from the water.

# CHAPTER II: PROVISIONS FOR EXPORT CREDITS AND TIED AID

## 3. MAXIMUM REPAYMENT TERM

The maximum repayment term, irrespective of country classification, is 12 years after delivery.

## 4. CASH PAYMENT

The Participants shall require a minimum cash payment of 20% of the contract price by delivery.

## 5. REPAYMENT OF PRINCIPAL AND PAYMENT OF INTEREST

a) The principal sum of an export credit shall be repaid in equal instalments at regular intervals of normally six months and a maximum of 12 months.

b) Interest shall be paid no less frequently than every six months and the first payment of interest shall be made no later than six months after the starting point of credit.

c) For export credits provided in support of lease transactions, equal repayments of principal and interest combined may be applied in lieu of equal repayments of principal as set out in paragraph a).

d) Interest due after the starting point of credit shall not be capitalised.

e) A Participant to this Sector Understanding intending to support a payment of interest on different terms than those set out in paragraph b) shall give prior notification at least ten calendar days before issuing any commitment, in accordance with Annex VII of the Arrangement.

## 6. MINIMUM PREMIUM

The provisions of the Arrangement in relation to minimum premium benchmarks shall not be applied until such provisions have been further reviewed by the Participants to this Sector Understanding.

## 7. PROJECT FINANCE

The provisions of Article 7 and of Annex VI to the Arrangement shall not be applied until such provisions have been further reviewed by the Participants to this Sector Understanding.

## 8. AID

Any Participant desiring to provide aid must, in addition to the provisions of the Arrangement, confirm that the ship is not operated under an open registry during the repayment term and that appropriate assurance has been obtained that the ultimate owner resides in the receiving country, is not a non-operational subsidiary of a foreign interest and has undertaken not to sell the ship without his government's approval.

# CHAPTER III: PROCEDURES

## 9. NOTIFICATION

For the purpose of transparency each Participant shall, in addition to the provisions of the Arrangement and the IBRD/Berne Union/OECD Creditor Reporting System, provide annually information on its system for the provision of official support and of the means of implementation of this Sector Understanding, including the schemes in force.

## 10. REVIEW

a) The Sector Understanding shall be reviewed annually or upon request by any Participant within the context of the OECD Working Party on Shipbuilding, and a report made to the Participants to the Arrangement.

b) To facilitate coherence and consistency between the Arrangement and this Sector Understanding and taking into account the nature of the shipbuilding industry, the Participants to this Sector Understanding and to the Arrangement will consult and co-ordinate as appropriate.

c) Upon a decision by the Participants to the Arrangement to change the Arrangement, the Participants to this Sector Understanding (the Participants) will examine such a decision and consider its relevance to this Sector Understanding. Pending such consideration the amendments to the Arrangement will not apply to this Sector Understanding. In case the Participants can accept the amendments to the Arrangement they shall report this in writing to the Participants to the Arrangement. In case the Participants cannot accept the amendments to the Arrangement as far as their application to shipbuilding is concerned they shall inform the Participants to the Arrangement of their objections and enter into consultations with them with a view to seeking a resolution of the issues. In case no agreement can be reached between the two groups, the views of the Participants as regards the application of the amendments to shipbuilding shall prevail.

# ATTACHMENT: COMMITMENTS FOR FUTURE WORK

In addition to the Future Work of the Arrangement, the Participants to this Sector Understanding agree:

a) To develop an illustrative list of types of ships which are generally considered non-commercially viable, taking into account the disciplines on tied aid set out in the Arrangement.

b) To review the provisions of the Arrangement in relation to minimum premium benchmarks with a view to incorporating them into this Sector Understanding.

c) To discuss, subject to the developments in relevant international negotiations, the inclusion of other disciplines on minimum interest rates including a special CIRR and floating rates.

d) To review the applicability to this Sector Understanding of provisions of the Arrangement in relation to Project Finance.

e) To discuss whether:

– the date of the first instalment of principal;

– the Weighted Average Life concept

may be used in relation to the repayment profile contained in Article 5 of this Sector Understanding.

# ANNEX II: SECTOR UNDERSTANDING ON EXPORT CREDITS FOR NUCLEAR POWER PLANTS

## CHAPTER I: SCOPE OF THE SECTOR UNDERSTANDING

### 1. SCOPE OF APPLICATION

a) This Sector Understanding sets out the provisions which apply to officially supported export credits relating to contracts for:

1) The export of complete nuclear power stations or parts thereof, comprising all components, equipment, materials and services, including the training of personnel directly required for the construction and commissioning of such nuclear power stations.

2) The modernisation of existing nuclear power plants in cases where both the overall value of the modernisation is at or above SDR 80 million and the economic life of the plant is likely to be extended by at least the repayment period to be awarded. If either of these criteria is not met, the terms of the Arrangement apply.

3) The supply of nuclear fuel and enrichment.

4) The provision of spent fuel management.

b) This Sector Understanding does not apply to:

1) Items located outside the nuclear power plant site boundary for which the buyer is usually responsible, in particular costs associated with land development, roads, construction village, power lines, switchyard① and water supply, as well as costs arising in the buyer's country from official approval procedures (*e. g.* site permit, construction permit, fuel loading permit).

2) Sub-stations, transformers and transmission lines located outside the nuclear power plant site boundary.

3) Official support provided for the decommissioning of a nuclear power plant.

# CHAPTER II: PROVISIONS FOR EXPORT CREDITS AND TRADE-RELATED AID

## 2. MAXIMUM REPAYMENT TERMS

a) The maximum repayment term for goods and services included in the provisions of Articles 1 a) 1) and 2) of this Sector Understanding is 18 years.

b) The maximum repayment term for the initial fuel load is four years from delivery. The maximum repayment term for subsequent

---

① However, in cases where the buyer of the switchyard is the same as the buyer of the power plant and the contract is concluded in relation to the original switchyard for that power plant, the terms and conditions for the original switchyard shall not be more generous than those for the nuclear power plant.

reloads of nuclear fuel is two years from delivery.

c) The maximum repayment term for spent fuel disposal is two years.

d) The maximum repayment term for enrichment and spent fuel management is five years.

## 3. REPAYMENT OF PRINCIPAL AND PAYMENT OF INTEREST

a) The Participants shall apply a profile of repayment of principal and payment of interest as specified in sub-paragraph 1) or 2) below:

1) Repayment of principal shall be made in equal instalments.

2) Repayment of principal and payment of interest combined shall be made in equal instalments.

b) Principal shall be repaid and interest shall be paid no less frequently than every six months and the first instalment of principal and interest shall be made no later than six months after the starting point of credit.

c) On an exceptional and duly justified basis, official support for goods and services mentioned in Articles 1) a) 1) and 2) of this Understanding may be provided on terms other than those set out in paragraphs a) and b) above. The provision of such support shall be explained by an imbalance in the timing of the funds available to the obligor and the debt service profile available under an equal, semi-annual repayment schedule, and shall comply with the following criteria:

1) The maximum repayment term shall be 15 years.

2) No single repayment of principal or series of principal payments within a six-month period shall exceed 25% of the principal sum of the credit.

3) Principal shall be repaid no less frequently than every 12 months. The first repayment of principal shall be made no later than 12 months after the starting point of credit and no less than 2% of the principal sum of the credit shall have been repaid 12 months after the starting point of credit.

4) Interest shall be paid no less frequently than every 12 months and the first interest payment shall be made no later than six months after the starting point of credit.

5) The maximum weighted average life of the repayment period shall not exceed nine years.

d) Interest due after the starting point of credit shall not be capitalised.

## 4. CONSTRUCTION OF CIRRs

The applicable CIRRs for official financing support provided in accordance with the provisions of this Sector Understanding are constructed using to the following base rates and margins:

| Repayment Term (years) | New nuclear power stations① | | All other contracts② | |
|---|---|---|---|---|
| | Base Rate (Government bonds) | Margin (bps) | Base Rate (Government bonds) | Margin (bps) |
| < 11 | Relevant CIRR in accordance with Article 20 of the Arrangement | | | |
| 11 to 12 | 7 years | 100 | 7 years | 100 |
| 13 | 8 years | 120 | 7 years | 120 |
| 14 | 9 years | 120 | 8 years | 120 |
| 15 | 9 years | 120 | 8 years | 120 |
| 16 | 10 years | 125 | 9 years | 120 |
| 17 | 10 years | 130 | 9 years | 120 |
| 18 | 10 years | 130 | 10 years | 120 |

## 5. ELIGIBLE CURRENCIES

The currencies that are eligible for official financing support are those which are fully convertible and for which data are available to construct the minimum interest rates mentioned in Article 4 of this Sector Understanding, and Article 20 of the Arrangement for repayment terms less than 11 years.

## 6. OFFICIAL SUPPORT FOR NUCLEAR FUEL AND FOR NUCLEAR FUEL RELATED SERVICES

Without prejudice to the provisions of Article 7 of this Sector Understanding, the Participants shall not provide free nuclear fuel or services.

---

① Article 1 a) 1) refers.

② Articles 1 a) 2) to 4) refer.

## 7. AID

The Participants shall not provide aid support.

# CHAPTER III: PROCEDURES

## 8. PRIOR NOTIFICATION

a) A Participant shall give prior notification in accordance with Article 48 of the Arrangement at least ten calendar days before issuing any commitment if it intends to provide support in accordance with the provisions of this Sector Understanding.

b) If the notifying Participant intends to provide support with a repayment term in excess of 15 years and/or in accordance with Article 3 c) of this Sector Understanding, it shall wait an additional ten calendar days if any other Participant requests a discussion during the initial ten calendar days.

c) A Participant shall inform all other Participants of its final decision following a discussion, to facilitate the review of the body of experience.

# CHAPTER IV: REVIEW

## 9. FUTURE WORK

The Participants agree to examine the following issues:

a) A minimum floating interest rate regime.

b) The maximum amount of official support for local costs.

## 10. REVIEW AND MONITORING

The Participants shall review regularly the provisions of the Sector Understanding and at the latest by the end of 2017.

# ANNEX III: SECTOR UNDERSTANDING ON EXPORT CREDITS FOR CIVIL AIRCRAFT

## *PART 1: GENERAL PROVISIONS*

### 1. PURPOSE

a) The purpose of this Sector Understanding is to provide a framework for the predictable, consistent and transparent use of officially supported export credits for the sale or lease of aircraft and other goods and services specified in Article 4 a) below. This Sector Understanding seeks to foster a level playing field for such export credits, in order to encourage competition among exporters based on quality and price of goods and services exported rather than on the most favourable officially supported financial terms and conditions.

b) This Sector Understanding sets out the most favourable terms and conditions on which officially supported export credits may be provided.

c) To this aim, this Sector Understanding seeks to establish a balanced equilibrium that, on all markets:

1) Equalises competitive financial conditions between the Participants,

2) Neutralises official support among the Participants as a factor in the choice among competing goods and services specified in Article 4 a) below, and

3) Avoids distortion of competition among the Participants to this Sector Understanding and any other sources of financing.

d) The Participants to this Sector Understanding (the Participants) acknowledge that the provisions included in this Sector Understanding have been developed for the sole purpose of this Sector Understanding and such provisions do not prejudice the other parts of the Arrangement on Officially Supported Export Credits (the Arrangement) and their evolution.

## 2. STATUS

This Sector Understanding is a Gentlemen's Agreement among its Participants and is Annex III to the Arrangement; it forms an integral part of the Arrangement and it succeeds the Sector Understanding which came into effect in July 2007.

## 3. PARTICIPATION

The Participants currently are: Australia, Brazil, Canada, the European Union, Japan, Korea, New Zealand, Norway, Switzerland and the United States. Any non-Participant may become a Participant in accordance with the procedures set out in Appendix I.

## 4. SCOPE OF APPLICATION

a) This Sector Understanding shall apply to all official support provided by or on behalf of a government, and which has a repayment term of two years or more, for the export of:

1) New civil aircraft and engines installed thereon, including buyer furnished equipment.

2) Used, converted, and refurbished civil aircraft and engines installed thereon, including, in each case, buyer furnished equipment.

3) Spare engines.

4) Spare parts for civil aircraft and engines.

5) Maintenance and service contracts for civil aircraft and engines.

6) Conversion, major modifications and refurbishment of civil aircraft.

7) Engine kits.

b) Official support may be provided in different forms:

1) Export credit guarantee or insurance (pure cover).

2) Official financing support:

– direct credit/financing and refinancing or

– interest rate support.

3) Any combination of the above.

c) This Sector Understanding shall not apply to official support for:

1) The exports of new or used military aircraft and related goods and services listed in paragraph a) above, including when used for

military purposes.

2) New or used flight simulators.

## 5. INFORMATION AVAILABLE TO NON-PARTICIPANTS

A Participant shall, on the basis of reciprocity, reply to a request from a non-Participant in a competitive situation on the financial terms and conditions offered for its official support as it would reply to a request from a Participant.

## 6. AID SUPPORT

The Participants shall not provide aid support, except for humanitarian purposes, through a Common Line procedure.

## 7. ACTIONS TO AVOID OR MINIMISE LOSSES

This Sector Understanding does not prevent its Participants from agreeing to less restrictive financial terms and conditions than those provided for by this Sector Understanding, if such action is taken after the export credit agreement and ancillary documents have already become effective and is intended solely to avoid or minimise losses from events which could give rise to non-payment or claims. A Participant shall notify all other Participants and the OECD Secretariat (the Secretariat), within 20 working days following the Participant's agreement with the buyer/borrower, of the modified financial terms and conditions. The notification shall contain information, including the motivation, on the new financial terms and conditions, using the reporting form set out in Appendix IV.

# *PART 2: NEW AIRCRAFT*

# CHAPTER I: COVERAGE

## 8. NEW AIRCRAFT

a) For the purpose of this Sector Understanding, a new aircraft is:

1) An aircraft, including buyer furnished equipment, and the engines installed on such aircraft owned by the manufacturer and not delivered nor previously used for its intended purpose of carrying passengers and/or freight and

2) Spare engines and spare parts when contemplated as part of the original aircraft order in accordance with the provisions of Article 20 a) below.

b) Notwithstanding the provisions of paragraph a) above, a Participant may support terms appropriate to new aircraft for transactions where, with the prior knowledge of that Participant, interim financing arrangements had been put in place because the provision of official support had been delayed; such delay shall not be longer than 18 months. In such cases, the repayment term and the final repayment date shall be the same as if the sale or lease of the aircraft would have been officially supported from the date the aircraft was originally delivered.

# CHAPTER II: FINANCIAL TERMS AND CONDITIONS

Financial terms and conditions for export credits encompass all the provisions set out in this Chapter, which shall be read in conjunction one with the other.

## 9. ELIGIBLE CURRENCIES

The currencies which are eligible for official financing support are euro, Japanese yen, UK pound sterling, US dollar, and other fully convertible currencies for which data are available to construct the minimum interest rates mentioned in Appendix III.

## 10. DOWN PAYMENT AND MAXIMUM OFFICIAL SUPPORT

a) For transactions with buyers/borrowers classified in Risk Category 1 (as per Table 1 of Appendix II), the Participants shall:

1) Require a minimum down payment of 20% of the net price of the aircraft at or before the starting point of credit;

2) Not provide official support in excess of 80% of the net price of the aircraft.

b) For transactions with buyers/borrowers classified in Risk Categories 2 to 8 (as per Table 1 of Appendix II), the Participants shall:

1) Require a minimum down payment of 15% of the net price of the aircraft at or before the starting point of credit;

2) Not provide official support in excess of 85% of the net price of the aircraft.

c) A Participant which applies Article 8 b) above shall reduce the maximum amount of official support by the amount of principal of the instalments deemed due from the starting point of the credit so as to ensure that, at the time of disbursement, the amount outstanding is the same as if such an officially supported export credit was provided at the time of delivery. In such circumstances, prior to delivery the Participant shall have received an application for official support.

## 11. MINIMUM PREMIUM RATES

a) The Participants providing official support shall charge, for the credit amount officially supported, no less than the minimum premium rate set out in accordance with Appendix II.

b) The Participants shall use, whenever necessary, the agreed premium rate conversion model to convert between *per annum* spreads calculated on the outstanding amount of the official support and single up-front premium rates calculated on the original amount of the official support.

## 12. MAXIMUM REPAYMENT TERM

a) The maximum repayment term shall be 12 years for all new aircraft.

b) On an exceptional basis, and with a prior notification, a maximum repayment term of up to 15 years shall be allowed. In this case, a surcharge of 35% to the minimum premium rates calculated in accordance with Appendix II shall apply.

c) There shall be no extension of the repayment term by way of sharing of rights in the security on a *pari passu* basis with commercial lenders for the officially supported export credit.

## 13. REPAYMENT OF PRINCIPAL AND PAYMENT OF INTEREST

a) The Participants shall apply a profile of repayment of principal and payment of interest as specified in sub-paragraph 1) or 2) below.

1) Repayment of principal and payment of interest combined shall be made in equal instalments:

– Instalments shall be made no less frequently than every three months and the first instalment shall be made no later than three months after the starting point of credit.

– Alternatively, and subject to a prior notification, instalments shall be made every six months and the first instalment shall be made no later than six months after the starting point of credit. In this case, a surcharge of 15% to the minimum premium rates calculated in accordance with Appendix II shall apply.

– In the case of a floating rate transaction, the principal amortising profile shall be set for the entire term, no more than five business days prior to the disbursement date, based on the floating or swap rate at that time.

2) Repayment of principal shall be made in equal instalments with interest payable on declining balances:

– Instalments shall be made no less frequently than every three months and the first instalment shall be made no later than three months after the starting point of credit.

– Alternatively, and subject to a prior notification, instalments shall be made every six months and the first instalment shall be made no later than six months after the starting point of credit. In this case, a surcharge of 15% to the minimum premium rates calculated in accordance with Appendix II shall apply.

b) Notwithstanding paragraph a) above, and subject to a prior notification, the repayment of principal may be structured to include a final payment of all outstanding amounts on a specified date. In such case, repayments of principal prior to the final payment will be structured as set out in paragraph a) above, based on an amortization period not greater than the maximum repayment term allowed for the goods and services being supported.

c) Notwithstanding paragraph a) above, repayment of principal may be structured on terms less favourable to the obligor.

d) Interest due after the starting point of credit shall not be capitalised.

## 14. MINIMUM INTEREST RATES

a) The Participants providing official financing support shall apply either a minimum floating interest rate or a minimum fixed interest rate, in accordance with the provisions of Appendix III.

b) For jet aircraft of a net price of at least USD 35 million, official financing support on CIRR basis shall only be provided in exceptional circumstances. A Participant intending to provide such support shall notify all other Participants at least 20 calendar days before final commitment, identifying the borrower.

c) Interest rate excludes any payment by way of premium referred to in Article 11 above, and fees referred to in Article 16 below.

## 15. INTEREST RATE SUPPORT

The Participants providing interest rate support shall comply with the financial terms and conditions of this Sector Understanding and shall require any bank or any other financial institution which is a party to the interest supported transaction to participate in that transaction only on terms that are consistent in all respects with the financial terms and conditions of this Sector Understanding.

## 16. FEES

a) Subject to the limits of the premium holding period, the Participants providing official support in the form of pure cover shall charge a premium holding fee on the un-drawn portion of the official support during the premium holding period, as follows:

1) For the first six months of the holding period: zero basis points *per annum*.

2) For the second six months of the holding period: 12.5 basis points *per annum*.

3) For the third and final six months of the holding period: 25 basis points *per annum*.

b) The Participants providing official support in the form of direct credit / financing shall charge the following fees:

1) Arrangement / Structuring fee: 25 basis points on the disbursed amount payable at the time of each disbursement.

2) Commitment and premium holding fee: 20 basis points *per annum* on the un-drawn portion of the officially supported export credit to be disbursed, during the premium holding period, payable in arrears.

3) Administration fee: five basis points *per annum* on the amount of official support outstanding payable in arrears. Alternatively, the Participants may elect to have this fee payable as an up-front fee, on the amount disbursed, at the time of each disbursement pursuant to the provisions of Article 11 b) above.

## 17. CO-FINANCING

Notwithstanding Articles 14 and 16 above, in a co-financing where official support is provided by way of direct credit and pure cover, and where pure cover represents at least 35% of the officially supported amount, the Participant providing direct credit shall apply the same financial terms and conditions, including fees, as those provided by the financial institution under pure cover, to generate an all-in cost equivalence between the pure cover provider and the direct lender. In such circumstances, the Participant providing such support shall report the financial terms and conditions supported, including fees, in accordance with the reporting form set out in Appendix IV.

# *PART 3: USED AIRCRAFT, SPARE ENGINES, SPARE PARTS, MAINTENANCE AND SERVICE CONTRACTS*

## CHAPTER I: COVERAGE

### 18. USED AIRCRAFT AND OTHER GOODS AND SERVICES

This Part of the Sector Understanding shall apply to used aircraft and to spare engines, spare parts, conversion, major modification, refurbishing, maintenance and service contracts in conjunction with both new and used aircraft and engine kits.

## CHAPTER II: FINANCIAL TERMS AND CONDITIONS

The financial terms and conditions to be applied, other than the maximum repayment term, shall be in accordance with the provisions set out in Part 2 of this Sector Understanding.

### 19. SALE OF USED AIRCRAFT

a) Subject to paragraph b) below, the maximum repayment term for used aircraft shall be established in accordance with the age of the aircraft, as set out in the following table:

| Age of Aircraft (years since the date of original manufacture) | Maximum Repayment Terms for Asset-Backed or Sovereign Transactions (years) | Maximum Repayment Terms for Transactions neither Asset-Backed nor Sovereign (years) |
|---|---|---|
| 1 | 10 | 8.5 |
| 2 | 9 | 7.5 |
| 3 | 8 | 6.5 |
| 4 | 7 | 6 |
| 5 ~ 8 | 6 | 5.5 |
| Over 8 | 5 | 5 |

b) The maximum repayment term for aircraft that have undergone conversion, provided the transaction meets all the requirements of Article 19 of Appendix II and provided further that official support, if any, provided in respect of such conversion was not provided in accordance with Article 21 a) below, shall be established in accordance with the period of time since the date of conversion and the age of the aircraft, as set out in the following table:

**Maximum Repayment Terms for Asset-Backed Converted Aircraft (years)**

| Period of Time Since the Date of Conversion (years) | Age of Aircraft (years since the date of original manufacture) | | | | | |
|---|---|---|---|---|---|---|
| | 1 | 2 | 3 | 4 | 5 ~ 8 | Over 8 |
| 0 (Newly converted) | 10 | 9 | 8 | 8 | 8 | 8 |
| 1 | 10 | 9 | 8 | 7 | 7 | 7 |
| 2 | — | 9 | 8 | 7 | 6 | 6 |
| 3 or more | — | — | 8 | 7 | 6 | 5 |

## 20. SPARE ENGINES AND SPARE PARTS

a) When purchased, or ordered in connection with the engines to be installed on a new aircraft, the official support for spare engines may be provided on the same terms and conditions as for the aircraft.

b) When purchased with new aircraft, the official support for spare parts may be provided on the same terms and conditions as for the aircraft up to a maximum 5% of the net price of the new aircraft and installed engines; paragraph d) below shall apply to official support for spare parts in excess of the 5% limit.

c) When spare engines are not purchased with a new aircraft, the maximum repayment term shall be eight years. For spare engines with a unit value of USD 10 million or more, provided the transaction meets all the requirements of Article 19 of Appendix II, the repayment term shall be 10 years.

d) When other spare parts are not purchased with a new aircraft, the maximum repayment term shall be:

1) Five years with a contract value of USD 5 million or more.

2) Two years with a contract value of less than USD 5 million.

## 21. CONTRACTS FOR CONVERSION/ MAJOR MODIFICATION/REFURBISHING

a) If a transaction for conversion:

1) Is valued at USD 5 million or more, and

– Meets all the requirements of Article 19 of Appendix II, a Participant may offer official support with a repayment term of up to eight years.

– Does not meet all the requirements of Article 19 of Appendix II, a Participant may offer official support with a repayment term of up to five years.

2) Is valued at less than USD 5 million, a Participant may offer official support with a repayment term of up to two years.

b) If a transaction is for a major modification, or refurbishment, a Participant may offer official support with a repayment term of up to:

1) Five years if the contract value is USD 5 million or more;

2) Two years, if the contract value is less than USD 5 million.

## 22. MAINTENANCE AND SERVICE CONTRACTS

The Participants may offer official support with a repayment term of up to three years.

## 23. ENGINE KITS

The Participants may offer official support with a repayment term of up to five years.

## *PART 4: TRANSPARENCYP ROCEDURES*

All communications shall be made between the designated contact points in each Participant country by means of instant communication, *e. g.* the OECD On-Line Information System (OLIS). Unless otherwise agreed, all information exchanged under this Part of the Sector Understanding shall be treated by all Participants as confidential.

### *SECTION 1: INFORMATION REQUIREMENTS*

## 24. INFORMATION ON OFFICIAL SUPPORT

a) Within one month after the date of a final commitment, a Participant shall submit the information required in Appendix IV to all other Participants, with a copy to the Secretariat.

b) In order to establish the margin benchmark in accordance with Appendix III Article 8 b), information on pure cover margins, as outlined in Appendix III Articles 8 c) and d), shall be submitted to the Secretariat no later than five days after the end of each month.

*SECTION 2: EXCHANGE OF INFORMATION*

## 25. REQUESTS FOR INFORMATION

a) A Participant may ask another Participant for information about the use of its officially supported export credits for the sale or lease of aircraft covered by this Sector Understanding.

b) A Participant which has received an application for official support may address an enquiry to another Participant, giving the most favourable credit terms and conditions that the enquiring Participant would be willing to support.

c) The Participant to which such an enquiry is addressed shall respond within seven calendar days and provide reciprocal information to the fullest extent possible. The reply shall include the best indication that the Participant can give of the decision it is likely to take. If necessary, the full reply shall follow as soon as possible.

d) Copies of all enquiries and responses shall be sent to the Secretariat.

## 26. FACE-TO-FACE CONSULTATIONS

a) In a competitive situation, a Participant may request face-to-face consultations with one or more Participants.

b) Any Participant shall agree within ten working days to such requests.

c) The consultations shall take place as soon as possible after the expiry of the ten working-day period.

d) The Chairman of the Participants shall co-ordinate with the Secretariat on any necessary follow-up action. The Secretariat shall promptly make available to all Participants the outcome of the consultation.

## 27. SPECIAL CONSULTATIONS

a) A Participant (the initiating Participant) that has reasonable grounds to believe that financial terms and conditions offered by another Participant (the responding Participant) are more generous than those provided for in this Sector Understanding shall inform the Secretariat; the Secretariat shall immediately make available such information to the responding Participant.

b) The responding Participant shall clarify the financial terms and conditions of the official support being considered within five working days following the issue of the information from the Secretariat.

c) Following clarification by the responding Participant, the initiating Participant may request that a special consultation with the responding Participant be organised by the Secretariat within five working days to discuss the issue.

d) The responding Participant shall wait for the outcome of the consultation which shall be determined on the day of such consultation before proceeding any further with the transaction.

*SECTION 3: COMMON LINES*

## 28. PROCEDURES AND FORMAT OF COMMON LINES

a) Common Line proposals shall be addressed to the Secretariat only. The identity of the initiator is not revealed on the Common Line register on the OLIS. However, the Secretariat may orally reveal the identity of the initiator to a Participant on demand. The Secretariat shall keep a record of such requests.

b) The Common Line proposal shall be dated and shall be in the following format:

1) Reference number, followed by Common Line.

2) Name of the importing country and buyer/borrower.

3) Name or description of the transaction as precise as possible to clearly identify the transaction.

4) Common Line proposal for the most generous terms and conditions to be supported.

5) Nationality and names of known competing bidders.

6) Bid closing date and tender number to the extent it is known.

7) Other relevant information, including reasons for proposing the Common Line and as appropriate, special circumstances.

## 29. RESPONSES TO COMMON LINE PROPOSALS

a) Responses shall be made within 20 calendar days, although the Participants are encouraged to respond to a Common Line proposal as quickly as possible.

b) A response may be acceptance, rejection, a request for additional information, a proposal for modification of the Common Line or an alternative Common Line proposal.

c) A Participant which remains silent or advises that it has no position shall be deemed to have accepted the Common Line proposal.

## 30. ACCEPTANCE OF COMMON LINES

a) After a period of 20 calendar days, the Secretariat shall inform all Participants of the status of the Common Line proposal. If not all Participants have accepted the Common Line, but no Participant has rejected it, the proposal shall be left open for a further period of eight calendar days.

b) After this further period, a Participant which has not explicitly rejected the Common Line proposal shall be deemed to have accepted the Common Line. Nevertheless, a Participant, including the initiating Participant, may make its acceptance of the Common Line conditional on the explicit acceptance by one or more Participants.

c) If a Participant does not accept one or more elements of a Common Line it implicitly accepts all other elements of the Common

Line.

## 31. DISAGREEMENT ON COMMON LINES

a) If the initiating Participant and a Participant which has proposed a modification or alternative cannot agree on a Common Line within the additional eight calendar-day period mentioned in Article 30 above, this period can be extended by their mutual consent. The Secretariat shall inform all Participants of any such extension.

b) A Common Line which has not been accepted may be reconsidered using the procedures in Articles 28 to 30 above. In these circumstances, the Participants are not bound by their original decision.

## 32. EFFECTIVE DATE OF COMMON LINE

The Secretariat shall inform all Participants either that the Common Line will go into effect or that it has been rejected; the agreed Common Line will take effect three calendar days after this announcement.

## 33. VALIDITY OF COMMON LINES

a) Unless agreed otherwise, a Common Line, once agreed, shall be valid for a period of two years from its effective date, unless the Secretariat is informed that it is no longer of interest, and that such situation is accepted by all Participants.

b) If a Participant seeks an extension within 14 calendar days of the original date of expiry and in the absence of disagreement, a Common Line shall remain valid for a further two-year period; subsequent extensions may be agreed through the same procedure.

c) The Secretariat shall monitor the status of Common Lines and shall keep the Participants informed accordingly, through the maintenance of the listing "The Status of Valid Common Lines" on OLIS. Accordingly, the Secretariat, *inter alia*, shall issue, on a quarterly basis, a list of Common Lines due to expire in the following quarter.

d) Upon the request of a non-Participant which produces competing aircraft, the Secretariat shall make available valid Common Lines to that non-Participant.

*SECTION 4: MATCHING*

## 34. MATCHING

a) Taking into account a Participant's international obligations, a Participant may match financial terms and conditions of official support offered by a non-Participant.

b) In the event of matching non-conforming terms and conditions offered by a non-Participant:

1) The matching Participant shall make every effort to verify such terms and conditions.

2) The matching Participant shall inform the Secretariat and all other Participants of the nature and outcome of such efforts, as well as of the terms and conditions it intends to support, at least ten calendar days before issuing any commitment.

3) If a competing Participant requests a discussion during this ten calendar-day period, the matching Participant shall wait an additional ten calendar days before issuing any commitment on such terms.

c) If a matching Participant modifies or withdraws its intention to support the notified terms and conditions, it shall immediately inform all other Participants accordingly.

# *PART 5: MONITORING AND REVIEW*

## 35. MONITORING

a) The Secretariat shall monitor the implementation of this Sector Understanding and report to the Participants on an annual basis.

b) Each transaction deemed eligible under Article 39 a) shall be reported in accordance with the provisions of Article 24 a) and Appendix IV.

c) Each transaction deemed eligible under Article 39 b) shall be reported in accordance with the provisions of Article 24 a) and Appendix IV, in addition to which:

1) The reporting Participant shall indicate the link between that transaction and the transition list.

2) The transition lists shall be monitored on a semi-annual basis; to that end, the Secretariat shall meet with each Participant, with a view to:

– Monitoring the number of firm orders registered on the transition lists which have been delivered.

– Updating for the following year the delivery schedule for transactions registered on the transition lists.

– Identifying orders registered on transition lists which have not been or shall not, for any reason, be delivered to the buyer listed on such transition lists. Any such order shall be deleted from the transition list and shall not be reallocated in any way to any other buyer.

## 36. REVIEW

The Participants shall review the procedures and provisions of this Sector Understanding, against the criteria, and at the times, set out in paragraphs a) and b) below.

a) The Participants shall undertake the review of this Sector Understanding as follows:

1) In the fourth calendar year following the effective date of this Sector Understanding and, regularly thereafter, in each case with three months prior notice given by the Secretariat.

2) At the request of a Participant after due consultation, provided that three months prior notice has been given by the Secretariat and the requesting Participant provides a written explanation of the reason for, and objectives of, the review as well as a summary of the consultations preceding its request.

3) Modalities of update of minimum premium rates and minimum interest rates are set out in Appendixes II and III respectively.

4) Fees set out in Article 16 shall be part of reviews.

b) The review set out in sub-paragraph a) 1) above shall consider:

1) The extent to which the purposes of this Sector Understanding,

as set out in Article 1 above, have been achieved and any other issue a Participant may wish to bring forward for discussion.

2) In view of the elements in sub-paragraph b) 1) above, whether amendments to any aspect of this Sector Understanding are justified.

c) In recognition of the importance of the review process, to ensure that the terms and conditions of this Sector Understanding continue to meet the needs of the Participants, each Participant reserves the right to withdraw from this Sector Understanding in accordance with Article 40 below.

## 37. FUTURE WORK

Consideration will be given to:

a) Examining Participants' practices in providing official support before the starting point of credit.

b) The provisions applicable to indirect loans.

c) An extension of maximum repayments terms under Article 19 for used aircraft that have undergone significant refurbishment prior to sale.

d) An extension of maximum repayment terms under Article 21 for larger contract values.

e) The provisions applicable to "refurbishing" (Article 21) and "services" (Article 22).

f) The Cape Town eligibility process.

g) The definition of "Interested Participant".

# *PART 6: FINAL PROVISIONS*

## 38. ENTRY INTO FORCE

The effective date of this Sector Understanding is 1 February 2011.

## 39. TRANSITIONAL ARRANGEMENTS

Notwithstanding Article 38 above, the Participants may provide official support on the terms and conditions set out as follows:

a) The Participants may provide official support on the terms and conditions set out in the Aircraft Sector Understanding in force as of 1 July 2007 ("the 2007 ASU") if the following conditions are fulfilled:

1) The goods and services shall be subject to a firm contract concluded not later than 31 December 2010.

2) The goods and services shall be physically delivered not later than 31 December 2012 for 2007 ASU Category 1 aircraft and 31 December 2013 for 2007 ASU Category 2 and 3 aircraft.

3) For each final commitment notified, a 20 basis points *per annum* commitment fee shall be charged from the earlier of the date of the final commitment or 31 January 2011 (2007 ASU Category 1 aircraft) /30 June 2011 (2007 ASU Category 2 and 3 aircraft), until the aircraft is delivered. This commitment fee shall be in lieu of the fees set out in Articles 17 a) and b) 2) of the 2007 ASU. This commitment fee shall be charged in addition to the minimum premium charged.

b) The Participants may provide official support on terms and conditions applicable prior to the effective date of this Sector Understanding if the following conditions are fulfilled:

1) The goods and services shall be subject to a firm contract concluded not later than 31 December 2010.

2) Such official support is limited to deliveries of 69 2007 ASU Category 1 aircraft per Participant and 92 2007 ASU Category 2 aircraft per Participant.

3) In order to benefit from the terms and conditions set out in this paragraph, aircraft mentioned in sub-paragraph b) 2) above shall be registered on lists (hereafter "transition lists") which shall be notified by the Participants to the Secretariat prior to the entry into force of this Sector Understanding. Such transition lists shall include:

– The aircraft models and numbers.

– Tentative delivery dates.

– Identity of buyers.

– The applicable regime (either the Aircraft Sector Understanding prevailing prior to the 2007 ASU, or the 2007 ASU).

4) Information under the first, second and fourth *tirets* above shall be shared with all Participants; information under the third *tiret* above shall be managed exclusively by the Secretariat and the Chairman.

5) For each aircraft on transition lists:

– If official support is committed under the Aircraft Sector

Understanding prevailing prior to the 2007 ASU, a commitment fee of 35 basis points *per annum* shall be charged from the earlier of the date of the final commitment or 31 March 2011, until the aircraft is delivered. In addition, the minimum premium charged shall be no less than 3% on an up-front basis.

– If official support is committed under the 2007 ASU, a commitment fee of 20 basis points per annum shall be charged from the earlier of the date of the final commitment or 30 June 2011, until the aircraft is delivered.

– The commitment fee set out in both *tirets* above shall be in lieu of the fees set out in Articles 17 a) and b) 2) of the 2007 ASU. This commitment fee shall be charged in addition to the minimum premium charged.

6) The Participants may provide officially supported export credits on the terms and conditions set out in the Aircraft Sector Understanding prevailing prior to the 2007 ASU only for deliveries of aircraft scheduled to occur on or prior to 31 December 2010, in accordance with firm contracts concluded not later than 30 April 2007 and notified to the Secretariat not later than 30 June 2007.

c) The implementation of this Article shall be monitored in accordance with Articles 35 b) and c).

## 40. WITHDRAWAL

A Participant may withdraw from this Sector Understanding by notifying the Secretariat in writing by means of instant communication, *e. g.* the OLIS. The withdrawal takes effect six months after receipt of the notification by the Secretariat. Withdrawal will not affect agreements reached on individual transactions entered into prior to the effective date of the withdrawal.

# APPENDIX I PARTICIPATION IN THE AIRCRAFT SECTOR UNDERSTANDING

1. The Participants encourage non-Participants that are developing a manufacturing capacity for civil aircraft to apply the disciplines of this Sector Understanding. In this context the Participants invite non-Participants to enter into a dialogue with them regarding the conditions of joining the ASU.

2. The Secretariat should ensure that a non-Participant interested in participating in this Sector Understanding is provided with full information on the terms and conditions associated with becoming a Participant to this Sector Understanding.

3. The non-Participant would then be invited by the Participants to take part in the activities in pursuance of this Sector Understanding and to attend, as an observer, the relevant meetings. Such an invitation would be for a maximum of two years and could be renewed once for a further two years. During this period the non-Participant shall be invited to provide a review of its export credit system, especially for the export of civil aircraft.

4. At the end of that period, the non-Participant shall indicate whether it wishes to become a Participant in this Sector Understanding and to follow its disciplines; in the case of such confirmation, the non-Participant shall contribute, on an annual basis, to the costs associated with the implementation of this Sector Understanding.

5. The interested non-Participant shall be considered a Participant 30 working days after the confirmation referred to in Article 4 of this Appendix.

# APPENDIX II MINIMUM PREMIUM RATES

This Appendix sets out the procedures to be used when determining the pricing of official support for a transaction subject to this Sector Understanding. Section 1 sets out the risk classification procedures; Section 2 sets out the minimum premium rates to be charged for new and used aircraft, and Section 3 sets out the minimum premium rates to be charged for spare engines, spare parts, conversion/major modification/refurbishing, maintenance and service contracts, and engine kits.

*SECTION 1: PROCEDURES FOR RISK CLASSIFICATION*

1. The Participants have agreed on a list of risk classifications (the List) for buyers/borrowers; such risk classifications reflect the senior unsecured credit rating of buyers/borrowers using a common rating scale such as that of one of the credit rating agencies (CRA).

2. The risk classifications will be made by experts nominated by the Participants against the risk categories set out in Table 1 of this Appendix.

3. The List shall be binding at any stage of the transaction (*e. g.* campaign and delivery), subject to the provisions of Article 15 of this Appendix.

## I. ESTABLISHMENT OF THE LIST OF RISK CLASSIFICATIONS

4. The List shall be developed and agreed among the Participants prior to the entry into force of this Sector Understanding; it shall be maintained by the Secretariat and made available to all the Participants on a confidential basis.

5. Upon request, the Secretariat may, on a confidential basis, inform an aircraft-producing non-Participant of the risk classification of a buyer/borrower; in this case, the Secretariat shall inform all Participants of the request. A non-Participant may, at any time, propose additions to the List to the Secretariat. A non-Participant proposing an addition to the List may participate in the risk-classification procedure as if it were an interested Participant.

## II. UPDATE OF THE LIST OF RISK CLASSIFICATIONS

6. Subject to the provisions of Article 15 of this Appendix, the List may be updated on an *ad hoc* basis in the event that either a Participant signals, in any form, its intention to apply another risk classification than that on the List, or a Participant needs a risk classification for a buyer/borrower that is not yet on the List[①][②].

---

① An explanation shall be provided where the proposed risk-rating of a buyer/borrower exceeds the risk rating of the host sovereign.

② For transactions with an export contract value of less than USD 5 million, a Participant not wishing to follow the risk classification procedure set out in Articles 6 to 8 of this Appendix shall apply the risk classification "8" for the buyer/borrower which is the subject of the transaction and shall notify the transaction in accordance with Article 24 a) of this Sector Understanding.

7. Any Participant shall, before any use of an alternative or new risk classification, send a request to the Secretariat for updating the List on the basis of an alternative or new risk classification. The Secretariat will circulate this request to all Participants within two working days, without mentioning the identity of the Participant who submitted the request.

8. A period of ten[1] working days is allowed for interested Participants either to agree to or to challenge any proposed change to the List; a failure to respond within this period is considered as an agreement to the proposal. If at the end of the ten-day period, no challenge has been made to the proposal, the proposed change in the List is deemed to have been agreed. The Secretariat will modify the List accordingly and send an OLIS message within five working days; the revised List shall be binding from the date of that message.

## III. RESOLUTION OF DISAGREEMENTS

9. In the event of a challenge to a proposed risk classification, interested Participants shall, at an expert level, make their best efforts to come to an agreement on the risk classification within a further period of ten working days after notification of a disagreement. All means necessary to resolve the disagreement should be explored, with the assistance of the Secretariat if necessary (*e. g.* conference calls or face-to-face consultations). If interested Participants agree to a risk classification within this ten working-day period, they shall inform the Secretariat of the outcome upon which the Secretariat will update the

---

① For transactions with an export contract value of less than USD 5 million, a five working-day period shall apply.

List accordingly and send an OLIS message in the following five working days. The adjusted List shall be binding from the date of that message.

10. In case the disagreement is not resolved among the experts within ten working days, the issue will be referred to the Participants for decision on an appropriate risk classification, in a period that shall not exceed five working days.

11. In the absence of a final agreement, a Participant may have recourse to a CRA to determine the risk classification of the buyer/borrower. In such cases, the Chairman of the Participants shall address a communication on behalf of the Participants to the buyer/borrower, within ten working days. The communication shall include the terms of reference for the risk assessment consultation as agreed among the Participants. The resulting risk classification will be registered in the List and become binding immediately following the Secretariat's OLIS message to finalise the update procedure within five working days.

12. Unless otherwise agreed, the cost of such recourse to a CRA shall be borne by the interested buyer/borrower.

13. During the procedures set out in Articles 9 to 11 of this Appendix, the prevailing risk classification (when available on the List) shall remain applicable.

## IV. VALIDITY PERIOD OF CLASSIFICATIONS

14. The valid risk classifications are the prevailing risk classifications as recorded in the List maintained by the Secretariat; indications and commitments of premium rates shall only be made in accordance with those risk classifications.

15. Risk classifications have a 12-month maximum validity period from the date recorded in the List by the Secretariat for the purpose of the Participants providing indication and final commitments of premium rates; the validity period for a specific transaction may be extended by an additional 18 months once a commitment or a final commitment has occurred and premium holding fees are charged. Risk classifications may be subject to revision during the 12-month validity period in case of material changes to the risk profile of the buyer/borrower, such as a modification of a rating delivered by a CRA.

16. Unless any Participant requests its update, at least 20 working days before the end of the relevant risk classification validity period, the Secretariat shall remove that risk classification from the next succeeding updated List. The Secretariat will circulate this update request to all Participants within two working days, without mentioning the identity of the Participant who submitted the request, and the procedures set out in Articles 9 to 11 of this Appendix shall apply.

## V. BUYER/BORROWER RISK CLASSIFICATION REQUEST

17. If, at the campaign stage, a buyer/borrower requests an indication of its risk classification and if it is not yet on the List, that buyer/borrower may ask for an indicative risk classification from a CRA at its own expense. This risk classification shall not be included in the List; it may be used by the Participants as a basis for their own risk assessment.

*SECTION 2: MINIMUM PREMIUM RATES FOR NEW AND USED AIRCRAFT*

## I. ESTABLISHMENT OF THE MINIMUM PREMIUM RATES

18. Articles 19 to 58 of this Appendix set out the minimum premium rates corresponding to the risk classification of a buyer/borrower (or, if a different entity, the primary source of repayment of the transaction).

19. The Participants may provide official support at or above the minimum premium rate provided that all the conditions below are fulfilled:

a) The transaction is asset-backed, meeting all of the following criteria:

1) A first priority security interest on or in connection with the aircraft and engines.

2) In the case of a lease structure, assignment and/or a first priority security interest in connection with the lease payments.

3) Cross default and cross collateralization of all aircraft and engines owned legally and beneficially by the same parties under the proposed financing, whenever possible under the applicable legal regime.

b) The transaction is structured to include, as a minimum, risk mitigants as set out in Table 1 below:

**Table 1** **Risk Mitigants**

| ASU Risk Category | Risk Ratings | Risk Mitigants | |
|---|---|---|---|
| | | TOTAL | Of which at least "A" |
| 1 | AAA to BBB – | 0 | 0 |
| 2 | BB + and BB | 0 | 0 |
| 3 | BB – | 1 | 1 |
| 4 | B + | 2 | 1 |
| 5 | B | 2 | 1 |
| 6 | B – | 3 | 2 |
| 7 | CCC | 4 | 3 |
| 8 | CC to C | 4 | 3 |

20. For purposes of Article 19 of this Appendix:

a) The Participants may select from the following risk mitigants:

*"A" risk mitigants:*

1) Reduced advance rate: each reduction of five percentage points from the advance rates referred to in Articles 10 a) and b) of this Sector Understanding is equivalent to one "A" risk mitigant. In this case, the Participant shall not provide official support in any form in excess of the reduced advance rate.

2) Straight line amortisation: repayment of principal in equal instalments is equivalent to one risk mitigant.

3) Reduced repayment term: a repayment term which does not exceed ten years is equivalent to one risk mitigant.

*"B" risk mitigants:*

1) Security deposit: each security deposit in an amount equal to

one quarterly instalment of principal and interest is equivalent to one risk mitigant. The security deposit can be in the form of cash or a standby letter of credit.

2) Lease payments in advance: lease payments in an amount equal to one quarterly instalment of principal and interest shall be paid one quarter in advance of each repayment date.

3) Maintenance reserves in a form and amount reflective of market best practices.

b) Subject to a prior notification, up to one of the "A" risk-mitigants may be replaced by a 15% surcharge on the applicable minimum premium rate.

21. Pursuant to Article 11 of this Sector Understanding, the minimum premium rates to be applied are composed of minimum risk-based rates (RBR) to which a market reflective surcharge (MRS) shall be added, in accordance with Articles 22 to 34 below.

22. As of the entry into force of this Sector Understanding, the RBRs are:

**Table 2 Risk-Based Rates**

| ASU Risk Category | Spreads (bps) | Upfront (%) |
|---|---|---|
| 1 | 89 | 4.98 |
| 2 | 98 | 5.49 |
| 3 | 116 | 6.52 |
| 4 | 133 | 7.49 |
| 5 | 151 | 8.53 |
| 6 | 168 | 9.51 |
| 7 | 185 | 10.50 |
| 8 | 194 | 11.03 |

23. The RBRs rates shall be reset on an annual basis, based on 4-year moving average of the annual Moody's Loss Given Default (LGD). The appropriate LGD for this reset is based on the 1st Lien Senior Secured Bank Loans, and shall be calculated as follows:

**Table 3**

| LGD Mapping | |
|---|---|
| 4 – year Moving Average | LGD Considered |
| ≥45% | 25% |
| ≥35% and < 45% | 23% |
| ≥30% and < 35% | 21% |
| < 30% | 19% |

24. A RBR adjustment factor shall be determined as follows:

$$\frac{\text{LGD Considered}}{19\%} = \text{RBR adjustment factor}$$

25. The RBR adjustment factor shall be multiplied by the RBRs set out in Table 2 above, in order to determine the reset RBRs.

26. The first reset process will take place in the first quarter of 2012 and the resulting RBRs will become effective as of 15 April 2012.

27. The RBRs resulting from subsequent reset processes will be effective as of 15 April of each following year. Once the RBRs resulting from the annual reset have been determined, the Secretariat shall inform immediately all Participants of the applicable rates and make them publicly available.

28. For each risk category, a Market Reflective Surcharge shall be calculated as follows:

$$MRS = B \times [(0.5 \times MCS) - RBR]$$

where:

– B is a blend coefficient varying from 0.7 to 0.35 according to each risk category as per Table 4 below.

– MCS is a 90 – day moving average of Moody's Median Credit Spreads (MCS) with an average life of 7 years.

29. Where risk categories include more than one risk rating, the spreads shall be averaged. In risk category 1, the BBB – spread shall be used.

30. The MCS spreads shall be discounted by 50% to account for the asset-security. The MCS discounted spreads shall then be adjusted by a blend factor ranging from 70% to 35% as per Table 4 below, applied on the difference between the MCS discounted spreads and the RBR. Any negative spreads resulting from the blending shall not be deducted.

**Table 4** **Blend Factors**

| Risk-Ratings | ASU Risk Category | Blend Factor (%) |
|---|---|---|
| AAA | 1 | 70 |
| AA | 1 | 70 |
| A | 1 | 70 |
| BBB + | 1 | 70 |
| BBB | 1 | 70 |
| BBB – | 1 | 70 |
| BB + | 2 | 65 |
| BB | 2 | 65 |

续表

| Risk – Ratings | ASU Risk Category | Blend Factor (%) |
|---|---|---|
| BB – | 3 | 50 |
| B + | 4 | 45 |
| B | 5 | 40 |
| B – | 6 | 35 |
| CCC | 7 | 35 |
| CC | 8 | 35 |
| C | 8 | 35 |

31. The MRS shall be updated on a quarterly basis, as follows:

– The first update process shall take place in the first quarter of 2011 and the resulting MCS shall become effective as of 15 April 2011; however, until 15April 2012, the outcome of updates of the MRS applying to Risk Category 1 shall become effective only if they result in an increase of such MRS.

– The subsequent update processes shall take place in the second, third and fourth quarters of 2011 (and thereon) and the resulting MCS shall become effective respectively on 15 July 2011, 15 October 2011 and 15 January 2012, and thereon.

– Following each update, the Secretariat shall inform immediately all Participants of the applicable MRS and the resulting minimum rates and make them publicly available prior to the date these rates become effective.

32. The MRS shall be applied only if and when it is positive and exceeds 25 basis points.

33. The increase in minimum premium rates resulting from the

MRS update shall not exceed 10% of the previous quarterly minimum premium rates. The minimum premium rates (which result from adding the risk-based rates and the market reflective surcharge) shall not exceed the risk-based rates by more than 100%.

34 – 1. In order to determine the minimum premium rates:

– The following formula shall be used:

$$\text{Net MPR} = \text{MPR} \times (1 + \text{RTAS}) \times (1 + \text{RFAS}) \times (1 + \text{RMRS}) \times (1 - \text{CTCD}) \times (1 + \text{NABS}) - \text{CICD}$$

Where:

- RTAS represents the repayment term adjustment surcharge set out in Article 12 b) of this Sector Understanding.
- RFAS represents the repayment frequency adjustment surcharge set out in Articles 13 a) 1) and 2) of this Sector Understanding.
- RMRS represents the risk mitigant replacement surcharge set out in Article 20 b) of this Appendix.
- CTCD represents the Cape Town Convention Discount set out in Article 36 of this Appendix.
- NABS represents the non-asset-backed surcharge set out in Articles 55 a) 4), 55 b) and 57 b) of this Appendix II, as applicable.
- CICD represents the conditional insurance coverage discount set out in Article 54 a) of this Appendix.

– Premium may be paid either upfront or, over the life of the facility, as spreads expressed in basis points per annum, or in any combination of upfront rates and spreads. The upfront rates and spreads shall be calculated using the premium rate conversion model (PCM) so that the premium payable for a given transaction has the same NPV whether payable upfront, as a spread over the life of the facility, or a combination thereof. In transactions where, prior to the commencement of cover, terms are agreed or stipulated, which entail a reduction in the weighted average life, an upfront rate (calculated using the PCM) may be charged, which in terms of the resulting premium payable, corresponds to that payable in NPV terms under the spreads.

34 – 2. The applicable minimum premium rates as of the initial effective date of this Sector Understanding (1 February 2011) are set out in Table 5 below.

**Table 5 Minimum Premium Rates**

**(12 – year repayment term, asset-backed transactions)**

| Risk Category | Risk Classification | Minimum Premium Rates | |
|---|---|---|---|
| | | Per Annum Spreads (bps) | Up – Front (%) |
| 1 | AAA to BBB – | 137 | 7.72 |
| 2 | BB + and BB | 184 | 10.44 |
| 3 | BB – | 194 | 11.03 |
| 4 | B + | 208 | 11.85 |
| 5 | B | 234 | 13.38 |
| 6 | B – | 236 | 13.50 |
| 7 | CCC | 252 | 14.45 |
| 8 | CC to C | 257 | 14.74 |

## II. REDUCTIONS OF THE MINIMUM PREMIUM

35. Subject to the provisions of Article 36 of this Appendix, a

reduction of the minimum premium rates established in accordance with sub-Section I above shall be allowed if:

a) The asset-backed transaction relates to an aircraft object within the meaning of the Cape Town Protocol on Matters Specific to Aircraft Equipment,

b) The operator of the aircraft object (and, if different, the borrower/buyer or lessor if, in the view of the Participant providing the official support, the structure of the transaction so warrants) is situated in a State which, at the time of disbursement in respect of the aircraft object, appears on the list of States which qualify for the reduction of the minimum premium rates ("Cape Town List"), and where applicable, in a territorial unit of that State that qualifies under Article 38 of this Appendix, and

c) The transaction relates to an aircraft object registered on the International Registry established pursuant to the Cape Town Convention, and the Aircraft Protocol thereto (Cape Town Convention or CTC).

36. The reduction of the minimum premium rates established in accordance with sub-Section I above shall not exceed 10% of the applicable minimum premium rate.

37. In order to be included on the Cape Town List, a State shall:

a) Be a Contracting Party to the Cape Town Convention;

b) Have made the qualifying declarations set out in Annex I to this Appendix; and

c) Have implemented the Cape Town Convention, including the qualifying declarations, in its laws and regulations, as required, in such a way that the Cape Town Convention commitments are appropriately translated into national law.

38. To qualify under Article 35 of this Appendix, a territorial unit shall:

a) Be a territorial unit to which the Cape Town Convention has been extended;

b) Be a territorial unit in respect of which the qualifying declarations set out in Annex I to this Appendix apply; and

c) Have implemented the Cape Town Convention, including the qualifying declarations, in its laws and regulations, as required, in such a way that the Cape Town Convention commitments are appropriately translated into national law.

39. An initial agreed Cape Town List shall be provided by the Participants to the Secretariat prior to the entry into force of this Sector Understanding. Updates to the Cape Town List shall be made in accordance with Articles 40 to 52 of this Appendix.

40. Any Participant or non-Participant which provides official support for aircraft may propose to the Secretariat the addition of a State to the Cape Town List. Such proposal shall include, with respect to such State:

a) All the relevant information in respect of the date of deposit of the Cape Town Convention ratification or accession instruments with the Depositary;

b) A copy of the declarations made by the State which is proposed to be added to the Cape Town List;

c) All relevant information in respect of the date on which the Cape Town Convention and the qualifying declarations have entered into force;

d) An analysis which outlines the steps that the State which is proposed to be added to the Cape Town List has taken to implement the Cape Town Convention including the qualifying declarations in its laws and regulations, as required to ensure that the Cape Town Convention commitments are appropriately translated into national law; and

e) A duly completed questionnaire, the form of which is attached at Annex 2 of this Appendix ("CTC Questionnaire") completed by at least one law firm qualified to give legal advice in relation to the relevant jurisdiction of the State which is proposed to be added to the Cape Town List. The completed CTC Questionnaire shall specify:

(i) The name (s) and office address (es) of the responding law firm (s);

(ii) The law firm's relevant experience, which could include experience in legislative and constitutional processes as they relate to the implementation of international treaties in the State, and specific experience in CTC related issues including any experience in advising either a government on implementation and enforcement of the Cape Town Convention or the private sector, or enforcement of creditor's rights in the State which is proposed to be added to the Cape Town List;

(iii) Whether the law firm is involved or intends to be involved in any transactions that may benefit from a reduction of minimum premium rates if the proposed State is added to the CTC list[①]; and

( iv ) The date on which the CTC Questionnaire has been completed.

41. The Secretariat shall circulate an OLIS message within five working days containing the proposal.

42. Any Participant or non-Participant which provides official support for aircraft may propose that a State be removed from the Cape Town List if they are of the view that such State has taken actions that are inconsistent with, or failed to take actions that are required by virtue of, that State's Cape Town Convention commitments. To that end, the Participant or non-Participant shall include in a proposal for removal from the Cape Town List, a full description of the circumstances that have given rise to the proposal for deletion, such as any State actions that are inconsistent with its Cape Town Convention commitments, or any failure to maintain or enforce legislation required by virtue of that State's Cape Town Convention commitments. The Participant or non-Participant who submits the proposal for removal from the Cape Town List shall provide any supporting documentation that may be available, and the Secretariat shall circulate an OLIS message within five working days containing such proposal.

43. Any Participant or non-Participant which provides official support for aircraft may propose the reinstatement of a State that has been previously removed from the Cape Town List, where such

① Together with information regarding any involvement ( provided with due respect for confidentiality duties).

reinstatement is justified by subsequent corrective actions or events. Such a proposal shall be accompanied by a description of the circumstances that gave rise to the removal of the State as well as a report of the subsequent corrective actions in support of reinstatement. The Secretariat shall circulate an OLIS message within five working days containing such proposal.

44. The Participants may either agree to or challenge a proposal brought forward under Articles 40 to 43 of this Appendix within 20 working days from the date of submission of the proposal ("Period 1").

45. If at the end of Period 1, no challenge has been made to the proposal, the proposed update to the Cape Town List is deemed to have been accepted by all Participants. The Secretariat will modify the Cape Town List accordingly and send an OLIS message within five working days. The updated Cape Town List shall take effect on the date of that message.

46. In the event of a challenge to the proposed update of the Cape Town List, the challenging Participant or Participants shall, within Period 1, provide a written explanation of the basis of the challenge. Following circulation by the OECD Secretariat to all Participants of the written challenge, the Participants shall make best efforts to come to an agreement within a further ten working day period ("Period 2").

47. The Participants shall inform the Secretariat of the outcome of their discussions. If an agreement is reached during Period 2, the Secretariat will, if necessary, update the Cape Town List accordingly and send an OLIS message in the following five working days. The updated Cape Town List shall take effect on the date of that message.

48. If no agreement is reached during Period 2, the Chairman of the Participants to this Sector Understanding (hereafter "the Chairman") will make her/his best efforts to facilitate a consensus between the Participants, within twenty working days ("Period 3") immediately following Period 2. If at the end of Period 3, no consensus is reached, a final resolution shall be achieved through the following procedures:

a) The Chairman shall make a written recommendation with respect to the proposed update of the Cape Town List. The Chairman's recommendation shall reflect the majority view emerging from the views openly expressed by at least the Participants which provide official support for aircraft exports. In the absence of a majority view, the Chairman shall make a recommendation based exclusively on the views expressed by the Participants and shall set out in writing the basis for the recommendation, including in the case of ineligibility, the eligibility criteria that were not met.

b) The Chairman's recommendation shall not disclose any information relating to Participants' views or positions expressed in the context of the process set out in Articles 40 to 49 of this Appendix, and

c) The Participants shall accept the recommendation of the Chairman.

49. If, following a proposal submitted under Article 40, the Participants or Chairman has determined that a State is not eligible to be added to the Cape Town List, a Participant or non-Participant may submit another proposal requesting that the Participants reconsider the State's eligibility. The proposing Participant or non-Participant shall address the reasons substantiating the original determination of

ineligibility. The proposing Participant or non-Participant shall also obtain and provide an updated CTC questionnaire. This new proposal shall be subject to the process set out in Articles 44 to 50.

50. In the event of any change to the list of qualified countries pursuant to the procedures set out in Article 48 of this Appendix, the Secretariat shall issue an OLIS message containing the updated Cape Town List within five working days of such change. The updated Cape Town List shall take effect on the date of that message.

51. The addition, withdrawal or reinstatement of a State to the Cape Town List after disbursement in respect of an aircraft shall not affect MPRs established regarding such aircraft.

52. In the context of the process set out in Articles 40 to 50 of this Appendix, the Participants shall not disclose any information relating to views or positions expressed.

53. The Participants shall monitor the implementation of Articles 40 to 52 of this Appendix and review it in the first half of 2012, annually thereafter or upon the request of any Participant.

54. The following adjustments to the applicable minimum premium rates may be applied:

a) A discount of five basis points (per annum spreads) or 0.29% (up-front) to the applicable minimum premium rates may be applied for officially supported transactions in the form of conditional insurance cover.

b) The minimum premium rates shall be applied on the covered principal amount.

## III. NON ASSET-BACKED TRANSACTIONS

55. Notwithstanding the provisions of Article 19 a) of this Appendix, the Participants may provide officially supported export credits for non-asset backed transactions, provided either of the following conditions is fulfilled:

a) In the case of non-sovereign transactions:

1) The maximum value of the export contract receiving official support is USD 15 million.

2) The maximum repayment term shall be 10 years,

3) No third party has a security interest in the assets being financed, and

4) A minimum surcharge of 30% shall be applied to the minimum premium rates established in accordance with sub-Section I above.

b) In the case of a transaction with a sovereign or backed by an irrevocable and unconditional sovereign guarantee, a minimum surcharge shall, in accordance with Table 6 below, be applied to the minimum premium rates set out in accordance with sub-Section I above.

**Table 6**

| Risk Category | Surcharge (%) |
|---|---|
| 1 | 0 |
| 2 | 0 |
| 3 | 0 |
| 4 | 10 |

续表

| Risk Category | Surcharge (%) |
|---|---|
| 5 | 15 |
| 6 | 15 |
| 7 | 25 |
| 8 | 25 |

56. The provisions of Articles 35 to 51 of this Appendix do not apply to officially supported export credits provided pursuant to Article 55 of this Appendix.

*SECTION 3: MINIMUM PREMIUM RATES FOR GOODS AND SERVICES OTHER THAN USED AIRCRAFT COVERED BY PART 3 OF THIS SECTOR UNDERSTANDING*

57. When providing official support for all goods and services other than used aircraft covered by Part 3 of this Sector Understanding, the minimum premium rates shall be as follows:

a) In the case of asset-backed transactions, the minimum premium rates shall be equal to the prevailing minimum spreads established in accordance with sub-Section I above and, in the case of pure cover, converted to upfront fees using the conversion model and the appropriate tenor.

b) In the case of non asset-backed transactions, the minimum premium rates shall be equal to the prevailing minimum spreads established in accordance with sub-Section I above to which a surcharge of 30% will be added, and, in the case of pure cover, converted to upfront fees using the conversion model and the appropriate tenor.

58. The provisions of Articles 35 to 54 of this Appendix shall

apply to official support for all goods and services other than used aircraft covered by Part 3 of this Sector Understanding.

# ANNEX 1: QUALIFYING DECLARATIONS

1. For the purpose of Section 2 of Appendix II, the term "qualifying declarations", and all other references thereto in this Sector Understanding, means that a Contracting party to the Cape Town Convention (Contracting Party):

a) Has made the declarations in Article 2 of this Annex, and

b) Has not made the declarations in Article 3 of this Annex.

2. The declarations for the purpose of Article 1 a) of this Annex are:

a) Insolvency: State Party declares that it will apply the entirety of Alternative A under Article XI of the Aircraft Protocol to all types of insolvency proceeding and that the waiting period for the purposes of Article XI (3) of that Alternative shall be no more than 60 calendar days.

b) Deregistration: State Party declares that it will apply Article XIII of the Aircraft Protocol.

c) Choice of Law: State Party declares that it will apply Article VIII of the Aircraft Protocol.

And at least one of the following (though both are encouraged):

d) Method for Exercising Remedies: State Party declares under

Convention Article 54 (2) that any remedies available to the creditor under any provision of the Convention which are not expressed under the relevant provisions thereof to require application to a court may be exercised without leave of the court (the insertion "without court action and" to be recommended (but not required) before the words "leave of the court");

e) Timely Remedies: State Party declares that it will apply Article X of the Aircraft Protocol in its entirety (though clause 5 thereof, which is to be encouraged, is not required) and that the number of working days to be used for the purposes of the time-limit laid down in Article X (2) of the Aircraft Protocol shall be in respect of:

1) The remedies specified in Articles 13 (1) (a), (b) and (c) of the Convention (preservation of the aircraft objects and their value; possession, control or custody of the aircraft objects; and immobilisation of the aircraft objects), not more than that equal to ten calendar days, and

2) The remedies specified in Articles 13 (1) (d) and (e) of the Convention (lease or management of the aircraft objects and the income thereof and sale and application of proceeds from the aircraft equipment), not more than that equal to 30 calendar days.

3. The declarations referred to in Article 1 b) of this Annex are the following:

a) Relief Pending Final Determination: State Party shall not have made a declaration under Article 55 of the Convention opting out of Article 13 or Article 43 of the Convention; provided, however, that, if State Party made the declarations set out under Article 2 d) of this Annex, the making of a declaration under Article 55 of the Convention shall not prevent application of the Cape Town Convention discount.

b) Rome Convention: State Party shall not have made a declaration under Article XXXII of the Aircraft Protocol opting out of Article XXIV of the Aircraft Protocol; and

c) Lease Remedy: State Party shall not have made a declaration under Article 54 (1) of the Convention preventing lease as a remedy.

4. Regarding Article XI of the Aircraft Protocol, for Member States of the European Union, the qualifying declaration set out in Article 2 a) of this Annex shall be deemed made by a Member State, for purposes hereof, if the national law of such Member State was amended to reflect the terms of Alternative A under Article XI of the Aircraft Protocol (with a maximum 60 calendar days waiting period). As regards the qualifying declarations set out in Articles 2 c) and e) of this Annex, these shall be deemed satisfied, for the purpose of this Sector Understanding, if the laws of the European Union or the relevant Member States are substantially similar to that set out in such Articles of this Annex. In the case of Article 2 c) of this Annex, the laws of the European Union (EC Regulation 593/2008 on the Law Applicable to Contractual Obligations) are agreed to be substantially similar to Article VIII of the Aircraft Protocol.

# ANNEX 2: CAPE TOWN CONVENTION QUESTIONNAIRE

## I. Preliminary Information

Please provide the following information:

1. The name and full address of the law firm completing the questionnaire.

2. The law firm's relevant experience, which could include experience in legislative and constitutional processes as they relate to the implementation of international treaties in the State, and specific experience in CTC related issues including any experience in advising either a government on implementation and enforcement of the Cape Town Convention or the private sector, or enforcement of creditor's rights in the State which is proposed to be added to the Cape Town List;

3. Whether the law firm is involved or intends to be involved in any transactions that may benefit from a reduction of minimum premium rates if the proposed State is added to the CTC list;①

4. The date on which this questionnaire was completed.

## II. Questions

1. *Qualifying declarations*

1.1 Has the State② made each of the qualifying declarations in accordance with the requirements of Annex 1 to Appendix II of the Sector Understanding on Export Credits for Civil Aircraft ("ASU")

---

① Together with information regarding any involvement (provided with due respect for confidentiality duties).

② For the purposes of this questionnaire the "State" is the country that is being proposed for addition to the Cape Town Convention List under Appendix II, Section 2, II of the ASU. Where appropriate, these questions shall also be answered in respect of the laws of the particular "territorial unit" of the State in which the relevant operator of an aircraft (or other relevant body as set out in Article 35 (b) Appendix II) is located and "national law" shall be read as including a reference to the relevant local law.

(each a "Qualifying Declaration")? In particular, regarding the declarations concerning "Method for Exercising Remedies" [Article 2 d)] and "Timely Remedies" [Article 2 e)], please specify if one or both of these have been made.

1. 2 Please describe the way in which the declarations made differ, if at all, from the requirements referred to in Question 1. 1.

1. 3 Please confirm that the State has not made any of the declarations listed in Article 3 of Annex 1 to Appendix II of the ASU.

2. *Ratification*

1. 1 Has the State ratified, accepted, approved or acceded to the Cape Town Convention and Aircraft Protocol ("Convention")? Please could you state the date of ratification/accession and briefly describe the State's process of accession to or ratification of the Convention?

1. 2 Do the Convention and Qualifying Declarations ("QD") made have the force of law in the whole territory of the State without any further act, implementing legislation or the passing of any further law or regulation?

1. 3 If so, please briefly explain the process that gives the Convention and QDs the force of law.

3. *Effect of national and local law*

1. 1 Describe and list, if applicable, the implementing legislation and regulation (s) with respect to the Convention and each QD made by the State.

1. 2 Would the Convention and QDs made, as translated into

national law① ("Convention and QDs"), overrule or have priority over any conflicting national law, regulation, order, judicial precedent or regulatory practice. If so, please describe the process by which this happens,② and if not, please provide details.

1.3 Are there any existing gaps in the implementation of the Convention and QDs? If so, please describe. ③

4. *Court and administrative decisions*

1.1 Please describe any matters, including judicial, regulatory, or administrative practice which could be expected to result in the courts, authorities or administrative bodies failing to give full force and effect to the Convention and QDs. ④⑤

---

① For the purposes of this questionnaire, "national law" refers to all national legislation of a State, including but not limited to, the Constitution and its Amendments, any federal, state and district law or regulation.

② For example, that (i) treaties prevail over other law as a matter of constitutional or similar framework law in State X, or (ii) legislation is required in State X, and has been enacted expressly setting out the priority of the Cape Town Treaty and /or superseding such other law, or (iii) the Cape Town Treaty or its implementing legislation is (a) more specific than other law (*lex specialis derogat legi generali*), and/or (b) later in time than such other law (*lex posterior derogat legi priori*), and as a result of (a) and/or (b) prevails over such other law.

③ For example, is there any reason why the rights and remedies granted to creditors under the Convention, including those granted under the QDs, would not (a) be recognized as being effective or (b) be sufficient by themselves, to enable such rights and remedies to be validly exercised in the State?

④ An example of an administrative action for the purposes of this question might be the failure by the State to put in place any procedures or resources to give effect to a provision of the Convention or a Qualifying Declaration. Another example would be the failure by a State to put in place proper procedures in its aircraft registry for recording IDERAs.

⑤ Please include in your analysis any precedent / decision relating to the recognition of rights of creditors, including ECAs, when relevant.

1.2 To your knowledge, has there been any judicial or administrative enforcement action taken by a creditor under the Convention? If so, please describe the action and indicate whether it was successful.

1.3 To your knowledge, since ratification/implementation, have the courts in that State refused in any instance to enforce loan obligations of a debtor or guarantor in the State contrary to the Convention and QDs?

1.4 To your knowledge, are there any other matters that may impact whether courts and administrative bodies should be expected to act in a manner consistent with the Convention and QDs? If so, please specify.

# Appendix III MINIMUM INTEREST RATES

The provision of official financing support shall not offset or compensate, in part or in full, for the appropriate premium rate to be charged for the risk of non-repayment pursuant to the provisions of Appendix II.

## 1. MINIMUM FLOATING INTEREST RATE

a) The minimum floating interest rate shall be, as appropriate, the EURIBOR, the Bank Bill Swap Rate, *i. e.* BBSY, the London Inter-Bank Offered Rate, *i. e.* LIBOR, as compiled by the British Bankers' Association (BBA) with the currency and the maturity corresponding to the frequency of interest payment of officially supported export credit, or the Canadian Dealer Offered Rate (CDOR), to which a margin benchmark calculated in accordance with Article 8 of this Appendix, shall be added.

b) The floating interest rate setup mechanism shall vary according to the repayment profile chosen, as follows:

1) When the repayment of principal and the payment of interest are combined in equal instalments, the relevant EURIBOR/BBSY/LIBOR/CDOR effective two business days prior to the loan drawdown date, according to the relevant currency and payment frequency shall be used to calculate the entire payment schedule, as if it were a fixed rate. The principal payment schedule shall then be fixed as well as the first interest payment. The second interest payment, and so on, shall be calculated based on the relevant EURIBOR/BBSY/LIBOR/CDOR effective two business days before the prior payment date over the outstanding principal balance initially established.

2) When the repayment of principal is made in equal instalments, the relevant EURIBOR/BBSY/LIBOR/CDOR, according to the relevant currency and payment frequency, effective two business days before the loan drawdown date and prior to each payment date shall be used to calculate the following interest payment over the outstanding principal balance.

c) Where official financing support is provided for floating rate loans, buyers/borrowers may have the option to switch from a floating rate to a fixed rate provided that the following conditions are fulfilled:

1) The option is restricted to switching to the swap rate only;

2) The option to switch shall only be exercised upon request, only

once, and shall be reported accordingly with a reference to the reporting form initially sent to the Secretariat pursuant to Article 24 of this Understanding.

## 2. MINIMUM FIXED INTEREST RATE

The minimum fixed interest rate shall be either:

a) The swap rate, concerning the relevant currency of the officially supported export credit and with a maturity equal to the interpolated rate for the two closest available annual periods to the weighted average life of the loan. The interest rate shall be set two business days prior to each drawdown date.

OR

b) The Commercial Interest Reference Rate (CIRR) established according to the provisions set out in Articles 3 to 7 of this Appendix,

to which, in both cases, the margin benchmark, calculated in accordance with Article 8 f) of this Appendix, shall be added.

## 3. CONSTRUCTION OF CIRR

a) A CIRR is established for any of the eligible currencies set out in Article 9 of this Sector Understanding and calculated by adding a fixed margin of 120 basis points to one of the following three yields (the base rates):

1) Five-year government bond yields for a repayment term up to and including nine years,

2) Seven-year government bond yields for over nine and up to and

including 12 years, or

3) Nine-year government bond yields for over 12 and up to and including 15 years.

b) CIRR shall be calculated monthly using data from the previous month and notified to the Secretariat, no later than five days after the end of each month. The Secretariat shall then inform immediately all Participants of the applicable rates and make them publicly available. CIRR shall take effect on the 15th day of each month.

c) A Participant or a non-Participant may request that a CIRR be established for the currency of a non-Participant. In consultation with the non-Participant, a Participant or the Secretariat on behalf of that non-Participant may make a proposal for the construction of the CIRR in that currency using the Common Line procedures set out in Articles 28 to 33 of this Sector Understanding.

## 4. VALIDITY PERIOD OF CIRR

a) Holding the CIRR: the CIRR applying to a transaction shall not be held for a period longer than six months from its selection (export contract date or any application date thereafter) to the credit agreement date. If the credit agreement is not signed within that limit, and the CIRR is reset for an additional six months, the new CIRR shall be committed at the rate prevailing at the date of reset.

b) After the credit agreement date, the CIRR shall be applied for drawing periods which do not exceed six months. After the first six-month drawing period, the CIRR is reset for the next six months; the new CIRR shall be the one prevailing at the first day of the new six-month period and cannot be lower than the CIRR originally selected (procedure to be replicated for each subsequent six-month period of drawings).

## 5. APPLICATION OF MINIMUM INTEREST RATES

Within the provisions of the credit agreement the borrower shall not be allowed an option to switch from an officially supported floating rate financing to a pre-selected CIRR financing, nor be allowed to switch between a pre-selected CIRR and the short term market rate quoted on any interest payment date throughout the life of the loan.

## 6. EARLY REPAYMENT OF FIXED INTEREST RATE LOANS

In the event of a voluntary, early repayment of a fixed interest rate loan as determined in Article 2 of this Appendix, or any portion thereof or when the CIRR applied under the credit agreement is modified into a floating or a swap rate, the borrower shall compensate the institution providing official financing support for all costs and losses incurred as a result of such actions, including the cost to the government institution of replacing the part of the fixed rate cash inflow interrupted by the early repayment.

## 7. IMMEDIATE CHANGES IN INTEREST RATES

When market developments require the notification of an amendment to a CIRR during the course of a month, the amended rate shall be implemented ten working days after notification of this amendment has been received by the Secretariat.

## 8. MARGIN BENCHMARK

a) A three-month LIBOR margin benchmark shall be calculated monthly in accordance with paragraph b), using data notified to the Secretariat in accordance with paragraph c), and shall take effect on the $15^{th}$ day of each month. Once calculated, the margin benchmark shall be notified by the Secretariat to the Participants and shall be made publicly available.

b) The three-month LIBOR margin benchmark shall be a rate equivalent to the average of the lowest 50% of the margins over: (i) three-month LIBOR charged for floating rate transactions and (ii) three-month LIBOR as interpolated by swapping the fixed rate issuance to a floating rate equivalent charged for fixed rate transactions or capital market issuances. In either case, the margins included in the monthly benchmark reports submitted by relevant Participants shall be those from the three full calendar months preceding the effective date set out in paragraph a) above. Transactions / issuances that are used in the calculation of the margin benchmark shall meet the following conditions:

1) 100% unconditional guarantee transactions denominated in US dollars; and

2) Official support provided in respect of aircraft valued at or above USD 35 million (or its equivalent in any other eligible currency).

c) Participants shall report a margin at the time it becomes known and that margin will remain on the Participant's margin benchmark report for three full calendar months. In the case of individual transactions with multiple pricing events, there shall be no attempt to match subsequent pricing events to *ex post* notifications.

d) Participants shall notify transactions as of the date on which the long-term margin is realised. For bank mandated deals (including PEFCO), the date on which the margin is realised would be the earliest of the following: (i) issuance of a final commitment by the Participant, (ii) setting of the margin post-commitment, (iii) loan drawdown, and (iv) setting of the long-term margin post-draw-down. In the case of several drawdowns occurring under the same bank mandate at the same margin, notification shall only be made in respect of the first aircraft. For loans funded by way of capital market issuance, the date on which the margin is realised shall be the date on which the long-term rate is set which is typically the bond issuance date. In the case of several drawdowns occurring under the same bond and at the same margin, notification shall only be made in respect of the first aircraft.

e) The three-month LIBOR margin benchmark shall be applicable to a floating rate transaction and shall be set at final commitment.

f) For a fixed rate transaction, the margin benchmark applicable to the transaction shall be determined by swapping the three-month LIBOR margin benchmark into an equivalent spread over the applicable fixed rate, as determined in Article 2 of this Appendix, on the final commitment date and shall be set as of that date.

g) The Participants shall monitor the margin benchmark and shall review the margin benchmark mechanism upon the request of any Participant.

# APPENDIX Ⅳ REPORTING FORM

## a) *Basic Information*

1. Notifying country

2. Notification date

3. Name of notifying authority/agency

4. Identification number

## b) *Buyer/Borrower/Guarantor Information*

5. Name and country of buyer

6. Name and country of borrower

7. Name and country of guarantor

8. Status of buyer/borrower/guarantor, *e. g.* sovereign, private bank, other private

9. Risk classification of buyer/borrower/guarantor

## c) *Financial Terms and Conditions*

10. In what form is official support provided, *e. g.* pure cover, official financing support

11. If official financing support is provided, is it a direct credit/refinancing/interest rate support

12. Description of the transaction supported, including the

manufacturer, aircraft model and number of aircraft; indication of whether the transaction falls under the transitional arrangements set out in Article 39 a) or b) of this Understanding.

13. Final commitment date

14. Currency of credit

15. Credit amount, according to the following scale in USD millions:

| Category | Credit Amount |
|---|---|
| I | 0 ~ 200 |
| II | 200 ~ 400 |
| III | 400 ~ 600 |
| IV | 600 ~ 900 |
| V | 900 ~ 1200 |
| VI | 1200 ~ 1500 |
| VII | 1500 ~ 2000 * |

* *Indicate the number of USD* 300 *million multiples in excess of USD* 2000 *million.*

16. Percentage of official support

17. Repayment term

18. Repayment profile and frequency – including, where appropriate, weighted average life

19. Length of time between the starting point of credit and the first repayment of principal

20. Interest rates:

– Minimum interest rate applied

– Margin benchmark applied

21. Total premium charged by way of:

– Up-front fees (in percentage of the credit amount) or

– Spreads (basis points *per annum* above the applied interest rate)

– As appropriate, please indicate separately the 15% surcharge applied in accordance with Appendix II Article 20 b).

22. In the case of direct credit/financing, fees charged by way of:

– Arrangement/Structuring fee

– Commitment/Premium holding fee

– Administration fee

23. Premium holding period

24. In the case of pure cover, premium holding fees

25. Transaction structuring terms: risk mitigants / premium surcharge applied

26. As appropriate, an indication of the impact of the Cape Town Convention on the premium rate applied

# APPENDIX V LIST OF DEFINITIONS

All-In Cost Equivalence: the net present value of premium rates, interest rate costs and fees charged for a direct credit as a percentage of the direct credit amount is equal to the net present value of the sum of premium rates, interest rate costs and fees charged under pure cover as a percentage of the credit amount under pure cover.

Asset-Backed: a transaction that meets the conditions set out in 19 a) of Appendix II.

Buyer/Borrower: includes (but is not limited to) commercial entities such as airlines and lessors, as well as sovereign entities (or if a different entity, the primary source of repayment of the transaction).

Buyer Furnished Equipment: equipment furnished by the buyer and incorporated in the aircraft during the manufacture/refurbishment process, on or before delivery, as evidenced by the Bill of Sale from the manufacturer.

Cape Town Convention: refers to the Cape Town Convention on International Interests in Mobile Equipment and the Protocol thereto on Matters specific to Aircraft Equipment.

Commitment: any statement, in whatever form, whereby the willingness or intention to provide official support is communicated to the recipient country, the buyer, the borrower, the exporter or the financial institution, including without limitation, eligibility letters, marketing letters.

Common Line: agreement of the Participants for a given transaction, or in special circumstances on specific financial terms and conditions for official support; such common line shall prevail over the relevant provisions of this Sector Understanding only for the transaction or in the circumstances specified in the common line.

Conditional Insurance Cover: official support which in the case of a default on payment for defined risks provides indemnification to the beneficiary after a specified waiting period; during the waiting period the beneficiary does not have the right to payment from the Participant. Payment under conditional insurance cover is subject to the validity and the exceptions of the underlying documentation and of the underlying transaction.

Conversion: A major change in the type design of an aircraft through its conversion into a different type of aircraft (including the conversion of a passenger aircraft into a water bomber, cargo aircraft, search and rescue, surveillance aircraft, or business jet), subject to certification by the responsible Civil Aviation Authority.

Country Risk Classification: the prevailing country risk classification of the Participants to the Arrangement on Officially Supported Export Credits as published on the OECD website.

Credit Rating Agency: one of the internationally reputable rating agencies or any other rating agency that is acceptable to the Participants.

Engine Kits: a set of parts introduced to improve reliability, durability and/or on-wing performance procurement through introduction of technology.

Export Credit: an insurance, guarantee or financing arrangement which enables a foreign buyer of exported goods and/or services to defer payment over a period of time; an export credit may take the form of a supplier credit extended by the exporter, or of a buyer credit, where the exporter's bank or other financial institution lends to the buyer (or its bank).

Final Commitment: a final commitment exists when the Participant commits to precise and complete financial terms and conditions, either through a reciprocal agreement or by a unilateral act.

Firm Contract: an agreement between the manufacturer and the person taking delivery of the aircraft or engines as buyer, or, in connection with a sale-leaseback arrangement, as lessee under a lease with a term of at least five years, setting forth a binding commitment (excluding those relating to then unexercised options), where non-performance entails legal liability.

Interested Participant: a Participant which (i) provides official support for airframe or aircraft engines completely or partially manufactured in its territory, (ii) has an existing substantial commercial interest or has experience with the buyer/borrower concerned, or (iii) has been requested by a manufacturer/exporter to provide official support to the buyer/borrower in question.

Interest Rate Support: can take the form of an arrangement between on the one hand a government, or an institution acting for or on behalf of a government and, on the other hand, banks or other financial institutions which allows the provision of fixed rate export finance at or above the relevant minimum fixed interest rate.

Major Modification/Refurbishing: operations of reconfiguration or upgrading of either a passenger or cargo aircraft.

Net Price: the price for an item invoiced by the manufacturer or supplier thereof, after accounting for all price discounts and other cash credits, less all other credits or concessions of any kind related or fairly allocable thereto, as stated in a binding representation by each of the aircraft and engine manufacturers-the engine manufacturer representation is required only when it is relevant according to the form of the purchase agreement - or service provider, as the case may be, and supported by documentation required by the provider of official support to confirm that net price. All import duties and taxes (*e. g.* VAT) are not included in the net price.

New Aircraft: see Article 8 a) of this Sector Understanding.

Non-Asset-Backed: a transaction that does not meet the conditions set out in 19 a) of Appendix II.

Non-Sovereign Transaction: a transaction that does not meet the description set out in Article 49 b) of Appendix II.

Premium Holding Period: subject to Article 35 b) of Appendix II, period during which a premium rate offered for a transaction is being maintained; not to exceed 18 months from the date of Final Commitment.

Premium Rate Conversion Model: model agreed by and made available to the Participants, to be used for the purpose of this Sector Understanding in order to convert up-front premium fees into spreads and *vice versa*, in which the interest rate and the discount rate used shall be 4.6%; such rate shall be reviewed regularly by the Participants.

Prior Notification: a notification made at least ten calendar days before issuing any commitment, using the reporting form set out in Appendix IV.

Pure Cover: Official support provided by or on behalf of a government by a way of export credit guarantee or insurance only, *i. e.* which does not benefit from official financing support.

Repayment Term: the period beginning at the Starting Point of Credit and ending on the contractual date of the final repayment of principal.

Sovereign Transaction: a transaction that meets the description set out in Article 55 b) of Appendix II.

Starting Point of Credit: for the sale of aircraft including helicopters, spare engines and parts, at the latest the actual date when the buyer takes physical possession of the goods, or the weighted mean date when the buyer takes physical possession of the goods. For services, the latest starting point of credit is the date of the submission of the invoices to the client or acceptance of service by the client.

Swap Rate: a fixed rate equal to the semi-annual rate to swap floating rate debt to fixed rate debt (Offer side), posted on any independent market index provider, such as Telerate, Bloomberg, Reuters, or its equivalent, at 11:00 am New York time, two business days prior to the loan drawdown date.

Weighted Average Life: the time it takes to retire one-half of the principal of a credit; this is calculated as the sum of time (in years) between the starting point of credit and each principal repayment weighted by the portion of principal repaid at each repayment date.

# ANNEX IV  SECTOR UNDERSTANDING ON EXPORT CREDITS FOR RENEWABLE ENERGY, CLIMATE CHANGE MITIGATION AND ADAPTATION, AND WATER PROJECTS

The purpose of this Sector Understanding is to provide adequate financial terms and conditions to projects in selected sectors identified including under international initiatives as significantly contributing to climate change mitigation, including renewable energy, greenhouse gas (GHG) emissions' reduction and high energy efficiency projects, climate change adaptation, as well as water projects. The Participants to this Sector Understanding agree that the financial terms and conditions of the Sector Understanding, which complements the Arrangement, shall be implemented in a way that is consistent with the Purpose of the Arrangement.

## CHAPTER I: SCOPE OF THE SECTOR UNDERSTANDING

### 1. SCOPE OF APPLICATION FOR PROJECTS IN RENEWABLE ENERGY SECTORS ELIGIBLE TO APPENDIX I

a) This Sector Understanding sets out the financial terms and conditions that apply to officially supported export credits relating to contracts in the eligible sectors listed in Appendix I of this Sector Understanding for:

1) The export of complete renewable energies plants or parts thereof, comprising all components, equipment, materials and services (including the training of personnel) directly required for the construction and commissioning of such plants.

2) The modernisation of existing renewable energies plants in cases where the economic life of the plant is likely to be extended by at least the repayment period to be awarded. If this criterion is not met, the terms of the Arrangement apply.

b) This Sector Understanding does not apply to items located outside the power plant site boundary for which the buyer is usually responsible, in particular, water supply not directly linked to the power production plant, costs associated with land development, roads, construction villages, power lines and switchyard, as well as costs arising in the buyer's country from official approval procedures (*e. g.* site permits, construction permit), except:

1) In cases where the buyer of the switchyard is the same as the buyer of the power plant and the contract is concluded in relation to the original switchyard for that power plant, the terms and conditions for the original switchyard shall not exceed those for the renewable energies power plant; and

2) The terms and conditions for sub-stations, transformers and transmission lines with a minimum voltage threshold of 60kV located outside the renewable energies power plant site boundary shall not be

more generous than those for the renewable energies power plant.

## 2. SCOPE OF APPLICATION FOR PROJECTS IN CLIMATE CHANGE MITIGATION SECTORS ELIGIBLE TO APPENDIX II

a) This Sector Understanding sets out the financial terms and conditions that apply to officially supported export credits relating to contracts in a sector listed in Appendix II of this Sector Understanding. This list of sectors and, when applicable, corresponding technology-neutral performance criteria used to define a project's eligibility, may be modified over time in accordance with the review provisions set out in Article 12 of this Sector Understanding.

b) Such contracts shall relate to the export of complete projects or parts thereof, comprising all components, equipment, materials and services (including the training of personnel) directly required for the construction and commissioning of an identifiable project, providing that:

1) The project should result in low to zero carbon emissions, or $CO_2$ equivalent, and/or in high energy efficiency;

2) The project should be designed to meet, as a minimum, the performance standards as set out in Appendix II; and

3) The terms and conditions provided shall be extended only to address specific financial disadvantages encountered by a project, and shall be based on the individual financial needs and specific market conditions of each project.

## 3. SCOPE OF APPLICATION FOR ADAPTATION PROJECTS ELIGIBLE TO APPENDIX III

a) This Sector Understanding sets out the financial terms and conditions that apply to officially supported export credits relating to contracts for projects which meet the criteria set out in Appendix III of this Sector Understanding.

b) Such contracts shall relate to the export of complete projects or parts thereof, comprising all components, equipment, materials and services (including the training of personnel) directly required for the execution and commissioning of an identifiable project, providing that:

1) The conditions set out in Appendix III are met;

2) The terms and conditions provided shall be extended only to address specific financial disadvantages encountered by a project, and shall be based on the individual financial needs and specific market conditions of each project.

c) This Sector Understanding applies to the modernisation of existing projects, to take into consideration adaptation concerns, in cases where the economic life of the project is likely to be extended by at least the repayment period to be awarded. If this criterion is not met, the terms of the Arrangement apply.

## 4. SCOPE OF APPLICATION FOR WATER PROJECTS

This Sector Understanding sets out the financial terms and

conditions that apply to officially supported export credits relating to contracts for the export of complete projects or parts thereof related to the supply of water for human use and wastewater treatment facilities:

a) Infrastructure for the supply of drinking water to municipalities, including to households and small businesses, *i. e.* water purification for the purpose of obtaining drinking water and distribution network (including leakage control).

b) Wastewater collection and treatment facilities, *i. e.* collection and treatment of household and industrial wastewater and sewage, including processes for the re-use or recycling of water and the treatment of sludge directly associated with these activities.

c) The modernisation of such facilities in cases where the economic life of the plant is likely to be extended by at least the repayment period to be awarded. If this criterion is not met, the provisions of the Arrangement apply.

# CHAPTER II: PROVISIONS FOR EXPORT CREDITS

## 5. MAXIMUM REPAYMENT TERMS

a) For officially supported export credits relating to contracts in the sectors listed in Appendix I, and for water projects defined in Article 4 of this Sector Understanding, the maximum repayment term is 18 years.

b) For officially supported export credits relating to contracts of a value of at least SDR 10 million in the project classes listed in Appendix

II, the maximum repayment term is set out as follows:

1) For contracts in Project Class A: 18 years.

2) For contracts in Project Class B and Project Class C: 15 years.

c) For officially supported export credits relating to contracts of a value of less than SDR 10 million in the project classes listed in Appendix II, the maximum repayment term is set out as follows:

1) For Category I countries as defined in Article 11 of the Arrangement, the maximum repayment term is five years, with the possibility of agreeing up to eight-and-a-half years when the procedures for prior notification set out in Article 10 of this Sector Understanding are followed.

2) For Category II countries, the maximum repayment term is ten years.

3) Notwithstanding sub-paragraphs 1) and 2) above, for non-nuclear power plants as defined in Article 13 of the Arrangement, the maximum repayment term is 12 years.

d) For officially supported export credits relating to contracts of a value of at least SDR 10 million for projects supported in conformity with Appendix III, the maximum repayment term is 15 years.

## 6. REPAYMENT OF PRINCIPAL AND PAYMENT OF INTEREST

a) The Participants shall apply a profile of repayment of principal and payment of interest as specified in sub-paragraphs 1) or 2) below:

1) Repayment of principal shall be made in equal instalments.

2) Repayment of principal and payment of interest combined shall be made in equal instalments.

b) Principal shall be repaid and interest shall be paid no less frequently than every six months and the first instalment of principal and interest shall be made no later than six months after the starting point of credit.

c) On an exceptional and duly justified basis, official support may be provided on terms other than those set out in paragraphs a) and b) above. The provision of such support shall be explained by an imbalance in the timing of the funds available to the obligor and the debt service profile available under an equal, semi-annual repayment schedule, and shall comply with the following criteria:

1) No single repayment of principal or series of principal payments within a six-month period shall exceed 25% of the principal sum of the credit.

2) Principal shall be repaid no less frequently than every 12 months. The first repayment of principal shall be made no later than 18 months after the starting point of credit and no less than 2% of the principal sum of the credit shall have been repaid 18 months after the starting point of credit.

3) Interest shall be paid no less frequently than every 12 months and the first interest payment shall be made no later than six months after the starting point of credit.

4) The maximum weighted average life of the repayment period

shall not exceed 60% of the maximum available tenor.

d) Interest due after the starting point of credit shall not be capitalised.

## 7. MINIMUM INTEREST RATES

A Participant providing official financing support for fixed rates loans shall apply the following minimum interest rates:

| Repayment term (years) | Standard minimum interest rates | | Minimum interest rates for projects with long construction periods, *i. e.* :<br>– New large hydro-power projects<br>– Appendix II Project Class A<br>– Appendix III Adaptation Projects | |
|---|---|---|---|---|
| | Government bonds (years) | Margin (bps) | Government bonds (years) | Margin (bps) |
| < 11 | Relevant CIRR in accordance with Article 20 of the Arrangement | | | |
| 11 to 12 | 7 | 100 | 7 | 100 |
| 13 | 7 | 120 | 8 | 120 |
| 14 | 8 | 120 | 9 | 120 |
| 15 | 8 | 120 | 9 | 120 |
| 16 | 9 | 120 | 10 | 125 |
| 17 | 9 | 120 | 10 | 130 |
| 18 | 10 | 120 | 10 | 130 |

## 8. ELIGIBLE CURRENCIES

The currencies that are eligible for official financing support are those which are fully convertible and for which data are available to construct the minimum interest rates mentioned in Article 7 of this Sector Understanding, and in Article 20 of the Arrangement for repayment terms less than 11 years.

## 9. LOCAL COSTS

a) For officially supported export credits relating to contracts of a value of at least SDR 10 million, official support provided for local costs shall not exceed 30% of the export contract value.

b) For officially supported export credits relating to contracts of a value of less than SDR 10 million:

1) For the sectors listed in Appendix I of this Sector Understanding, official support provided for local costs shall not exceed 45% of the export contract value.

2) For the sectors listed in Appendix II and for water projects defined in Article 4 of this Sector Understanding, official support provided for local costs shall not exceed 30% of the export contract value.

c) Where official support for local cost exceeds 15% of the export contract value, such official support shall be subject to prior notification, pursuant to Article 10 of this Sector Understanding, specifying the nature of the local costs being supported.

# CHAPTER III: PROCEDURES

## 10. PRIOR NOTIFICATION

a) A Participant intending to provide support in accordance with the provisions of this Sector Understanding, shall give prior notification at least ten calendar days before issuing any commitment, in accordance with:

1) Article 48 of the Arrangement if the support is extended pursuant to Article 1, 2 or 4 of this Sector Understanding;

2) Article 47 of the Arrangement if the support is extended pursuant to Article 3 of this Sector Understanding.

b) For projects falling in the Project Classes listed in Appendix II of this Sector Understanding, such notifications shall include an enhanced description of the project in order to demonstrate how the project complies with the criteria for support, as set out in Article 2 b) of this Sector Understanding.

c) For projects supported in conformity with Appendix III of this Sector Understanding, such notification shall include:

1) An enhanced description of the project in order to demonstrate how the project complies with the criteria for support, as set out in Article 3 b) of this Sector Understanding, and

2) Access to the outcome of the independent third-party review required in Appendix III.

d) Notwithstanding paragraph a) 1) above, if the notifying Participant intends to provide support with a repayment term in excess of 15 years and/or in accordance with Article 6 c) of this Sector Understanding, it shall give prior notification at least ten calendar days before issuing any commitment in accordance with Article 47 of the Arrangement.

e) A Participant shall inform all other Participants of its final decision following a discussion, to facilitate the review of the body of experience.

# CHAPTER IV: MONITORING AND REVIEW

## 11. FUTURE WORK

The Participants agree to examine the following issues:

a) Term-adjusted risk-premia.

b) Conditions for low emission/high energy efficiency fossil fuel power plants including definition of CCS-readiness.

c) Net zero energy buildings.

d) Smart grids.

e) Fuel cell projects.

## 12. MONITORING AND REVIEW

a) The Secretariat shall report annually on the implementation of this Sector Understanding.

b) The Participants shall regularly review the scope and other provisions of this Sector Understanding and at the latest by the end of 2017.

c) Appendix II of this Sector Understanding shall be reviewed at regular intervals, including upon the request of a Participant, with the view to assessing whether any Project Class and/or Type should be added to, or removed from, or whether any thresholds should be changed in, that Appendix. Proposals for new Project Classes and/or Types shall be supported by information on how projects within such a Class/Type should fulfil the criteria set out in Article 2 b) and shall follow the methodology set out in Appendix IV of this Sector Understanding.

d) The Participants shall undertake a review of Appendix III of this Sector Understanding no later than by 30 June 2018, with a view to assessing the international initiatives related to adaptation, market conditions, and the body of experience developed from the notification process to determine if the definitions, project criteria, terms and conditions should be continued and or amended.

e) After 31 December 2018, the terms and conditions related to Appendix III shall be discontinued unless the Participants agree otherwise.

# APPENDIX I: RENEWABLE ENERGIES SECTORS

The following renewable energies sectors shall be eligible for the financial terms and conditions set out in this Sector Understanding provided that their impacts are addressed in accordance with the 2012 Recommendation on Common Approaches on Officially Supported Export Credits and Environmental and Social Due Diligence① (as subsequently amended by Members of the OECD Working Group on Export Credits and Credit Guarantee (ECG) and adopted by the OECD Council):

① It is understood that the 2012 Recommendation applies equally to projects that are not eligible for these financial terms and conditions.

a) Wind energy. ①

b) Geothermal energy.

c) Tidal and tidal stream power.

d) Wave power.

e) Osmotic power.

f) Solar photovoltaic power.

g) Solar thermal energy.

h) Ocean thermal energy.

i) Bio-energy: all sustainable landfill gas, sewage treatment plant gas, biogas energy or fuel derived from biomass energy installations. "Biomass" shall mean the biodegradable fraction of products, waste and residues from agriculture (including vegetal and animal substances), forestry and related industries, as well as the biodegradable fraction of industrial and municipal waste.

j) Hydro power.

k) Energy efficiency in Renewable Energies projects.

---

① The maximum repayment term for jack-up rigs used in the installation of wind turbines shall be 12 years.

# APPENDIX Ⅱ: CLIMATE CHANGE MITIGATION SECTORS

| PROJECT CLASS | DEFINITION | RATIONALE | STANDARDS USED | REPAYMENT TERMS |
|---|---|---|---|---|
| PROJECT CLASS A: CARBON CAPTURE AND STORAGE | | | | |
| TYPE 1: Fossil Fuel Power Plants with Operational Carbon Capture and Storage (CCS) | A process consisting of the separation of $CO_2$ stream from the emissions produced by fossil fuel generation sources, transport to a storage site, for the purposes of environmentally safe and permanent geological storage of $CO_2$. | To achieve low carbon emission levels for fossil fuel power sources. | Carbon intensity shall achieve a level equal to or less than 350 metric ton $CO_2$ per GWh vented to atmosphere①;<br>Or<br>In the case of all projects, a capture and storage rate that would reduce the plant's carbon emissions by 65% or greater;<br>Or<br>The capture rate has to be at least 85% of $CO_2$ emitted by the equipment included in the application for officially supported export credits. The 85% is to apply at normal operating conditions. | 18 years |

① In the case of a plant fuelled by natural gas, significantly lower carbon intensity is expected to be achieved.

续表

| PROJECT CLASS | DEFINITION | RATIONALE | STANDARDS USED | REPAYMENT TERMS |
|---|---|---|---|---|
| PROJECT CLASS A: CARBON CAPTURE AND STORAGE | | | | |
| TYPE 2:<br>CCS Projects as such | A process consisting of the separation of $CO_2$ from industrial or energy generation sources, transport to a storage site, for the purposes of environmentally safe and permanent geological storage of $CO_2$. | To significantly reduce carbon emissions from existing sources. | In the case of all projects, a capture and storage rate that would reduce the industrial or energy generation carbon emissions by 65% or greater;<br>Or<br>The capture rate has to be at least 85% of $CO_2$ emitted by the equipment included in the application for officially supported export credits. The 85% is to apply at normal operating conditions. | 18 years |
| PROJECT CLASS B: FOSSIL FUFL SUBSTITUTION | | | | |
| TYPE 1:<br>Waste to Energy | Unit dedicated to generating energy by thermal treatment (including gasification) of mixed stream solid waste. | To offset GHG emissions from the use of conventional power and by reducing future GHG such as methane that would normally emanate from the waste. | In the case of a steam cycle, a boiler (or steam generator) energy conversion efficiency of at least 75% based on low heating value (LHV)①.<br>In the case of gasification, a gasifier efficiency of at least 65% LHV②. | 15 years |

① Boiler (or steam generator) energy conversion efficiency = (Net heat exported by the steam / heat or calorific value [LHV] provided by the fuel) (x 100%).

② Gasifier efficiency = (Calorific value of gas per kg of fuel used / average net calorific value (LHV) of one kg of fuel) (x 100%).

续表

| PROJECT CLASS | DEFINITION | RATIONALE | STANDARDS USED | REPAYMENT TERMS |
|---|---|---|---|---|
| PROJECT CLASS B: FOSSIL FUFL SUBSTITUTION | | | | |
| TYPE 2:<br>Hybrid Power Plants | A power plant that generates electric power from both a renewable energy source and a fossil fuel source. | To meet the requirement of plant availability, a fossil fuel generating source is required for those periods when power from the renewable energy source is not available or sufficient. The fossil fuel source enables the usage of renewable energy in the hybrid plant, thereby achieving a significant carbon reduction compared with standard fossil fuel plant. | Model 1:<br>Two separate generation sources: one Renewable Energy and one fossil fuel.<br>Project shall be designed such that at least 50% of its projected total annual energy output originates from the plant's renewable energy source.<br>Model 2:<br>Single generation source using the combination of renewable and fossil fuel. The project shall be designed such that at least 75% of the useful energy produced is derived from the renewable source. | 15 years |

续表

| PROJECT CLASS | DEFINITION | RATIONALE | STANDARDS USED | REPAYMENT TERMS |
| --- | --- | --- | --- | --- |
| PROJECT CLASS C: ENERGY EFFICIENCY | | | | |
| TYPE 1: Combined Heat & Power projects | Simultaneous generation of multiple forms of energy (electrical, mechanical and thermal) in a single integrated system. Output of the CHP plant shall include electric or mechanical energy and heat for commercial industrial and/or residential use. | Up to two thirds of the primary energy used to generate electricity in conventional thermal power plants is lost in the form of heat. Combined heat and power (CHP) generation can therefore be an effective GHG mitigation option. CHP is possible with all heat machines and fuels (including biomass and solar thermal) from a few kW-rated to 1000MW steam-condensing power plants①. | Overall efficiency of at least 75% based on low heating value (LHV)②. | 15 years |

① IPCC Fourth Assessment Report: Climate Change 2007, http://www.ipcc.ch/publications_and_data/ar4/wg3/en/ch4s4-3-5.html

② The total system efficiency ($\eta_0$) of a CHP system is the sum of the net useful power output ($W_E$) and net useful thermal outputs ($\Sigma Q_{TH}$) divided by the total fuel input ($Q_{FUEL}$), as shown below: $\eta_0 = \frac{W_E + \sum Q_{TH}}{Q_{FUEL}}$

续表

| PROJECT CLASS | DEFINITION | RATIONALE | STANDARDS USED | REPAYMENT TERMS |
|---|---|---|---|---|
| PROJECT CLASS C: ENERGY EFFICIENCY | | | | |
| TYPE 2:<br>District heating and/or cooling | Network which carries/distributes thermal energy from energy producing unit to end use. | To improve the efficiency of heating of districts by building piping networks for steam and/or hot water with substantial thermal efficiency, both by minimising losses of piping and converters, and by increasing the amount of utilisation of waste heat.<br>District cooling is an integrative technology that can make significant contributions to reducing emissions of carbon dioxide and air pollution and to increasing energy security *e. g. via* substitution of individual air-conditioners. | The district piping thermal conductivity shall be less than 80% of the relevant thermal conductivity required by the European standard EN253: 2009 (*to be reviewed when this standard is updated*). | 15 years |

# APPENDIX III: ELIGIBILITY CRITERIA FOR CLIMATE CHANGE ADAPTATION PROJECTS

A project is eligible for the financial terms and conditions set out in this Sector Understanding if:

a) Climate change adaptation is the principal objective of the project, and it is explicitly indicated and explained as such in the project plan and supporting documents, as being fundamental to the design of the project.

b) The project's proposal shall include an analysis and identification of specific and relevant climate change-related risks and vulnerabilities, and how the proposed measures or technologies will directly address them.

c) There is an independent third-party review conducted on the project, either separately or as an integral part of the project plan which is made publicly available, such as published on the website of the national authority. The review shall evaluate the specific and relevant climate change-related risks and vulnerabilities and how the proposed measures contained within the project will directly address them.

d) The useful life of the project exceeds 15 years.

# APPENDIX IV: METHODOLOGY TO BE USED WHEN ETERMINING THE ELIGIBILITY OF SECTORS RELATING TO ARTICLE 2 OF THIS SECTOR UNDERSTANDING

When proposing that Project Class or Type be added to Appendix II of this Sector Understanding, Participants shall provide a detailed description of the proposed Project Class or Type and information on how such projects fulfil the criteria set out in Article 2 b) of this Sector Understanding; such information shall include:

a) An evaluation of the direct contribution of the Project Class or Type to climate change mitigation, including a comparison of the sector performance, based on measurable data regarding carbon emissions or $CO_2$ equivalent and/or in high energy efficiency, with conventional and in-use newer technological approaches; this comparison shall, in all cases, be based on quantitative measures, such as a decrease in emissions per unit produced.

b) A description of the technical and performance standards of the Project Class or Type proposed sector, including information on any relevant, existing Best Available Techniques (BAT); if appropriate, this description shall explain how the technology is an improvement on the existing BAT.

c) A description of the financial barriers in the proposed Project Class or Type, including any financial needs and market conditions, and identify the provisions under this Sector Understanding that are expected to enable such projects to proceed.

# APPENDIX V: LIST OF DEFINITIONS

Best Available Techniques: as per the definition of EU Directive 96/61/EC (Article 2. 1), "Best Available Techniques" shall mean the most effective and advanced stage in the development of activities and their methods of operation which indicate the practical suitability of particular techniques for providing in principle the basis for emission limit values designed to prevent and, where that is not practicable, generally to reduce emissions and the impact on the environment as a whole:

a) "techniques" shall include both the technology used and the way in which the installation is designed, built, maintained, operated and decommissioned.

b) "available" techniques shall mean those developed on a scale which allows implementation in the relevant industrial sector, under economically and technically viable conditions, taking into consideration the costs and advantages, whether or not the techniques are used or produced inside the Member State in question, as long as they are reasonably accessible to the operator.

c) "best" shall mean most effective in achieving a high general level of protection of the environment as a whole.

Greenhouse Gases: greenhouse gases are defined to include carbon dioxide, methane, nitrous oxide, hydrofluorocarbons, perfluorocarbons and sulphur hexafluoride.

Large Hydro Power Project: as per the definition of the International Commission on Large Dams (ICOLD). ICOLD defines a large dam as a dam with a height of 15m or more from the foundation. Dams that are between 5 and 15m high and have a reservoir volume of more than 3 million $m^3$ are also classified as large dams.

# ANNEX V SECTOR UNDERSTANDING ON EXPORT CREDITS FOR RAIL INFRASTRUCTURE

The Participants to this Sector Understanding agree that the financial terms and conditions of the Sector Understanding, which complements the Arrangement, shall be implemented in a way that is consistent with the Purpose of the Arrangement.

## CHAPTER I: SCOPE OF THE SECTOR UNDERSTANDING

### 1. SCOPE OF APPLICATION

This Sector Understanding sets out the financial terms and conditions that apply toofficially supported export credits relating to contracts for rail infrastructure assets essential to operating trains, including rail control (*e.g.* signalling and other rail IT), electrification, tracks, rolling stock, and related construction work.

## CHAPTER II: PROVISIONS FOR EXPORT CREDITS

### 2. MAXIMUM REPAYMENT TERMS

a) For officially supported export credits relating to contracts included within the scope of application of this Sector Understanding, the maximum repayment term is set out as follows:

1) For contracts in Category I countries (as defined in Article 11 of the Arrangement): 12 years.

2) For contacts in Category II countries (as defined in Article 11 of the Arrangement): 14 years.

b) To qualify for the repayment terms set out in paragraph a) above, the following conditions shall apply:

1) The transaction shall involve an overall contract value of more than SDR 10 million; and

2) The repayment terms shall not exceed the useful life of the rail infrastructure asset financed; and

3) For transactions in Category I countries, the transaction involves/is characterised by:

– Participation in a loan syndication with private financial institutions that do not benefit from Official Export Credit Support, whereby:

i) The Participant is a minority partner with *pari passu* status throughout the life of the loan; and

ii) Official export credit support provided by the Participants comprises less than 50% of the syndication.

– Premium rates for any official support that do not undercut available private market financing and that are commensurate with the corresponding rates being charged by other private financial institutions that are participating in the syndication.

c) A Participant may request a waiver of the condition set out in paragraph b) 3) above, through use of a Common Line, in accordance with Articles 58 to 63 of the Arrangement. In such cases. The Participant proposing the Common Line shall provide, either in the proposed Common Line or in each individual transaction thereafter notified, a comprehensive explanation for the support, including specific data on pricing, and a rationale for the need to waive the provisions of paragraph b) 3) above.

## 3. REPAYMENT OF PRINCIPAL AND INTEREST

The repayment of principal and interest shall be provided according to Article 14 of the Arrangement except that the maximum weighted average life of the repayment period under paragraph d) 4) of that Article shall be:

a) For transaction in a Category I countries, six-and-a-quarter years; and

b) For transaction in a Category II countries, seven-and-a-quarter years.

## 4. MINIMUM FIXED INTEREST RATES

A Participant providing official financing support for fixed rate loans shall apply, as minimum interest rates:

a) For repayment terms of up to and including 12 years, the relevant Commercial Interest Reference Rates (CIRRs) constructed in accordance with Article 20 of the Arrangement.

b) For repayment terms in excess of 12 years, the relevant Commercial Interest Reference Rates (CIRRs) constructed in accordance with Article 20 of the Arrangement, to which a surcharge of 20 basis points shall be added for all currencies.

# CHAPTER III: PROCEDURES

## 5. PRIOR NOTIFICATION

a) A Participant shall give prior notification in accordance with Article 47 of the Arrangement at least ten calendar days before issuing any commitment if it intends to provide support for a transaction in a Category I country. Such notifications shall include a comprehensive explanation for the official support, including specific data on pricing.

b) A Participant shall give prior notification in accordance with Article 48 of the Arrangement at least ten calendar days before issuing any commitment if it intends to provide support for:

1) A transaction in a Category II country; or

2) A transaction supported pursuant to a Common Line set out in accordance with Article 2 c) of this Sector Understanding. Such prior notification may be made concurrently with, and subject to the approval of, the Common Line proposal.

## 6. VALIDITY OF COMMON LINES

Notwithstanding the provisions of Article 63 a) of the Arrangement, all agreed Common Lines shall cease to be valid on 31

December 2018, unless the Participants agree to the extension of this Sector Understanding in accordance with Article 7 d) of this Sector Understanding.

# CHAPTER IV: MONITORING AND REVIEW

## 7. MONITORING AND REVIEW

a) The Secretariat shall report annually on the implementation of this Sector Understanding.

b) After 31 December 2017, and subject to paragraph c) below, the less than 50% syndication requirement set out in sub-paragraph ii) of the first *tiret* of Article 2 b) 3) of this Sector Understanding shall be replaced by a maximum 35% syndication requirement unless the Participants agree otherwise.

c) The Participants shall undertake a review of this Sector Understanding by no later than 30 June 2017 with a view to assessing the market conditions and other factors to determine whether the terms and conditions should be continued and or amended.

d) After 31 December 2017, the terms and conditions of this Sector Understanding shall be discontinued unlessthe Participants agree otherwise.

# ANNEX VI TERMS AND CONDITIONS APPLICABLE TO PROJECT FINANCE TRANSACTIONS

## CHAPTER I: GENERAL PROVISIONS

### 1. SCOPE OF APPLICATION

a) This Annex sets out terms and conditions that Participants may support for project finance transactions that meet the eligibility criteria set out in Appendix 1.

b) Where no corresponding provision exists in this Annex, the terms of the Arrangement shall apply.

## CHAPTER II: FINANCIAL TERMS AND CONDITIONS[①]

### 2. MAXIMUM REPAYMENT TERMS

The maximum repayment term is 14 years.

---

① a) The financial terms and conditions set out in Articles 2 and 3 d) shall apply to transactions for which a final commitment is issued on or before 31 December 2015.

b) After 31 December 2015, the financial terms and conditions set out in Articles 2 and 3 d) shall be discontinued unless the Participants agree otherwise.

c) If discontinued, the provisions of Articles 2 and 3 d) will be replaced by the following:

Article 2 – The maximum repayment term is 14 years, except when official export credit support provided by the Participants comprises more than 35% of the syndication for a project in a High Income OECD country, the maximum repayment term is ten years.

Article 3 d) – The weighted average life of the repayment period shall not exceed seven-and-a-quarter years, except when official export credit support provided by the Participants comprises more than 35% of the syndication for a project in a High Income OECD country, the weighted average life of the repayment period shall not exceed five-and-a-quarter years.

## 3. REPAYMENT OF PRINCIPAL AND PAYMENT OF INTEREST

The principal sum of an export credit may be repaid in unequal instalments, and principal and interest may be paid in less frequent than semi-annual instalments, as long as the following conditions are met:

a) No single repayment of principal or series of principal payments within a six-month period shall exceed 25% of the principal sum of the credit.

b) The first repayment of principal shall be made no later than 24 months after the starting point of credit and no less than 2% of the principal sum of the credit shall have been repaid 24 months after the starting point of credit.

c) Interest shall be paid no less frequently than every 12 months and the first interest payment shall be made no later than six months after the starting point of credit.

d) The weighted average life of the repayment period shall not exceed seven-and-a-quarter years.

e) The Participant shall give prior notification according to Article 5 of this Annex.

## 4. MINIMUM FIXED INTEREST RATES

Where Participants are providing official financing support for fixed rate loans:

a) For repayment terms of up to and including 12 years,

Participants shall apply the relevant Commercial Interest Reference Rates (CIRRs) constructed in Accordance with Article 20 of the Arrangement.

b) For repayment terms in excess of 12 years, a surcharge of 20 basis points on the CIRR shall apply for all currencies.

# CHAPTER III: PROCEDURES

## 5. PRIOR NOTIFICATION FOR PROJECT FINANCE TRANSACTIONS

A Participant shall notify all Participants of the intent to provide support according to the terms and conditions of this Annex at least ten calendar days before issuing any commitment. The notification shall be provided in accordance with Annex VII of the Arrangement. If any Participant requests an explanation in respect of the terms and conditions being supported during this period, the notifying Participant shall wait an additional ten calendar days before issuing any commitment.

# APPENDIX 1: ELIGIBILITY CRITERIA FOR PROJECT FINANCE TRANSACTIONS

## I. BASIC CRITERIA

The transaction involves/is characterised by:

a) The financing of a particular economic unit in which a lender is satisfied to consider the cash flows and earnings of that economic unit as the source of funds from which a loan will be repaid and to the assets of the economic unit as collateral for the loan.

b) Financing of export transactions with an independent (legally and economically) project company, *e. g.* special purpose company, in respect of investment projects generating their own revenues.

c) Appropriate risk-sharing among the partners of the project, *e. g.* private or creditworthy public shareholders, exporters, creditors, off-takers, including adequate equity.

d) Project cash flow sufficient during the entire repayment period to cover operating costs and debt service for outside funds.

e) Priority deduction from project revenues of operating costs and debt service.

f) A non-sovereign buyer/borrower with no sovereign repayment guarantee (not including performance guarantees, *e. g.* off-take arrangements).

g) Asset-based securities for proceeds/assets of the project, *e. g.* assignments, pledges, proceed accounts;

h) Limited or no recourse to the sponsors of the private sector shareholders/sponsors of the project after completion.

## II. ADDITIONAL CRITERIA FOR PROJECT FINANCE TRANSACTIONS IN HIGH INCOME OECD COUNTRIES

The transaction involves/is characterised by:

a) Participation in a loan syndication with private financial institutions that do not benefit from Official Export Credit Support, whereby:

1) The Participant is a minority partner with *pari passu* status throughout the life of the loan and;

2) Official export credit support provided by the Participants comprises less than 50% of the syndication.

b) Premium rates for any official support that do not undercut available private market financing and that are commensurate with the corresponding rates being charged by other private financial institutions that are participating in the syndication.

# ANNEX VII INFORMATION TO BE PROVIDED FOR NOTIFICATIONS

The information listed in Section I below shall be provided for all notifications made under the Arrangement (including its Annexes). In addition, the information specified in Section II shall be provided, as appropriate, in relation to the specific type of notification being made.

## I. INFORMATION TO BE PROVIDED FOR ALL NOTIFICATIONS

a) *Basic Information*

1. Notifying country

2. Notification date

3. Name of notifying authority/agency

4. Reference number

5. Original notification or revision to previous notification (revision number as relevant)

6. Tranche number (if relevant)

7. Reference number of credit line (if relevant)

8. Arrangement Article (s) under which the notification is being made

9. Reference number of notification being matched (if relevant)

10. Description of support being matched (if relevant)

11. Destination Country

b) *Buyer/Borrower/Guarantor Information*

12. Buyer Country

13. Buyer Name

14. Buyer Location

15. Buyer Status

16. Borrower Country (if different from the buyer)

17. Borrower Name (if different from the buyer)

18. Borrower Location (if different from the buyer)

19. Borrower Status (if different from the buyer)

20. Guarantor Country (if relevant)

21. Guarantor Name (if relevant)

22. Guarantor Location (if relevant)

23. Guarantor Status (if relevant)

c) *Information on Goods and/or Services Being Exported and the Project*

24. Description of the goods and/or services being exported

25. Description of the project (if relevant)

26. Location of the project (if relevant)

27. Tender closing date (if relevant)

28. Expiry date of credit line (if relevant)

29. Value of contract (s) supported, either the actual value (for all lines of credit and project finance transactions or for any individual transaction on a voluntary basis) or according to the following scale in millions of SDRs:

| Category | From | To |
|---|---|---|
| I: | 0 | 1 |
| II: | 1 | 2 |
| III: | 2 | 3 |
| IV: | 3 | 5 |
| V: | 5 | 7 |
| VI: | 7 | 10 |
| VII: | 10 | 20 |
| VIII: | 20 | 40 |
| IX: | 40 | 80 |
| X: | 80 | 120 |
| XI: | 120 | 160 |
| XII: | 160 | 200 |
| XIII: | 200 | 240 |
| XIV: | 240 | 280 |
| XV: | 280 | * |

* *Indicate the number of SDR* 40 *million multiples in excess of SDR* 280 *million, e. g. SDR* 410 *million would be notified as Category XV* + 3.

30. Currency of contract (s)

d) *Financial Terms and Conditions of the Official Export Credit Support*

31. Credit value; the actual value for notifications involving lines of credit and project finance transactions or for any individual transaction on a voluntary basis, or according to the SDR scale

32. Currency of credit

33. Down payment (percentage of the total value of the contracts supported)

34. Local Costs (percentage of the total value of the contracts supported)

35. Starting point of credit and reference to the applicable sub-paragraph of Article 10

36. Length of the repayment period

37. Interest rate base

38. Interest rate or margin

## II. ADDITIONAL INFORMATION TO BE PROVIDED, AS APPROPRIATE, FOR NOTIFICATIONS MADE IN RELATION TO SPECIFIC PROVISIONS

a) *Arrangement, Article* 14 *d*) 5)

1. Repayment profile

2. Repayment frequency

3. Length of time between the starting point of credit and the first repayment of principal

4. Amount of interest capitalised before the starting point of credit

5. Weighted average life of the repayment period

6. Explanation of the reason for not providing support according to Article 14 paragraphs a) through c)

b) *Arrangement*, *Articles* 24, 27, 30 *and* 31

1. Country risk classification of the obligor's country

2. Selected buyer risk category of the obligor

3. Length of the disbursement period

4. Percentage of cover for political (country) risk

5. Percentage of cover for commercial (buyer) risk

6. Quality of cover (*i. e.* below standard, standard, above standard)

7. MPR based on the country risk classification of the obligor's country absent any third party guarantee, involvement of a multilateral/regional institution, risk mitigation and/or buyer risk enhancements

8. Applicable MPR

9. Actual premium rate charged (expressed in MPR format as a percentage of the principal)

c) *Arrangement*, *Article* 24 c) *third tiret*

1. Benchmark (s) applied (see Annex IX).

d) *Arrangement*, *Article* 24 e) *first tiret*

1. Country risk classification of the guarantor's country

2. Selected buyer risk classification of the guarantor

3. Confirmation that all of the criteria listed in Annex X have been met.

4. Percentage of the total amount at risk (*i. e.* principal and interest) that is covered by the guarantee (*i. e.* total or partial amount)

5. Indication as to whether any financial relationship exists between the guarantor and the obligor

6. In the case that there is a relationship between the guarantor and the obligor:

– The type of relationship (*e. g.* parent-subsidiary, subsidiary-parent, common ownership)

– Confirmation that the guarantor is legally and financially independent and can fulfil the obligor's payment obligation

– Confirmation that the guarantor would not be affected by events, regulations or sovereign intervention in the obligor's country

e) *Arrangement*, *Article* 27 *e*)

1. Selected buyer risk category of the obligor

2. Accredited CRA foreign currency rating (s)

3. Rationale for buyer risk category better than accredited CRA rating

f) *Arrangement*, *Article* 30

1. Country risk mitigation technique used

2. Confirmation that the criteria listed in Annex XII have been met

3. For Technique 1, the applicable country risk classification resulting from the use of the technique

4. For Technique 2:

– the local currency used

– the value of the LCF applied

g) *Arrangement*, *Article* 31

1. The BRCE (s) applied

2. The CEF applied for each credit enhancement

3. The total CEF to be applied

h) *Arrangement*, *Articles* 49 *and* 50

1. Form of tied aid (*i. e.* development aid or premixed credit or

associated finance)

2. Overall concessionality level of the tied and partially untied aid financing calculated in accordance with Article 40

3. DDR used for concessionality calculation

4. Treatment of cash payments in the calculation of the concessionality level

5. Restrictions on use of credit lines

i) *Annex I*, *Article* 5 *e*)

1. Indication of:

– The date of the first payment of interest, if later than six months after the starting point of credit

– The frequency of payment of interest, if less frequent than every six months

j) *Annex II*, *Article* 8

1. Enhanced description of the export contract, *i. e.* new nuclear power station, modernisation of an existing nuclear power plant, supply of nuclear fuel and enrichment, or provision of spent fuel management.

2. Repayment of principal and payment of interest according to: Article 3 a) 1), Article 3 a) 2) or Article 3 c) of Annex II.

3. Where official support is provided in accordance with Article 3 c) of Annex II, please provide:

– Repayment profile

– Repayment frequency

– Length of time between the starting point of credit and the first repayment of principal

– Amount of interest capitalised before the starting point of credit

– Weighted average life of the repayment period

– Explanation of the reason for not providing support in accordance with Articles 3 a) and b) of Annex II.

4. Minimum interest rate applied in accordance with Article 4 of Annex II.

k) *Annex IV*, *Article* 10

1. Enhanced description of the project:

– New renewable energies and water plant, or modernisation of an existing renewable energies and water plant, including the specific sector as listed in Appendix I of Annex IV, or

– If a hydro-power project, whether a new large hydro-power project (as defined in Appendix IV of Annex IV), or

– For projects falling in the Project Classes listed in Appendix II of Annex IV, a demonstration of how the project complies with the criteria for support, as set out in Article 2 b) of Annex IV, or

– For projects supported in conformity with Appendix III of Annex IV:

• An enhanced description of the project in order to demonstrate how the project complies with the criteria for support, as set out in Article 3 b) or c) respectively of Annex IV, and

• Access to the outcome of the independent third-party review required in Appendix III of Annex IV.

2. Repayment profile of principal and payment of interest according to: Article 6 a) 1), Article 6 a) 2) or Article 6 c) of Annex IV.

3. Where official support is provided in accordance with Article 6 c) of Annex IV, please provide:

– Repayment profile

– Repayment frequency

– Length of time between the starting point of credit and the first repayment of principal

– Amount of interest capitalised before the starting point of credit

– Weighted average life of the repayment period

– Explanation of the reason for not providing support in accordance with Articles 6 a) and b) of Annex IV.

4. Minimum interest rate applied in accordance with Article 7 of Annex IV.

l) *Annex V, Article* 5

1. Comprehensive explanation for the terms and conditions of the

official support provided, including:

– Explanation of why the Rail Infrastructure terms and conditions are being provided

– How the repayment terms offered do not exceed the useful life of the rail infrastructure financed

2. For transactions in Category I countries:

– Total debt syndication amount for the project, including official and private lenders

– Total amount of the debt syndication from private lenders

– Percentage of the debt syndication provided by the Participants

– Confirmation that the Participant is involved in a loan syndication with private financial institutions that do not benefit from official export credit support, whereby (i) the Participant is a minority partner with *pari passu* status throughout the life of the loan and (ii) official export credit support provided by the Participants comprises less than 50% of the syndication

– Specific data on pricing to explain how premium rates charged for official support do not undercut available private market financing and are commensurate with the corresponding rates being charged by other private financial institutions that are participating in the syndication.

m) *Annex VI*, *Article* 5

1. Explanation of why project finance terms are being provided

2. Contract value in relation to turnkey contract, portion of sub-contracts, etc.

3. Enhanced project description

4. Type of cover provided prior to the starting point of credit

5. Percentage of cover for political risk prior to the starting point of credit

6. Percentage of cover for commercial risk prior to the starting point of credit

7. Type of cover provided after the starting point of credit

8. Percentage of cover for political risk after the starting point of credit

9. Percentage of cover for commercial risk after the starting point of credit

10. Length of the construction period (if applicable)

11. Length of the disbursement period

12. Weighted average life of the repayment period

13. Repayment profile

14. Repayment frequency

15. Length of time between the starting point of credit and the first repayment of principal

16. Percentage of principal repaid by the mid-point of credit

17. Amount of interest capitalised before the starting point of credit

18. Other fees received by the ECA, *e. g.* commitment fees (optional, except in the case of transactions with buyers in High Income OECD Countries)

19. Premium rate (optional, except in the case of projects in High Income OECD Countries)

20. Confirmation (and explanation as necessary) that the transaction involves/is characterised by:

– The financing of a particular economic unit in which a lender is satisfied to consider the cash flows and earnings of that economic unit as the source of funds from which a loan will be repaid and to the assets of the economic unit as collateral for the loan.

– Financing of export transactions with an independent (legally and economically) project company, *e. g.* special purpose company, in respect of investment projects generating their own revenues.

– Appropriate risk-sharing among the partners of the project, *e. g.* private or creditworthy public shareholders, exporters, creditors, off-takers, including adequate equity.

– Project cash flow sufficient during the entire repayment period to cover operating costs and debt service for outside funds.

– Priority deduction from project revenues of operating costs and debt service.

– A non-sovereign buyer/borrower with no sovereign repayment guarantee

– Asset-based securities for proceeds/assets of the project, *e. g.* assignments, pledges, proceed accounts;

– Limited or no recourse to the sponsors of the private sector shareholders/sponsors of the project after completion

n) *Annex VI, Article* 5, *for projects in High Income OECD Countries*

1. Total debt syndication amount for the project, including official and private lenders

2. Total amount of the debt syndication from private lenders

3. Percentage of the debt syndication provided by the Participants

4. Confirmation that:

– In respect of participation in a loan syndication with private financial institutions that do not benefit from official export credit support, the Participant is a minority partner with *pari passu* status throughout the life of the loan.

– The premium rate reported under item *m*) 19 above does not undercut available private market financing and is commensurate with the corresponding rates being charged by other private financial institutions that are participating in the syndication.

# ANNEX VIII CALCULATION OF THE MINIMUM PREMIUM RATES

## MPR Formula

The formula for calculating the applicable MPR for an export credit involving an obligor/guarantor in a country classified in Country Risk Categories 1 – 7 is:

$$MPR = \{[(a_i \times HOR + b_i) \times max(PCC, PCP)/0.95] \times (1 - LCF) + [c_{in} \times PCC/0.95 \times HOR \times (1 - CEF)]\} \times QPF_i \times PCF_i \times BTSF$$

where:

- $a_i$ = country risk coefficient in country risk category $i$ ($i$ = 1 – 7)
- $c_{in}$ = buyer risk coefficient for buyer category $n$ ($n$ = SOV+, SOV/CCO, CC1 – CC5) in country risk category $i$ ($i$ = 1 – 7)
- $b_i$ = constant for country category risk category $i$ ($i$ = 1 – 7)
- HOR = horizon of risk
- PCC = commercial (buyer) risk percentage of cover
- PCP = political (country) risk percentage of cover
- CEF = credit enhancements factor

- $QPF_i$ = quality of product factor in country risk category $i$ ($i$ = 1 - 7)
- $PCF_i$ = percentage of cover factor in country risk category $i$ ($i$ = 1 - 7)
- BTSF = better than sovereign factor
- LCF = local currency factor

## Applicable Country Risk Classification

The applicable country risk classification is determined according to Article 24 e) of the Arrangement, which in turn determines the country risk coefficient (ai) and constant (bi) that are obtained from the following table:

| | 1 | 2 | 3 | 4 | 5 | 6 | 7 |
|---|---|---|---|---|---|---|---|
| a | 0.090 | 0.200 | 0.350 | 0.550 | 0.740 | 0.900 | 1.100 |
| b | 0.350 | 0.350 | 0.350 | 0.350 | 0.750 | 1.200 | 1.800 |

## Selection of the Appropriate Buyer Risk Category

The appropriate buyer risk category is selected from the following table, which provides the combinations of country and buyer risk categories that have been established and the agreed concordance between buyer risk categories CC1-CC5 and the classifications of accredited CRAs. Qualitative descriptions of each buyer risk category (SOV + to CC5) have been established to facilitate the classification of obligors (and guarantors) and are provided in Annex XI.

| Country Risk Category | | | | | | |
|---|---|---|---|---|---|---|
| 1 | 2 | 3 | 4 | 5 | 6 | 7 |
| SOV + | SOV + | SOV + | SOV + | SOV + | SOV + | SOV + |
| SOV / CC0 | SOV / CC0 | SOV / CC0 | SOV / CC0 | SOV / CC0 | SOV / CC0 | SOV / CC0 |
| CC1 AAA to AA – | CC1 A + to A – | CC1 BBB + to BBB – | CC1 BB + to BB | CC1 BB – | CC1 B + | CC1 B |
| CC2 A + to A – | CC2 BBB + to BBB – | CC2 BB + to BB | CC2 BB – | CC2 B + | CC2 B | CC2 B – or worse |
| CC3 BBB + to BBB – | CC3 BB + to BB | CC3 BB – | CC3 B + | CC3 B | CC3 B – or worse | |
| CC4 BB + to BB | CC4 BB – | CC4 B + | CC4 B | CC4 B – or worse | | |
| CC5 BB – or worse | CC5 B + or worse | CC5 B or worse | CC5 B – or worse | | | |

The selected buyer risk category, in combination with the applicable country risk category determines the buyer risk coefficient ($c_{in}$) that is obtained from the following table:

| Buyer Risk Category | Country Risk Category | | | | | | |
|---|---|---|---|---|---|---|---|
| | 1 | 2 | 3 | 4 | 5 | 6 | 7 |
| SOV + | 0. 000 | 0. 000 | 0. 000 | 0. 000 | 0. 000 | 0. 000 | 0. 000 |
| SOV / CC0 | 0. 000 | 0. 000 | 0. 000 | 0. 000 | 0. 000 | 0. 000 | 0. 000 |
| CC1 | 0. 110 | 0. 120 | 0. 110 | 0. 100 | 0. 100 | 0. 100 | 0. 125 |
| CC2 | 0. 200 | 0. 212 | 0. 223 | 0. 234 | 0. 246 | 0. 258 | 0. 271 |
| CC3 | 0. 270 | 0. 320 | 0. 320 | 0. 350 | 0. 380 | 0. 480 | n/a |
| CC4 | 0. 405 | 0. 459 | 0. 495 | 0. 540 | 0. 621 | n/a | n/a |
| CC5 | 0. 630 | 0. 675 | 0. 720 | 0. 810 | n/a | n/a | n/a |

## Horizon of Risk (HOR)

The Horizon of Risk (HOR) is calculated as follows:

For standard repayment profiles (*i. e.* equal semi-annual repayments of principal):

HOR = (length of the disbursement period ×0.5) + the length of the repayment period

For non-standard repayment profiles:

HOR = (length of the disbursement period ×0.5) + (weighted average life of the repayment period – 0.25) / 0.5

In the above formulas, the unit of measurement for time is years.

## Percentage of Cover for Commercial (Buyer) Risk (PCC) and Political (Country) Risk (PCP)

The Percentages of Cover (PCC and PCP) expressed as a decimal value (*i. e.* 95% is expressed as 0.95) in the MPR formula.

## Buyer Risk Credit Enhancements

The value of the credit enhancement factor (CEF) is 0 for any transaction that is not subject to any buyer risk credit enhancements. The value of the CEF for transactions that are subject to buyer risk credit enhancements is determined according to Annex XII, subject to the restrictions set out in Article 31 c) of the Arrangement and may not exceed 0.35.

## Quality of Product Factor (QPF)

The QPF is obtained from the following table:

| Product Quality | Country Risk Category | | | | | | |
|---|---|---|---|---|---|---|---|
| | 1 | 2 | 3 | 4 | 5 | 6 | 7 |
| Below Standard | 0.9965 | 0.9935 | 0.9850 | 0.9825 | 0.9825 | 0.9800 | 0.9800 |
| Standard | 1.0000 | 1.0000 | 1.0000 | 1.0000 | 1.0000 | 1.0000 | 1.0000 |
| Above Standard | 1.0035 | 1.0065 | 1.0150 | 1.0175 | 1.0175 | 1.0200 | 1.0200 |

## Percentage of Cover Factor (PCF)

The PCF is determined as follows:

For ( max (PCC, PCP) ≤0.95, PCF = 1)

For ( max (PCC, PCP) > 0.95, PCF = 1 + ( ( max (PCC, PCP) − 0.95) / 0.05 ) × ( percentage of cover coefficient )

The percentage of cover coefficient is obtained from the following table:

| Country Risk Category | | | | | | | |
|---|---|---|---|---|---|---|---|
| | 1 | 2 | 3 | 4 | 5 | 6 | 7 |
| Percentage of cover coefficient | 0.00000 | 0.00337 | 0.00489 | 0.01639 | 0.03657 | 0.05878 | 0.08598 |

## Better than Sovereign Factor (BTSF)

When an obligor is classified in the "better than sovereign" (SOV+) buyer risk category, BTSF = 0.9, otherwise BTSF = 1

## Local Currency Factor (LCF)

For transaction making use of local currency country risk mitigation, the value of the LCF may not exceed 0. 2. The value of the LCF for all other transactions is 0.

# ANNEX IX MARKET BENCHMARKS FOR TRANSACTIONS IN CATEGORY ZERO COUNTRIES

## Un-covered Portion of Export Credits or the non-ECA Covered Part of a Syndicated Loan

The price indicated by private banks/institutions with respect to the uncovered portion of the export credit in question (or sometimes as the non-ECA covered part of a syndicated loan) may represent the best match to ECA cover. Pricing on such un-covered portions or non-covered parts should only be used if provided on commercial terms (*e. g.* this would exclude IFI funded portions).

## Name-Specific Corporate Bonds

Corporate bonds reflect name specific credit risk. Care should be used in matching in terms of the ECA contract characteristics, such as term of maturity, and currency denomination, and any credit enhancements. If primary corporate bonds (*i. e.* all-in yield upon issuance) or secondary corporate bonds (*i. e.* the option adjusted spread over the appropriate curve, which is usually the relevant currency swap curve) are used, those for the obligor should be used in the first instance; if not available, primary or secondary corporate bonds for comparable borrowers and comparable transactions should be used.

## Name-Specific Credit Default Swaps

Credit Default Swaps ( CDS ) are a form of protection against default. The CDS spread is the amount paid per period by the buyer of the CDS as a percentage of notional principal, and is usually expressed in basis points. The CDS buyer effectively buys insurance against default by making payments to the seller of the CDS for the life of the swap, or until the credit event occurs. A CDS curve for the obligor should be used in the first instance; if not available, CDs curves for comparable borrowers and comparable transactions should be used.

## Indexed Credit Default Swaps

An indexed Credit Default Swap is a compilation of registered CDS for an industry sector, or part of it, or for a geographical area. The CDS spreads thus compiled reflects the credit risk of the particular market segment that the index is capturing. Its relevance may be greatest in cases where no name-specific CDS is available or when the market for a name-specific CD is illiquid.

## Loan Benchmarks

Primary loan benchmarks ( *i. e.* pricing upon issuance ) or secondary loan benchmarks ( *i. e.* the current yield on the loan expected by the financial institution purchasing the loan from another financial institution). All fees must be known for primary loan benchmarks so that the all-in yield can be calculated. If loan benchmarks are used, those for the obligor should be used in the first instance; if not available, those for comparable borrowers and comparable transactions should be used.

## Benchmark Market Curves

Benchmark market curves reflect the credit risk of a whole sector or class of buyers. This market information may be relevant when name specific information is not available. In general, the quality of the information inherent to these markets depends upon their liquidity. In any case, one should look for market instruments that provide the closest match in terms of the ECA contract characteristics, such as date, credit rating, term of maturity, and currency denomination.

## Weighted Average Cost of Financing Resources (WACFR)

From the buyer's financial statements it may be possible to gauge the WACFR. Care must be taken when using this method to ensure that the average cost of finance resources of a company reflects the real conditions under which the finance has been provided.

# ANNEX X CRITERIA AND CONDITIONS GOVERNING THE APPLICATION OF A THIRD PARTY REPAYMENT GUARANTEE AND THE CLASSIFICATION OF MULTILATERAL OR REGIONAL INSTITUTIONS

## PURPOSE

This Annex provides the criteria and conditions that govern the application of third party repayment guarantees, including the repayment guarantee of a classified multilateral or regional institution according to Article 24 e) of the Arrangement. It also provides the criteria by which multilateral or regional institutions should be assessed when determining if an institution should be classified in connection with Article 28 of the Arrangement.

## APPLICATION

*Case* 1: *Guarantee for the Total Amount at Risk*

When security in the form of a repayment guarantee from an entity is provided for the total amount at risk (*i. e.* principal and interest), the applicable Country Risk Classification and Buyer Risk Category may be that of the guarantor when the following criteria are met:

– The guarantee covers the entire duration of the credit.

– The guarantee is irrevocable, unconditional and available on-demand.

– The guarantee is legally valid and capable of being enforced in the guarantor country's jurisdiction.

– The guarantor is creditworthy in relation to the size of the guaranteed debt.

– The guarantor is subject to the monetary control and transfer regulations of the country in which it is located.

For classified Multilateral or Regional Institutions acting as guarantors, the following criteria apply:

– The guarantee covers the entire duration of the credit.

– The guarantee is irrevocable, unconditional and available on-demand.

– The guarantor is legally committed for the total amount of the credit.

– The repayments are made directly to the creditor.

If the guarantor is a subsidiary/parent of the guaranteed entity, Participants shall, on a case-by-case basis, determine whether: (1) in consideration of the relationship between the subsidiary/parent and the degree of legal commitment of the parent, the subsidiary/parent is legally and financially independent and could fulfil its payment obligations; (2) the subsidiary/parent could be affected by local events/regulations or sovereign intervention; and (3) the Head Office would in the event of a default regard itself as being liable.

*Case 2: Guarantee Limited in Amount*

When security in the form of a repayment guarantee from an entity is provided for a limited amount at risk (*i. e.* principal and interest), the applicable Country Risk Classification and Buyer Risk Category may be that of the guarantor for the portion of the credit subject to the guarantee, providing that all other criteria listed under Case 1 are met.

For the unguaranteed portion, the applicable Country Risk Classification and Buyer Risk Category is that of the obligor.

*Classification of Multilateral or Regional Institutions*

Multilateral and regional institutions shall be eligible for classification if the institution is generally exempt from the monetary control and transfer regulations of the country in which it is located. Such institutions shall be classified in Country Risk Categories 0 through 7 on a case-by-case basis according to an assessment of the risk of each on its own merits and in consideration of whether:

– the institution has statutory and financial independence;

– all of the institution's assets are immune from nationalisation or confiscation;

– the institution has full freedom of transfer and conversion of funds;

– the institution is not subject to government intervention in the country where it is located;

– the institution has tax immunity; and

– there is an obligation of all its Member countries to supply additional capital to meet the institution's obligations.

The assessment should also take into consideration the historical payment record in situations of country credit risks default either in the country where it is located or in an obligor's country; and any other factors which may be deemed appropriate in the assessment process.

The list of classified multilateral and regional institutions is not closed and a Participant may nominate an institution for review according to the above-listed considerations. The classifications of multilateral and regional institutions shall be made public by the Participants.

# ANNEX XI BUYER RISK CATEGORIES QUALITATIVE DESCRIPTIONS

## Better than Sovereign (SOV +)

This is an exceptional classification. The entity achieving such a classification is one with an exceptionally strong credit profile which could be expected to fulfil its payment obligations during a period of sovereign debt distress or even default. International Credit Rating Agencies issue regular reports listing Corporate and Counterparty Ratings that exceed the Sovereign's Foreign Currency Rating. Except when the risk sovereign has been identified through the Sovereign Risk Assessment Methodology as being significantly higher than country risk, Participants proposing that an entity be classified as better than sovereign shall reference such better than sovereign ratings in support of their recommendation. In order to be classified as better than its host sovereign, an entity would be expected to display several or normally a majority of the following characteristics or equivalents:

- A strong credit profile;

- substantial foreign exchange earnings relative to its currency debt burden;

- production facilities and cash generation ability from subsidiaries or operations offshore, especially those domiciled in highly rat ed sovereigns, *i. e.* multinational enterprises;

• a foreign owner or a strategic partner which could be relied on as a source of financial support in the absence of a formal guarantee;

• a history of preferential treatment of the entity by the sovereign, including exemption from transfer and convertibility constraints and surrender requirements for export proceeds, and favourable tax treatment;

• committed credit lines from highly rated international banks, especially credit lines without a material adverse change (MAC) clause which enable banks to withdraw committed facilities in the event of a sovereign crisis or other risk events; and

• assets held offshore, especially liquid assets, often as a result of rules allowing exporters to trap and maintain cash balances offshore that are available for debt service.

Normally the SOV + buyer risk category is not applicable to:

• Publicly owned entities and utilities, sub-sovereigns as line ministries, regional governments, etc;

• financial institutions domiciled in the sovereign's jurisdiction; and

• entities primarily selling to the domestic market in local currency.

## Sovereign (SOV)

Sovereign obligors/guarantors are entities that are explicitly legally mandated to enter into a debt payment obligation on the behalf of the

Sovereign State, typically Ministry of Finance or Central bank[1]. A risk designated as sovereign is one where:

- the obligor/guarantor is legally mandated to enter into a debt payment obligation on behalf of the Sovereign and thereby commits the full faith and credit of the sovereign; and

- in the event of rescheduling of sovereign risk, the debt in question would be included in the rescheduling and payment obligations acquired by the sovereign by virtue of the rescheduling.

## Equivalent to the Sovereign (CC0): Exceptionally Good Credit Quality

The "equivalent to sovereign" category embraces two basic types of obligors/guarantors:

- Public entities where due diligence reveals that either the buyer has the implicit full faith and credit/support of the sovereign or that the likelihood of sovereign liquidity and solvency support is very high, both in relation to recovery prospects as well as default risk. Non-sovereign public entities equivalent to the sovereign would also include companies owned by the government with a monopoly or near monopoly on operations in a sector (*e. g.* power, oil, gas).

- Corporate entities with an exceptionally strong credit profile, displaying features in terms of both default and recovery prospects which indicate that the risk could be seen as being equivalent to sovereign.

---

[1] Most typically this would be a risk on the central bank or Ministry of Finance. For central government entities other than the finance ministry, due diligence shall be undertaken to affirm that the entity commits the full faith and credit of the sovereign.

Candidates could include strong blue chip corporates or very important banks for which the likelihood of sovereign liquidity and solvency support is high.

Exceptionally good credit quality implies that the risk of payment interruption is expected to be negligible and that the entity has an exceptionally strong capacity for repayment and this capacity is not likely to be affected by foreseeable events. The credit quality is typically manifested in a combination of some, if not all, of the following characteristics of the entity's business and financial profile:

- exceptionally good to very good cash and income generation
- exceptionally good to very good liquidity levels
- exceptionally low to very low leverage
- excellent to very strong business profile with proven and very strong management abilities

The entity is also characterised by ahigh quality of financial and ownership disclosure, unless there is a very high likelihood of support from a parent (or sovereign) with a buyer risk classification that is equal to or better than what corresponds to this buyer risk category.

Depending on the classification of the country in which the obligor/guarantor is domiciled, it is likely that an obligor/guarantor classified in buyer risk category CC0 would be rated between AAA (Country Category 1) and B (Country Category 7) by accredited CRAs.

## Very Good Credit Quality (CC1)

The risk of payment interruption is expected to be low or very low.

The obligor/guarantor has a very strong capacity for repayment and this capacity is not likely to be affected by foreseeable events. The obligor/guarantor has a limited or very limited susceptibility to adverse effects of changes in circumstances and economic conditions. The credit quality is typically manifested in a combination of some, if not all, of the following characteristics of the business and financial profile:

- very good to good cash and income generation
- very good to good liquidity levels
- very low to low leverage
- very strong business profile with proven management abilities

The entity is also characterised by a high quality of financial and ownership disclosure, unless there is a very high likelihood of support from a parent (or sovereign) with a buyer risk classification that is equal to or better than what corresponds to this buyer risk category.

Depending on the classification of the country in which the obligor/guarantor is domiciled, it is likely that an obligor/guarantor classified in buyer risk category CC1 would be rated between AAA (Country Category 1) and B (Country Category 7) by accredited CRAs.

## Good to Moderately Good Credit Quality, Above Average (CC2)

The risk of payment interruption is expected to be low. The obligor/guarantor has a good to moderately good capacity for repayment and this capacity is not likely to be affected by foreseeable events. The obligor/guarantor has a limited susceptibility to adverse effects of changes in circumstances and economic conditions. The credit quality is typically manifested in a combination of some, if not all, of the following characteristics of the business and financial profile:

- good to moderately good cash and income generation
- good to moderately good liquidity levels
- low to moderately low leverage
- moderately strong business profile with proven management abilities

The entity is also characterised by a high quality of financial and ownership disclosure, unless there is a very high likelihood of support from a parent (or sovereign) with a buyer risk classification that is equal to or better than what corresponds to this buyer risk category.

Depending on the classification of the country in which the obligor/guarantor is domiciled, it is likely that an obligor/guarantor classified in buyer risk category CC2 would be rated between A+ (Country Category 1) and B- or worse (Country Category 7) by accredited CRAs.

## Moderate Credit Quality, Average (CC3)

The risk of payment interruption is expected to be moderate or moderately low. The obligor/guarantor has a moderate or moderately good capacity for repayment. There is a possibility of credit risk developing as the obligor/guarantor faces major ongoing uncertainties or exposure to adverse business, financial or economic conditions which could lead to inadequate capacity to meet timely payments. However, business or financial alternatives may be available to allow financial commitments to be met. The credit quality is typically manifested in a combination of some, if not all, of the following characteristics of the business and financial profile.

- moderately good to moderate cash and income generation
- moderately good to moderate liquidity levels
- moderately low to moderate leverage
- moderate business profile with proven management abilities

The entity is also characterised by an adequate quality of financial and ownership disclosure, unless there is a very high likelihood of support from a parent (or sovereign) with a buyer risk classification that is equal to or better than what corresponds to this buyer risk category.

Depending on the classification of the country in which the obligor/guarantor is domiciled, it is likely that an obligor/guarantor classified in buyer riskcategory CC3 would be rated between BBB + (Country Category 1) and B – or worse (Country Category 6) by accredited CRAs.

## Moderately Weak Credit Quality, Below Average (CC4)

The risk of payment interruption is expected to be moderately weak. The obligor/guarantor has a moderate to moderately weak capacity for repayment. There is a possibility of credit risk developing as the obligor/guarantor faces major ongoing uncertainties or exposure to adverse business, financial or economic conditions which could lead to inadequate capacity to meet timely payments. However, business or financial alternatives may be available to allow financial commitments to be met. The credit quality is typically manifested in a combination of some, if not all, of the following characteristics of the business and financial profile:

- moderate to moderately weak cash and income generation
- moderate to moderately weak liquidity levels
- moderate to moderately high leverage
- moderately weak business profile with limited track record of management abilities

The entity is also characterised by an adequate quality of financial and ownership disclosure, unless there is a very high likelihood of support from a parent (or sovereign) with a buyer risk classification that is equal to or better than what corresponds to this buyer risk category.

Depending on the classification of the country in which the obligor/guarantor is domiciled, it is likely that an obligor/guarantor classified in buyer risk category CC4 would be rated between BB + (Country Category 1) and B – or worse (Country Category 5) by accredited CRAs.

## Weak Credit Quality (CC5)

The risk of payment interruption is expected to be high to very high. The obligor/guarantor has a moderately weak to weak capacity for repayment. The obligor/guarantor currently has the capacity to meet repayments but a limited margin of safety remains. However, there is a likelihood of developing payment problems as the capacity for continued payment is contingent upon a sustained, favourable business and economic environment. Adverse business, financial, or economic conditions will likely impair capacity or willingness to repay. The credit quality is typically manifested in a combination of some, if not all, of the following characteristics of the business and financial profile:

- moderately weak to weak to very weak cash and income generation
- moderately weak to weak liquidity levels
- moderately high to high leverage
- weak business profile with limited or no track record of management abilities

The entity is also characterised by a poor quality of financial and ownership disclosure, unless there is a very high likelihood of support from a parent (or sovereign) with a buyer risk classification that is equal to or better than what corresponds to this buyer risk category.

Depending on the classification of the country in which the obligor/guarantor is domiciled, it is likely that an obligor/guarantor classified in buyer risk category CC5 would be rated between BB – (Country Category 1) and B – or worse (Country Category 4) by accredited CRAs.

# ANNEX XII CRITERIA AND CONDITIONS GOVERNING THE APPLICATION OF COUNTRY RISK MITIGATION TECHNIQUES AND BUYER RISK CREDIT ENHANCEMENTS

## PURPOSE

This Annex provides detail on the use of country risk mitigation techniques listed in Article 30 a) of the Arrangement and the buyer risk credit enhancements listed in Article 31 a) of the Arrangement; this includes the criteria, conditions and specific circumstances which apply to their use as well as the impact on the MPRs.

## COUNTRY RISK MITIGATION TECHNIQUES

1. *Offshore Future Flow Structure Combined with Offshore Escrow Account*

*Definition*:

A written document, such as a deed or a release or trustee arrangement, sealed and delivered to a third party, *i. e.* a person not party to the instrument, to be held by such third party until the fulfilment of certain conditions and then to be delivered by him to the other party to take effect. If the following criteria are satisfied subject to consideration of the additional factors listed, this technique can reduce or eliminate the transfer risks, mainly in the higher risk country categories.

*Criteria*:

– The escrow account is related to a foreign exchange-earning project and the flows into the escrow account are generated by the project itself and/or by other offshore export receivables.

– The escrow account is held offshore, *i. e.* located outside of the country of the project where there are very limited, transfer or other country risks (*i. e.* in a High Income OECD country or High Income Euro Area country).

– The escrow account is located in a first class bank which is not directly orindirectly controlled by interests of the obligor or by the country of the obligor.

– The funding of the account is secured through long-term or other appropriate contracts.

– The combination of the sources of revenues (*i. e.* generated by the project itself and/or the other sources) of the obligor flowing through the account are in hard currency and can reasonably be expected to be collectively sufficient for the service of the debt for the entire duration of the credit, and come from one or more creditworthy foreign customers located in better risk countries than the country in which the project is located (*i. e.* normally High Income OECD countries or High Income Euro Area countries).

– The obligor irrevocably instructs the foreign customers to pay directly into the account (*i. e.* the payments are not forwarded through an account controlled by the obligor or through its country).

– The funds which have to be kept within the account are equal to at least six months of debt service. Where flexible repayment terms are being applied under a project finance structure, an amount equivalent to the actual six months debt service under such flexible terms are to be kept within the account; this amount may vary over time depending on the debt service profile.

– The obligor has restricted access to the account (*i. e.* only after payment of the debt service under the credit).

– The revenues deposited in the account are assigned to the lender as direct beneficiary, for the entire life of the credit.

– The opening of the account has received all the necessary legal authorisations from the local and any other appropriate authorities.

– The escrow account and contractual arrangements may not be conditional and/or revocable and/or limited in duration.

*Additional Factors to be taken into Consideration*:

– The technique applies subject to a case-by-case consideration of the above characteristics and, *inter alia*, with regard to:

– the country, the obligor (*i. e.* either public or private), the sector, the vulnerability in relation to the commodities or services involved, including their availability for the entire duration of the credit, the customers;

– the legal structures, *e. g.* whether the mechanism is sufficiently immune against the influence of the obligor or its country;

– the degree to which the technique remains subject to government interference, renewal or withdrawal;

– whether the account would be sufficiently protected against project related risks;

– the amount which will flow into the account and the mechanism for the continuation of appropriate provision;

– the situation with regard to the Paris Club (*e.g.* possible exemption);

– the possible impact of country risks other than the transfer risk;

– the protection against the risks of the country where the account is located;

– the contracts with the customers, including their nature and duration; and

– the global amount of the expected foreign earnings in relation to the total amount of the credit.

*Impact on the MPR*

The application of this country risk mitigation technique may result in a one category improvement in the applicable country risk classification for the transaction, except for transactions in Country Risk Category 1.

2. *Local Currency Financing*

*Definition*:

Contract and financing negotiated in convertible and available local, other than hard, currencies and financed locally that eliminates or mitigates the transfer risk. The primary debt obligation in local currency would, in principle, not be affected by the occurrence of the first two country credit risks.

*Criteria*:

– The ECA liability and claims payment orthe payment to the Direct Lender are expressed/ made throughout in local currency.

– The ECA is normally not exposed to the transfer risk.

– In the normal course of events, there will be no requirement for local currency deposits to be converted into hard currency.

– The borrower's repayment in his own currency and in his own country is a valid discharge of the loan obligation.

– If a borrower's income is in local currency the borrower is protected against adverse exchange rate movements.

– Transfer regulations in the borrower's country should not affect the borrower's repayment obligations, which would remain in local currency.

*Additional Factors to be taken into Consideration*:

The technique applies on a selective basis in respect of convertible and transferable currencies, where the underlying economy is sound. The Participant ECA should be in a position to meet its obligations to pay claims expressed in its own currency in the event that the local currency becomes either "non-transferable" or "non-convertible" after the ECA takes on liability. (A Direct Lender would however carry this exposure.)

*Impact on the MPR*

The application of this risk mitigation technique may result in a discount of no more than 20% to the country credit risk portion of the MPR (*i. e.* a local currency factor [LCF] with a value of no more than 0.2).

## BUYER RISK CREDIT ENHANCEMENTS

The following table provides definitions of the buyer risk credit enhancements that may be applied, along with their maximum impact on the applicable MPRs through the CEF in the MPR formula.

| Credit Enhancement | Definition | Maximum CEF |
|---|---|---|
| Assignment of Contract Proceeds or Receivables | In the event a borrower has contracts with strong off-takers, whether offshore or local, a legally enforceable assignment of the contract provides rights to enforce the borrower's contracts and/or make decisions under major contracts in the place of the borrower after a default under the loan. A direct agreement with a third party in a transaction (a local government agency in a mining or energy transaction) allows Lenders to approach a government to seek remedies for expropriation or other violation of contractual obligations related to the transaction.<br>An existing company operating in a difficult market or sector may have receivables related to the sale of production with a company or companies located in a more stable environment. Receivables would generally be in a hard currency but may not be the subject of a specific contractual relationship. Assignment of these receivables could provide asset security in the accounts of the Borrower, giving the Lender a preferential treatment in the cash flow generated by the Borrower. | 0.10 |

续表

| Credit Enhancement | Definition | Maximum CEF |
|---|---|---|
| Asset Based Security | Control of an asset shown by: (1) mortgage on very mobile and valuable piece of property and (2) property that has entire value in itself. An asset based security is one that can be reacquired with relative ease such as a locomotive, medical equipment or construction equipment. In valuing such a security, the ECA should take into consideration the legal ease of recovery. In other words, there is more value when the security interest in the asset is perfected under an established legal regime and less value where the legal ability to recover the asset is questionable. The precise value of an asset-based security is set by the market, with the relevant "market" being deeper than a local market because the asset can be moved to another jurisdiction. NOTE: The application of an asset based security credit enhancement applies to the buyer risk, where the asset based security is held internally within the country in which the transaction is domiciled. | 0.25 |
| Fixed Asset Security | A fixed asset security is most typically component equipment which may be constrained by its physicality such as turbine or manufacturing machinery integrated into an assembly line. The intent and value of the fixed asset security is to provide the ECA with more leverage over the use of the asset in recouping losses in the event of default. The value of a fixed asset security varies dependant on economic, legal, market and other factors. | 0.15 |

续表

| Credit Enhancement | Definition | Maximum CEF |
|---|---|---|
| Escrow Account | Escrow accounts involve debt service reserve accounts held as security for the lenders or other forms of cash receivable accounts held as security for the lenders by a party not controlled or sharing common ownership with the buyer/obligor. The escrowed amount must be deposited or escrowed in advance. The value of such security is nearly always 100% of the nominal amount in such cash accounts. Permits greater control over use of cash, ensures that debt is serviced before discretionary spending. NOTE: The application of an escrow account credit enhancement applies to the buyer risk, where the escrow account is held internally within the country in which the transaction is domiciled. Cash security significantly diminishes the risk of default for the covered instalments. | escrowed amount as % of credit up to a maximum of 0. 10 |

# ANNEX XIII CHECKLIST OF DEVELOPMENTAL QUALITY

## CHECKLIST OF DEVELOPMENTAL QUALITY OF AIDFINANCED PROJECTS

A number of criteria have been developed in recent years by the DAC to ensure that projects in developing countries that are financed totally or in part by Official Development Assistance (ODA) contribute to development. They are essentially contained in the:

- DAC Principles for Project Appraisal, 1988;
- DAC Guiding Principles for Associated Financing and Tied and Partially Untied Official Development Assistance, 1987; and
- Good Procurement Practices for Official Development Assistance, 1986.

## CONSISTENCY OF THE PROJECT WITH THE RECIPIENT COUNTRY'S OVERALL INVESTMENT PRIORITIES (PROJECT SELECTION)

Is the project part of investment and public expenditure programmes already approved by the central financial and planning authorities of the recipient country?

(Specify policy document mentioning the project, *e.g.* public investment programme of the recipient country.)

Is the project being co-financed with an international development finance institution?

Does evidence exist that the project has been considered and rejected by an international development finance institution or another DAC Memberon grounds of low developmental priority?

In the case of a private sector project, has it been approved by the government of the recipient country?

Is the project covered by an intergovernmental agreement providing for a broader range of aid activities by the donor in the recipient country?

## PROJECT PREPARATION AND APPRAISAL

Has the project been prepared, designed and appraised against a set of standards and criteria broadly consistent with the DAC Principles for Project Appraisal (PPA)? Relevant principlesconcern project appraisal under:

a) Economic aspects (paragraphs 30 to 38 PPA).

b) Technical aspects (paragraph 22 PPA).

c) Financial aspects (paragraphs 23 to 29 PPA).

In the case of a revenue producing project, particularly if it is producing for a competitive market, has the concessionary element of the aid financing been passed on to the end-user of the funds? (paragraph 25 PPA).

a) Institutional assessment (paragraphs 40 to 44 PPA).

b) Social and distributional analysis (paragraphs 47 to 57 PPA).

c) Environmental assessment (paragraphs 55 to 57 PPA).

## PROCUREMENT PROCEDURES

What procurement mode will be used among the following?

(For definitions, see Principles listed in Good Procurement Practices for ODA).

a) International competitive bidding (Procurement Principle III and its Annex 2: Minimum conditions for effective international competitive bidding).

b) National competitive bidding (Procurement Principle IV).

c) Informal competition or direct negotiations (Procurement Principles V A or B).

Is it envisaged to check price and quality of supplies (paragraph 63 PPA)?

# ANNEX XIV LIST OF DEFINITIONS

For the purpose of the Arrangement:

a) Commitment: any statement, in whatever form, whereby the willingness or intention to provide official support is communicated to the recipient country, the buyer, the borrower, the exporter or the financial institution.

b) Common Line: an understanding between the Participants to agree, for a given transaction or in special circumstances, on specific financial terms and conditions for official support. The rules of an agreed Common Line supersede the rules of the Arrangement only for the transaction or in the circumstances specified in the Common Line.

c) Concessionality Level of Tied Aid: in the case of grants the concessionality level is 100%. In the case of loans, the concessionality level is the difference between the nominal value of the loan and the discounted present value of the future debt service payments to be made by the borrower. This difference is expressed as a percentage of the nominal value of the loan.

d) Decommissioning: closing down or dismantling of a nuclear power plant.

e) Export Contract Value: the total amount to be paid by or on behalf of the purchaser for goods and/or services exported, *i.e.* excluding local costs as defined hereafter; in the case of a lease, it excludes the portion of the lease payment that is equivalent to interest.

f) Final Commitment: for an export credit transaction (either in the form of a single transaction or a line of credit), a final commitment exists when the Participant commits to precise and complete financial terms and conditions, either through a reciprocal agreement or by a unilateral act.

g) Initial Fuel Load: the initial fuel load shall consist of no more than the initially installed nuclear core plus two subsequent reloads, together consisting of up to two-thirds of a nuclear core.

h) Interest Rate Support: an arrangement between a government and banks or other financial institutions which allows the provision of fixed rate export finance at or above the CIRR.

i) Line of Credit: a framework, in whatever form, for export credits that covers a series of transactions which may or may not be linked to a specific project.

j) LocalCosts: expenditure for goods and services in the buyer's country that are necessary either for executing the exporter's contract or for completing the project of which the exporter's contract forms a part. These exclude commission payable to the exporter's agent in the buying country.

k) Pure Cover: official support provided by or on behalf of a government by way of export credit guarantee or insurance only, *i. e.* which does not benefit from official financing support.

l) Repayment Term: the period beginning at the starting point of credit, as defined in this Annex, and ending on the contractual date of the final repayment of principal.

m) Starting Point of Credit:

1) *Parts or components (intermediate goods) including related services*: in the case of parts or components, the starting point of credit is not later than the actual date of acceptance of the goods or the weighted mean date of acceptance of the goods (including services, if applicable) by the buyer or, for services, the date of the submission of

the invoices to the client or acceptance of services by the client.

2) *Quasi-capital goods, including related services-machinery or equipment, generally of relatively low unit value, intended to be used in an industrial process or for productive or commercial use*: in the case of quasi-capital goods, the starting point of credit is not later than the actual date of acceptance of the goods or the weighted mean date of acceptance of the goods by the buyer or, if the exporter has responsibilities for commissioning, then the latest starting point is at commissioning, or for services, the date of the submission of the invoices to the client or acceptance of the service by the client. In the case of a contract for the supply of services where the supplier has responsibility for commissioning, the latest starting point is commissioning.

3) *Capital goods and project services-machinery or equipment of high value intended to be used in an industrial process or for productive or commercial use*:

– In the case of a contract for the sale of capital goods consisting of individual items usable in themselves, the latest starting point is the actual date when the buyer takes physical possession of the goods, or the weighted mean date when the buyer takes physical possession of the goods.

– In the case of a contract for the sale of capital equipment for complete plant or factories where the supplier has no responsibility for commissioning, the latest starting point is the date at which the buyer is to take physical possession of the entire equipment (excluding spare parts) supplied under the contract.

– If the exporter has responsibility for commissioning, the latest starting point is at commissioning.

– For services, the latest starting point of credit is the date of the submission of the invoices to the client or acceptance of service by the client. In the case of a contract for the supply of services where the supplier has responsibility for commissioning, the latest starting point is commissioning.

4) *Complete plants or factories – complete productive units of high value requiring the use of capital goods*:

– In the case of a contract for the sale of capital equipment for complete plant or factories where the supplier has no responsibility for commissioning, the latest starting point of credit is the date when the buyer takes physical possession of the entire equipment (excluding spare parts) supplied under the contract.

– In case of construction contracts where the contractor has no responsibility for commissioning, the latest starting point is the date when construction has been completed.

– In the case of any contract where the supplier or contractor has a contractual responsibility for commissioning, the latest starting point is the date when he has completed installation or construction and preliminary tests to ensure it is ready for operation. This applies whether or not it is handed over to the buyer at that time in accordance with the terms of the contract and irrespective of any continuing commitment which the supplier or contractor may have, *e. g.* for guaranteeing its effective functioning or training local personnel.

– Where the contract involves the separate execution of individual parts of a project, the date of the latest starting point is the date of the starting point for each separate part, or the mean date of those starting points, or, where the supplier has a contract, not for the whole project but for an essential part of it, the starting point may be that appropriate to the project as a whole.

– For services, the latest starting point of credit is the date of the submission of the invoices to the client or the acceptance of service by the client. In the case of a contract for the supply of services where the supplier has responsibility for commissioning, the latest starting point is commissioning.

n) Tied Aid: aid which is in effect (in law or in fact) tied to the procurement of goods and/or services from the donor country and/or a restricted number of countries; it includes loans, grants or associated financing packages with a concessionality level greater than zero percent.

This definition applies whether the "tying" is by formal agreement or by any form of informal understanding between the recipient and the donor country, or whether a package includes components from the forms set out in Article 34 of the Arrangement that are not freely and fully available to finance procurement from the recipient country, substantially all other developing countries and from the Participants, or if it involves practices that the DAC or the Participants consider equivalent to such tying.

o) Untied Aid: aid which includes loans or grants whose proceeds are fully and freely available to finance procurement from any country.

p) Weighted Average Life of the Repayment Period: the time that it takes to retire one-half of the principal of a credit. This is calculated as the sum of time (in years) between the starting point of credit and each principal repayment weighted by the portion of principal repaid at each repayment date.